Missing

Francis Mond
1895–1918

Missing

The Need for Closure after the Great War

Richard van Emden

Pen & Sword
MILITARY

AN IMPRINT OF PEN & SWORD BOOKS LTD.
YORKSHIRE - PHILADELPHIA

First published in Great Britain in 2019 by
Pen & Sword Military
An imprint of
Pen & Sword Books Ltd
Yorkshire - Philadelphia

Hardback ISBN 978 1 52676 096 8
Paperback ISBN 978 1 52676 100 2

Printed and bound in England
By TJ International Ltd.

Pen & Sword Books Ltd incorporates the Imprints of Pen & Sword
Archaeology, Atlas, Aviation, Battleground, Discovery, Family History,
History, Maritime, Military, Naval, Politics, Railways, Select, Transport,
True Crime, Fiction, Frontline Books, Leo Cooper, Praetorian Press,
Seaforth Publishing, Wharncliffe and White Owl.

For a complete list of Pen & Sword titles please contact

PEN & SWORD BOOKS LIMITED
47 Church Street, Barnsley, South Yorkshire, S70 2AS, England
E-mail: enquiries@pen-and-sword.co.uk
Website: www.pen-and-sword.co.uk

or

PEN AND SWORD BOOKS
1950 Lawrence Rd, Havertown, PA 19083, USA
E-mail: uspen-and-sword@casematepublishers.com
Website: www.penandswordbooks.com

To
Alex Chung

Contents

Maps

Glossary

ADS	Advanced Dressing Station
AIF	Australian Imperial Force
BEMC	Battle Exploit Memorials Committee
BHQ	Battalion/Brigade Headquarters
BWGA	British War Graves Association
CID	Committee for Imperial Defence
CO	commanding officer
Coy	company
CWGC	Commonwealth War Graves Commission
DGR&E	Directorate of Grave Registration and Enquiries
GHQ	General Headquarters
GRC	Graves Registration Commission
GRU	Graves Registration Unit
IGC	Indian Graves Commission
IWGC	Imperial War Graves Commission
KIA	killed in action
LC	Labour Company
NCO	non-commissioned officer
MC	military cemetery
MFS	Maurice Farman Shorthorn
OC	officer commanding
OP	observation post
OTC	Officer Training Corps
RAOC	Royal Army Ordnance Corps
RAS	Reserve Aeroplane Squadron
RFC	Royal Flying Corps
YMCA	Young Men's Christian Association

Introduction

Now the wooden crosses have been gathered in and burned; the dead are housed in stately gardens.

Stephen Graham, *The Challenge of the Dead,* 1921

Nothing appeared to matter anymore when the news broke: wealth, business, social status, all of it became instantaneously trivial. In May 1918, the Mond family was just the next in line to receive the worst possible news, making Emile and Angela indistinguishable from countless other doting parents suffering the same mind-numbing shock: their son had been killed at the Front. With every death came an explanation of sorts, a narrative of circumstances, bravery and lasting respect. He was the best and sorely missed, sympathies were offered up in hastily penned notes from a commanding officer or perhaps a close pal, and written to reassure parents that death was instant, no pain felt, even if that were untrue. At first, Emile and Angela's story appeared to fit roughly the same blueprint, with two letters from eyewitnesses, but the Mond story did not develop the way most did. Theirs would be different.

The Monds' eldest son, Francis, serving with the Royal Air Force, had been shot down and killed. His body was recovered, identified, but then lost in curious circumstances, adding a disturbing twist to the family's narrative of bereavement. Angela's response: to embark on a search for her boy's remains that took her to the doors of government and to the killing fields of the Western Front. Her search was unrelenting and exhaustive, haunted by the high probability of ultimate failure. Her extraordinary and previously untold story is the backbone of this book, which will examine the much wider narrative of how the nation dealt with its dead and its collective search for peace.

At 11.00 am on 11 November 1918, there was an immediate and irreparable rupture between the living and the dead. Those who carried on, the survivors of the Great War, suddenly faced the prospect of building new post-war lives while giving meaning to the valiant service of their peers, their friends, who had died. How could they commemorate nearly 750,000 lost souls? How was it possible to pay fitting homage to such self-sacrifice? The weight of responsibility lay heavily on the shoulders of the British government and the public alike: it was axiomatic that by their sheer number, and the manner in which they had given their lives, the dead made their own pressing and overwhelming demands for remembrance.

During the war, and for the first time, senior politicians and military commanders understood that bodies could not simply be rolled into mass graves and forgotten, as they had been after Waterloo and other short, thunderclap battles. After 1918, the dead would have to be honoured on a scale commensurate with the sacrifice. And over half the dead were missing; men with no known graves, individuals who could not be denied their own visible memorials. Their physical bodies were gone, torn apart in many cases; for them, the 'fortune of war', as poet and author Rudyard Kipling wrote, had denied a 'known and honoured burial'.

The nation, exhausted by conflict, was presided over by an exchequer with dwindling income and depleted coffers; yet who would openly suggest short-changing the dead, penny-pinching over heroes at such a time as this? The dead would have their dwellings, graves preserved for eternity in cemeteries across the globe, maintained and cared for in perpetuity. And those who could not be found would be given inscribed permanence on the panels of vast memorials built on hallowed land, and when the ravages of time began to erase those names, a guarantee that they would be conscientiously recut. The commitment had been wholehearted, but within a few years, even before the great memorials were unveiled, the Exchequer would seek economies, pressing those charged with caring for the dead to find ways of making savings, astonishingly even to the point of part-abandoning the cemeteries upon which so much work had been lavished.

At home, personal peace remained elusive for survivors; for those who served and for the families of the fallen. With so many men missing and the awfulness of not knowing the circumstances of their fate, too many families were left to obsess about their loss for the rest of their lives. Angela Mond's story was different in one sense only: she knew her son was dead, of that there was no doubt, and yet, through some unresolved error, her son was denied a known grave. Her anguish was similar to that of hundreds of thousands of others: the desire for resolution – never closure – and a grave to visit.

Angela came from an affluent family with wealth built up through invention and business acumen. She had the means and the time to continue her unyielding search for Francis. She could call on contacts and request help in a way few could match. But wealth could be its own curse, condemning families to open-ended investigations with almost no chance of success, while paralysing lives that would otherwise continue, albeit under a veil. Angela directed her energies into her quest as part of her own process of dealing with grief, but she could never assuage her feelings of loss.

Amongst those families who remained bereft with no definite news of loved ones, there would be many questions in the new post-war world: how systematic would the search for the missing be? What lengths would the authorities go to, to identify recovered bodies? How long realistically would the nation sanction further searches? Never long enough, many would ultimately feel, leaving mothers, fathers and widows to vainly hope that one day, a missing soldier might miraculously arrive at the railway station or walk in at the back door left permanently unlocked. And not just for years, but for decades.

This is the story of the army's hunt for legions of missing men. How were they sought? How many were found and identified and what were the implications for families when that search was wound down? Tens of thousands of British people felt compelled to visit France and Belgium to see where their loved ones died; here we will explore what happened to the battlefields of Northern France and Belgium in the immediate post-war years. How did the battlefields' recovery from the ravages of war bring solace to the survivors and the bereaved? Was there a risk that in making cemeteries like 'stately gardens', a vital warning from history would be forgotten or downplayed? In telling the story of Britain's military cemeteries on the Western Front, this book will look at their design and horticulture, and examine the extraordinary lengths to which the gardeners of the Imperial War Graves Commission went to create an Eden for their dead comrades.

The mobilisation of Britain for an international war had ensured that almost every family in the country was wedded to the cause, and shared in the losses. What then was the role of British citizens in this process of remembrance? What pressure did they bring to ensure that all faiths and classes played their part in an act of national devotion on the Western Front? This was to be a far more difficult and controversial task than is generally appreciated today. How would the cemeteries be acquired and paid for? Who would decide on their design and layout? Would all families greet the egalitarian treatment of the dead in cemeteries with equanimity? What of the French and Belgian civilians who returned to their land within the battle zone? Were they to be allowed to restart their lives largely uninhibited or would their tolerance be tested too, as plots of *their* land were purchased and parcelled off for other people's cemeteries and their ploughing disrupted by the narrow paths that led to them, and by the occasionally careless attitude of visitors?

And what too of the men who had fought – the veterans? There were difficult choices to be made: to try to forget about the past as much as possible, to move on and look only to the future, or to remember the dead and never forget? Some soldiers stayed on in France after the Armistice, joining grizzly exhumation parties looking for the missing and, when their work was done, remaining on the Western Front, working with the Imperial War Graves Commission, helping to establish new cemeteries – gardeners for life in the service of the dead. Many former soldiers could never return, haunted by the misery of crystal-clear memory and, too often, lacking wealth and opportunity. Those who did return were not always happy with civilians whom they judged less as pilgrims than as tourists, there to gawp and keen on souvenirs. These old soldiers were as committed to the memory of dead pals as the mothers and fathers were to their dead sons or wives to their husbands. Their lifelong search for communion with comrades was as resolute as Angela Mond's search for the body of her son.

* * *

I first became aware of Angela Mond's story after reading a short, privately published book focusing on private memorials on the Western Front, memorials paid for by grieving families. The author had consulted a file about the Mond case held in the archive of the Commonwealth War Graves Commission (CWGC) in Maidenhead. Five years ago, I also went to look and I realised immediately that this story was truly remarkable, unique in its circumstances. I knew, too, that I would need more material were I to make Angela's story the centrepiece of a book. I contacted the family and spoke to Helen Cippico, the great-granddaughter of Angela and the custodian of much of what survives, including a collection of photographs, letters and documents belonging to the Mond family. After discussing my thoughts and ideas, Helen handed me the entire archive.

I mention this only because I believe that to fully appreciate the backdrop to Angela's devoted search, it is important to appreciate Francis: who he was before the war and his service in the Royal

Flying Corps (renamed as the Royal Air Force after 1 April 1918). Central to this family archive is a small collection of letters he wrote while on active service, all bar two penned in the seven weeks leading up to his death, indeed, the last letter written just five days before he was killed. These letters are superbly descriptive and evocative of their time. Francis was young, like so many of his comrades, mostly teenagers or men in their early twenties, all of whom lived under extraordinary physical and mental stress while fighting in France. They served at a crucial time when the outcome of the war appeared to be in the balance, the nation's survival at stake; it was duty and comradeship that kept these pilots flying. That most of them knew they were unlikely to come home alive or unscathed is a great testament to their courage, their willingness to put their lives on the line, and reason enough for their parents to cherish the memory of their dead sons in whatever way they saw fit.

No one is alive who can recall meeting Francis, and only two members of the extended family can still remember meeting his mother and father. One, Angela's granddaughter, Ursula, is interviewed at the end of this book. Who Francis was, his personality, remains a little elusive, though certain traits can be discerned from his letters. He was self-assured, sometimes insensitive, he was fun-loving yet thoughtful, and above all, he was exceptionally brave.

Missing is illustrated with a collection of images, some of them taken by Francis himself, and almost all have never been published before.

Chapter One

'The instructors were pre-war regular officers of the rank of Captain; they had flown in France, had actually been fired at in the air, had survived engine failures, forced landings, rifle fire and thunderstorms. We regarded them as living evidence that the Age of Heroes had come again.'

Duncan Grinnell-Milne, *Wind in the Wires*, 1933

Lieutenant Francis Mond
16 Squadron, Royal Flying Corps
France, 10 September 1915
The Trenches

Dear Mother
When you see in the papers 'A hostile aeroplane was brought down by our own aircraft guns', I wonder what you think it's like?

Well, I'll try and explain. I saw one shot down in front of me from 8,000 feet yesterday afternoon.

It was one of the most fascinating and nauseating spectacles I've ever seen. It was with extraordinary mixed feelings I saw the poor wretches literally tumble to destruction – at least one – as the pilot was obviously killed already. Just as we came out of the communication trench into the fire-trench (front line) we saw a Hun going along just his side of the lines – parallel to them. Then our 'Archie' [anti-aircraft fire] got onto him – got his line and elevation at once – but too far behind. Then each successive shot got nearer, and we kept saying, 'Lord, I bet that made him sit up!' Then, 'That got him – no, it didn't.'

Then one burst exactly over him, just halfway along the machine – we never said a word – hoped and prayed it had him fair and square.

Then the machine put its nose down a bit, did a half turn and a sort of a lurch – a drunken lurch – then put its nose right down vertically and began to spin round faster and faster. It didn't get very fast, however, but having got up a certain momentum simply spun round and round and round vertically – round its own axis.

About 5,000 feet something came away – possibly a wing tip, or one of the passengers – it was simply appalling – it took such ages to fall – like a wounded bird at first – then, well, it was simply too fascinating – and yet utterly repulsive. We hoped and prayed he'd 'flatten out' – the technical term for pulling its nose up out of the 'spinning nosedive' it was doing. But it simply went down and down, turning all the time, its black crosses plainly visible to the naked eye every time the top-side of the wings came round, the engine roaring all the time, simply pulling the thing down, a sure sign the pilot was killed or insensible, as if the controls had been severed, accounting for a spin, one would instinctively shut off the engine, which was not done. He fell just inside their own lines, about 100 yards behind – unfortunately. We just saw a bit of white behind a hedge and some trees through a periscope.

They [the artillery] waited for the Huns to begin to collect round, and then a battery of field guns put about 50 rounds slap into it in about a couple of minutes. Bang – whizzzzzz – plonk! Bang – whizzzzzz – plonk! The shells just cleared our heads as they came over our own parapet, from the rear of course. The trenches were only a couple of hundred yards away from each other.

Well, it was a thing to see, but I don't want to see it again. It was the most wonderful, <u>marvellous</u> shooting you'll ever see, only about 12 rounds and then all over – nothing in this world could possibly save them.

Our men sent up a terrific cheer as he fell – we hadn't the heart to – knowing what it well meant!

After that, we wandered about, to Neuve Chapelle, right over the village, about a hundred or two hundred yards behind the lines, you had to look pretty slippy for snipers – pffssssss – fweeppppp (hit a tree). Pffssssss – pppssss (a ricochet) – each awakening a hollow echo among the ruins. The graveyard adjoining the church had the roof on one of its graves blown clean off, and the lid of the coffin of what was once apparently a woman, – yellow and constructed like the opened mummies in the British Museum, in its torn winding sheet.

But perhaps the most pathetic sights are the improvised graveyards where the dead soldiers and officers are buried, a rough wooden cross with name, rank, regiment neatly put on, and perhaps pencilled in afterwards, R.I.P.

Particularly pathetic, and only too common when the fighting has been thick: 'Here Lies The Body Of An Unknown Soldier'.

Well, *au revoir*, – best love to all, from Francis.

The content of this letter was probably not the sort of thing Angela Mond would be keen on receiving when Francis, her son, was himself a pilot in the Royal Flying Corps. The detailed description of an aeroplane crippled in mid-air, the pilot and observer falling to their deaths and the likelihood that at least one was alive as the aircraft spiralled to the ground, was traumatic and heart-rending. Even Francis was both fascinated and nauseated by the spectacle, so why did he think his mother would want to read such an account? Here was the death of her own son foretold, a description not only meticulous but accompanied by pencil-drawn images of the enemy plane's last descent. 'Each shot is a <u>successive</u> one,' he wrote, drawing the plane flying horizontally with puffs of bursting anti-aircraft shells getting ever closer. 'i.e., the machine has moved on as each shell bursts – You can see the one that got him. Then the [picture of a plane turning] and then [picture of a plane dropping almost vertically] from 8,000 feet'. If Angela Mond did not fret constantly about her son, if she did not already wake up at night wondering if he would survive the following day, there is every reason to think that she would now.

Why would a son write such a letter home? Of course, young men – Francis was aged twenty – are prone to insensitivity, convinced of their own invincibility. 'I have absolute faith in my safe return to you all,' he would write in a letter home. The answer probably lies somewhere between the discombobulating effect of life on the Western Front in 1915, and the deeply traumatising aftermath of a crash and near-death experience that Francis had himself suffered just four days earlier. Francis was deeply traumatised, although he remained articulate: 'I'm feeling pretty fit again thanks – but I think they're sending me back for a rest for a short while, which will be welcome! Where to, I don't know yet.' His cheeriness hid the real truth. His squadron commander had noticed something different in Francis. After three months' active service on the Western Front, this pilot needed to recuperate. But there must have been something more than that, some incident unspecified, for within a week, Francis Mond was on his way home, not for a week's leave but to hospital, where he was diagnosed with neurasthenia – shell shock.

* * *

Saturday, 1 March 1913: Court of Summary Jurisdiction, Cambridge
Defendant: Francis Mond
Does it follow that a policeman will always magically appear when least wanted, if, as the maxim predicts, 'there's never one when

you do'? Francis Mond may have idly chewed over the thought as he waited outside the Court of Summary Jurisdiction. He may have reflected on his bad luck that Sunday afternoon, 20 February, when, riding his motorcycle at an alleged excessive speed in Harston village high street, his path crossed with that of 32-year-old Police Constable Henry Martin.

PC Martin was off-duty, standing in his front garden when he heard not one motorcycle but three 'coming from the direction of Cambridge [and] at a tremendous rate', he told the court. Hearing the noise, he walked to his gate to see two men passing, followed by a third. 'One [motor]cyclist was looking round as if looking for the defendant. Defendant then came by at between 45 and 50 miles an hour.'

This was not the first court session 17-year-old Francis Mond had attended, but it was the first time he had the confidence to properly contest the charges. The previous October, the teenage undergraduate from Peterhouse College, Cambridge had pleaded guilty to 'riding a motorcycle at a speed dangerous to the public' within the city and was fined £1 and costs. During those proceedings, Francis claimed that there had not been much traffic about and, in any case, he did not believe he was going at an excessive speed. The policeman who stopped him, Francis argued, had been 'rather led by the fact he [Francis] had on a racing cap, and that the machine was making a lot of noise'. The policeman, PC Wade, estimated Francis's speed at 40mph, Francis at markedly less, 25mph. Nevertheless, he accepted his punishment.

Six months later, perhaps worried that the court might take a dim view of a second appearance, he stood his ground. There had been a rash of such incidents in recent months as one over-exuberant undergraduate after another had been summoned before the courts to be rapped over the knuckles; enough in number, it seemed, for the local newspapers to take an interest. At least one journalist was there to hear the evidence, scribbling down notes.

At 4.45 witness thought he heard the same motorcycle, and went to the road. It was the same man – he had taken the number as he passed before. Witness stopped defendant, and defendant produced his licence. Witness told defendant he thought he was going quite 45 miles an hour, when he went by before. Defendant asked him to say it was only 35, because there was no mercy for him in Cambridge.

Defendant: 'How was it you could see my number if I was going 50 miles an hour?'

Witness: 'I always take the letter from the front and the number from the back.'

Defendant: 'You can't possibly say what speed I was going; you had no means of judging.'

Witness: 'All I can say is that it was the fastest I have seen anyone go.'

Joseph Jacklin, groom, Harston, also said he thought defendant was going at 50 miles an hour: 'He was going like an express train.'

Harry Gawthrop, Harston, also said he thought defendant was going at 50 miles an hour. He was going at a dangerous pace, and there were children in the road.

This was an interesting detail. PC Martin had a 5-year-old daughter and was unlikely to look kindly on anyone speeding through his village when there were children about, and certainly not twice in one day.

Addressing the magistrate, defendant said the road he was going along was perfectly straight, and it was before he got to the village where there was a corner. When he got to the corner he slowed down considerably. He contested that any of the witnesses had any means of judging his speed. It was purely guesswork that he was going 50 miles an hour. He contested that it was anything like that pace. There was no traffic on the road, and if there were any children they were at the side of the road.

Defendant, who had been fined for driving to the common danger in the Borough, was convicted and fined 30s. and costs.

The following day, the local paper ran Francis's court appearance with punchy, attention-grabbing headlines:

'Fastest I have seen'
'Undergraduate Motorist Fined'
'No Mercy in Cambridge'

Francis may have felt justified in contesting PC Martin's estimate of his speed. There was a tight corner as he entered the village and he probably slowed, but from what initial speed? Moreover, estimating speed would be more difficult at a time when there were so few cars on the road. Aircraft too were in their infancy and a novelty when seen, and only trains moved at genuine pace. People simply were not used to seeing anything pass quickly down a public highway. The motorcycle was era-changing and new: Norton, Triumph and Harley Davidson had begun production of these heady, liberating machines only in the previous decade, and as industry innovation brought faster and more reliable machines to the market, so motorcycle racing had gripped the imagination of young men ... that is, young men with some money.

Francis Mond was eager to embrace this new technology and so he became all too familiar with the inside of a courtroom: on 24 April 1913 at Cambridge, for 'wilfully' causing an obstruction, he was fined five shillings; on 21 March 1914, caught speeding on Brockley Hill on a motorcycle, fined thirty shillings and costs; and on 4 June 1914 at Cambridge, caught speeding along Garrett Hostel Lane. Fined again.

His court appearances did not seem to affect his prospects and, in particular, his military career. For three years, while at Rugby

School, he had done what most of his peers felt was their duty, serving in the school's Officer Training Corps, and although his 'general efficiency' as a cadet was judged as only 'fair', he did better in the OTC Band. At university, he joined the Territorial Army and, in the same month that he was fined for speeding, he was commissioned into the 6th London Brigade, Royal Field Artillery. He joined this unit on the outbreak of war, volunteered for overseas service but remained in England. Francis's thrill at speed, his enthusiasm for new technology, must have made horse-drawn artillery seem antiquated and unromantic. He had driven cars and motorcycles at seventeen, so what was enchanting about slow, methodical horses? Not very much, it seemed: Francis actively sought to change to the newly formed Royal Flying Corps, to join, as many romantically saw them, the new knights of the air.

*   *   *

Like so many of his generation studying at Oxford or Cambridge universities, Francis Mond was born into wealth, and as far as wealth went, Francis had few equals. He grew up in an affluent and influential family whose fortune had been built in the second half of the nineteenth century. Brunner Mond Chemicals had been established in 1873 in a venture between two successful industrial chemists: an Englishman of part Swiss extraction, John Brunner, and Ludwig Mond, of German birth but who, owing to low-level but persistent anti-Semitism in his native country, had chosen to move to Britain in 1862, eventually being naturalised in 1880. With its factory in Cheshire, Brunner Mond grew to become the most successful British chemical company of the era, later merging to form ICI after the Great War. The Mond family did not sit on their wealth but were noted instead for their benevolence, being the first significant company in Britain to introduce the idea of a week's paid holiday for all its employees as well as introducing the eight-hour working day in its factories. The family were also generous benefactors to the arts.

Francis's father, Emile Schweich-Mond, a chemical engineer and a nephew of Ludwig, joined the Brunner Mond Board as well as the Board of the Mond Nickel Company. In the early 1890s, through a friend, the fêted Victorian artist Sigismund Goetze, Emile met Angela, Sigismund's sister, and they married in October 1894.

Emile and Angela Mond's main London home was at 22 Hyde Park Square, just a few minutes' walk from Hyde Park and Marble Arch. Here Francis was born in July 1895, to be followed by Philip in 1897, Alfred in 1901, May in 1904 and finally, Stephen in 1907. Francis, of all the children, possessed the greatest natural gifts. He inherited his mother's musical appreciation and a superb musical talent. At Rugby School (1909–12) he was a good artist and a keen ornithologist and he shone academically, although he appears rarely in school literature and seems to have generally kept a low profile. His housemaster at the time was Parker Brooke, the father of the poet Rupert, and briefly, for a term in 1910, after the death of Brooke senior, Rupert was installed as Francis's housemaster.

It is possible that his time at Rugby was not especially happy. There is evidence of some anti-German feeling amongst the pupils, including overt bullying, and while Francis's younger brother Philip was also sent to Rugby, the third son, Alfred, went instead to Charterhouse.

Back in London, Francis's parents entertained frequently. Angela lived at the epicentre of London's social whirl. Her address book read like a Who's Who of established city life, including the names of the Balfour, Bonham Carter and Snowden families; Sir Edwin Lutyens, the great architect, is there, at '13 Mansfield Street, W1', as is the American-English retail magnate, Harry Gordon Selfridge, at 'Brook House, Park Lane'. Angela knew attachés, diplomats and ambassadors. Her sister, Violet, was a frequent visitor with her husband (Emile's cousin), Alfred Mond, later Sir Alfred Mond a

Liberal MP in the wartime Lloyd George coalition government and a post-war minister in Cabinet.

The Cippico family, a well-connected Italian dynasty from Rome, were also close friends. Contessa Cippico's son, Aldo, spent much of his childhood in the company of Emile and Angela's children, eventually marrying May Mond. He recalled with affection the happiness of his future in-laws' pre-war family life.

Angela who had ambitions for her husband's future career acted as a Society hostess, lionizing great names in the world of politics, arts and 'bel canto' singing. She gave regular evening musical parties in their honour. As to politics, Angela particularly favoured diplomats posted to the French embassy, for sentimental reasons and because she had always had a penchant for French art and history. As a further decoration at these brilliant gatherings, she could always count on the presence of 'family', Emile's first cousin Alfred Mond, and his wife ... and also on Rufus Isaacs [Sir, later 1st Marquess of Reading], another cousin who, a great barrister in his own right, later became Viceroy of India.

While the Mond family was fully engaged in London society life, they sought rural sanctuary at their country estate, Greyfriars, near Storrington, set at the foot of the Sussex South Downs. Aldo Cippico remembered how the house nestled close under the chalk hills, and was 'surrounded on all sides by broad fields and shady coppices. It really was a beautiful estate,' he recalled.

There were spacious oak-panelled rooms on the ground floor, with an imposing oak staircase rising up from the main hall to the bedrooms above and gave the place an atmosphere of quiet and simple luxury. ... At the far end of the house a vast billiard room had been added on to the main structure and was much used. Along one wall a deep bay with leaded windows was the nook where afternoon tea was made every day.

Here, close family and friends were entertained, with 'Angela officiating behind a huge brown teapot and kettle'. In the evening, the family settled down in front of the fireplace to play backgammon or card games, bridge and whist. The family were extremely happy, Aldo remembered, with the younger children, May and Stephen, enjoying:

> the wild freedom of the rolling unspoiled country ... climbing to the top of the Downs, chasing butterflies or each other against the wind. Or else we could be found busily extracting marine fossils, shells and sea-urchins, from an abandoned chalk-pit. ...
>
> Some mornings we of the younger generation used to play tennis down on the grass-court west of the house and I can still remember the almost intimidated awe which filled my mind when registering the solemn arrival of the butler, tall, elegant and majestic descending the steps leading to the court with slow ceremonial steps, bearing in his outstretched hands a large silver salver with glasses of iced lemonade and ginger-beer for our morning refreshment.

In the years before the Great War, this halcyon world, built on years of hard work and ingenuity, seemed unassailable.

* * *

8 March 1915, Farnborough Aerodrome

Francis Mond's transfer request from the artillery to the Royal Flying Corps was agreed in October 1914, though he remained with his regiment while he awaited further instructions, even managing to squeeze in another court appearance for speeding in a car and failing to produce a driving licence. In January 1915, he received orders to attend a medical examination, which he passed, and in early March, as a flying officer cadet, he was directed to the Farnborough aerodrome for days of theoretical instruction in the art of flying and then, all being well, a first flight with an instructor in a Maurice Farman Longhorn.

The Royal Flying Corps was not quite three years old. Formed in April 1912 as the aerial eyes of the British Army, its primary function was observation, assisting the artillery in accurate battery work, and providing aerial reconnaissance, spotting enemy troop movements, transport routes, new defensive works and ammunition dumps; everything that remained, in essence, hidden from those, such as the infantry, whose work remained rooted on the ground.

Accurate aerial observation was critical to the success of ground operations in the Great War and the compilation of trench maps. It was therefore also critical that each side brought down the other's aircraft. Fighter planes were born to protect cumbersome observation aircraft and to wrestle with the enemy for air supremacy. Pilots who flew fighter aircraft were glamorous individuals, but those who flew reconnaissance aircraft, photographing the battle-field below, were in many ways the real heroes. Vulnerable to attack from the air and from anti-aircraft fire from the ground, they flew missions that entailed keeping their planes perfectly level and steady so that they could photograph the ground, flying up and down the trench lines in predictable patterns, taking images on glass plates within cameras strapped to the side of their aircraft, images that could be exposed and developed back on the ground and overlapped so as to give an impression of the wider battlefield. Their importance to successfully prosecuting the war was never in doubt, so that the number of images these pilots would take increased from a few tens of thousands in 1915 to millions in 1918.

Aeroplanes of all varieties were prone to air-failure, with more pilots killed in accidents than in combat. There were no parachutes, not, as is popularly believed, to stop pilots jumping at the first sign of danger, but because parachutes were unwieldy and too heavy for such lightweight wood, wire and fabric-built aircraft – aircraft that could be literally blown backwards in a heavy headwind.

Airfields typically consisted of wooden and brick hangers, Nissen huts and tents, grass landing strips, fields where hedgerows were grubbed up when necessary, trees felled as required. The men who took to the skies were pilots but also pioneers; men of extraordinary courage who were willing to place their lives in the flimsy airframe of planes including, amongst the best known, the Maurice Farman Longhorn.

A fellow pilot, Duncan Grinnell-Milne, with whom Francis would serve in France, recalled these early days and the risks young men took flying primitive, dangerous aircraft, many young would-be pilots returning to their regiments deflated after 'a few days' trial', and too many errors.

> In the sheds was a collection of aircraft, most of them inter-esting museum pieces in which we were to be instructed, and two dangerous-looking single-seaters with which, I was glad to hear, we were to have no dealings whatsoever. There were about half a dozen of us novices and the same number of older pupils. The instructors were pre-war regular officers of the rank of Captain; they had flown in France, had actually been fired at in the air, had survived engine failures, forced landings, rifle fire and thunderstorms. We regarded them as living evidence that the Age of Heroes had come again.

During the morning, one of the museum pieces was wheeled from its shed and set down upon the edge of the turf.

> Officially it was called after its inventor: A Maurice Farman biplane; but it was better known as a 'Longhorn'. ... To the uninitiated eye the Longhorn presented a forest of struts and spars, with floppy white fabric dropped over all, and enough

piano wire to provide an impenetrable entanglement. At the sight of the craft before us, we put our heads on one side like puzzled terriers.

The Longhorn was a flimsy but reliable aircraft to train on, albeit with a weak 70hp engine and a takeoff speed of under 40mph. 'It was a Renault [engine] of uncertain strength,' wrote Grinnell-Milne. 'When running slowly it made a noise suggesting a pair of alarm-clocks ticking upon a marble mantelpiece.' It would be the training aircraft for Grinnell-Milne and Mond for the next six weeks.

From the moment Francis arrived at Farnborough for elementary training, all flights were noted and meticulously kept in his logbook. On a windless March morning, four days after arriving at the aerodrome, he flew for the first time in a Longhorn: a fifteen-minute flight including one and a half circuits of the aerodrome and two landings.

That first flight was always an experience to remember, Grinnell-Milne wrote:

The pilot and his passenger settled down into their elevated seats, adjusted goggles, helmets, and took a long look round as though it might be their last. After listening awhile to the engine, the pilot waved hands, attendant mechanics removed the wooden blocks from beneath the wheels and the machine moved forward, lurching slightly over the uneven ground like a cow going out to pasture.

That same day, in the afternoon, Francis took a twenty-five-minute hop to Brooklands, via Woking, and then, a day later, he flew 'as [a] passenger with camera', completing three circuits of the aerodrome. By 24 March, Francis was 'ready for the front seat', taking control of the aircraft, four times trundling down the grass runway, lifting off momentarily and landing again. By 1 April, with three hours and twenty-six minutes dual-control flying under his belt, Francis was adjudged to be competent enough to fly solo. It was a salutary moment for any young pilot, as Grinnell-Milne recalled, when one morning he caught the eye of an instructor:

'How much dual-control have you done?' he asked.

'Three hours and twenty minutes,' I answered, hopeful that so small an amount would induce him to give me more at once.

'H'm …' he muttered, still looking at me fixedly. 'Do you think you could go solo?'

The question staggered me. All my past lies flashed before me, whirled in my head and merged into one huge thumping fib.

'Yes,' I answered and at once regretted it. … My hour had struck before I was prepared. I knew nothing whatever about flying, and it was far too early in the morning and it was cold and I hadn't had breakfast. I was doomed and I knew it. I felt like asking for a priest.

Given that just six minutes' flying time separated the two pilots, it is almost inconceivable that Francis did not feel similar emotions. His logbook reveals no great drama as he undertook two seven-minute flights, lifting off twice in a straight line and making 'one bad landing'. Four days later and he flew around the aerodrome for twenty minutes at 1,000 feet: 'bumpy' was his only logbook comment. After five hours' total flying time, he made an 'Attempt for ticket', but failed. 'Bad landing and off the mark,' he noted. A week later he tried again. 'Obtained ticket. Perfect evening,' resulting in an immediate move to Hounslow and the next stage of instruction.

Francis Mond's logbook reveals little – an occasional bumpy landing and twice the engine cut out, which must have been unnerving. The pilots were taught the dangers of flying: dive too steeply and the wings could be wrenched off; bank too steeply and the plane could drop into an irremediable tailspin; a loop would be fatal in many aircraft not built for the strain. There were many vital lessons to be learnt and all pilots listened attentively. Grinnell-Milne recollected:

> The whole business was unpleasantly suggestive of tight-rope walking, the margins of safety were so narrow. ... If you went too fast something fell off or snapped; if any slower you stalled, spun, dived, slipped one way or another and ended for a certainty breaking your neck. And then there was the question of the engine. At full power it was just enough to get one safely off the ground and to climb high enough for turning, but if you ran at too great a speed the engine would overheat, and at the slightest loss of power the nose of the machine had to be pushed well down to maintain flying-speed. A tricky business.

Throughout April, Francis's flight times gradually extended and altitude increased to 5,800 feet by mid-May. He moved from Hounslow to Dover, then onwards to the Central Flying School at Upavon, where pilots' knowledge of aeronautics and Morse code were tested. In early June, Francis successfully completed all exams, becoming a qualified pilot and flying officer. He was now entitled to wear the RFC badge and uniform, with the famous Wings sewn onto his tunic. He was officially detached from the Artillery and attached to the RFC.

In the beautiful early summer weather, Francis made several sorties over Larkhill, Tidworth and Bulford, as likely as not watching the daily infantry and artillery manoeuvres taking place across Salisbury Plain. In mid-June, he moved to Gosport in Hampshire, from where he was able to visit Greyfriars, his family's country home, where he dazzled all those assembled there. Francis looked every bit the hero pilot, as family friend Aldo Cippico remembered.

> That Summer was exceptionally fine. Day after day of warm blissful sunshine and cool scented breezes. Francis was at

Greyfriars, a fine-looking fellow, not tall but possessed of an easy grace of movement and gesture. With his deep china-blue eyes and his brand-new Royal Flying Corps uniform he was my constant envy. War had suddenly sobered him. ... Be that as it may, he was now a very romantic figure to us.

Perhaps Francis already knew that he was soon to embark for France and active service. His training finished, there was the opportunity to fly over Greyfriars, his parents' country home. From Gosport he flew to Chichester, Arundel, then Storrington, where, Aldo recalled, 'everyone rushed out to the lawn to wave excitedly'. From Storrington, Francis flew to Shoreham via Worthing, and then back over Storrington for a second 'visit'. 'He flew his Farman biplane over Greyfriars and then suddenly the machine gave up the ghost at the critical moment and his stick-and-canvas contraption belly-flopped down on an embankment in a nearby field.' The plane was wrecked. Fortunately, neither he nor his co-pilot, Lieutenant Wood, was injured.

A camera was sought, and pictures taken. It may have proved a little delicate to explain why he had 'belly-flopped' right outside his parents' house: eyebrows must have been raised back at Gosport, though he appears to have suffered no sanction. A week's further testing and final flights and he was ordered to leave for Folkestone on 23 June, crossing to Calais and entraining for St Omer, the headquarters of the RFC. A brief stop and Francis was posted to 'C' Flight, 16 Squadron, based at Chocques.

Grinnell-Milne would be posted to the same squadron as Francis, albeit nearly three months later. He recalled his arrival at the squadron as a new boy would at school: curious, nervous and ignored. 'There were a very few officers about and the one or two I met were strangely distant, offhand or unable to speak.' When he finally met his flight commander he was quizzed as to his flying experience, replying that he had done thirty-three and a half hours.

'How much?' he [the flight-commander] exclaimed, but he meant 'how little'. And he went on to declare violently that it was a disgrace to send pilots to a squadron on active service who did not have fifty, no, a hundred hours to their credit. What types had I flown? Longhorn? Of course, but that was no damn' use! Caudron? Good Lord – that was worse than nothing. Ah, so I had flown a B.E., had I? what sort of B.E.? Not the latest type, with the new undercarriage and the 90 horse-power engine? No? Well then – no good.

It is not unlikely that Francis was met with similar shocked incredulity for he had flown precisely the same aircraft and had even less flying time under his belt – just twenty-nine hours and forty-two minutes.

*   *   *

16 July: Richebourg St Vaast, FRANCE
Combat Report
Pilot 2nd Lt FL Mond and Observer Capt F.W.K. Davies
7.20 am
No 16 Squadron
Type: M.F.S. [Maurice Farman Shorthorn]
Number 5019
Armament 1 Lewis Gun & Thansen Automatic
Locality between Lavantie & Fromelles
Height 9,000ft
Duty: Patrol

D.F.W. [Reconnaissance] Machine, 2 seater. Machine gun. About 8,000ft flying S.S.W.

Towards Armentières, while patrolling the lines, we saw a machine coming along in the opposite direction over the enemy's side of the lines (we were on our own side). I turned and headed him off, and found he was an enemy machine. He then saw us and turned for home. We followed him over the lines and the observer opened fire, and we continued chasing him some five miles over the enemy's side of the lines until our ammunition was exhausted. He tried to put his nose down and was zig-zagging and firing back over the tail at us. We were fired at by anti-aircraft guns on recrossing the line.

While continuing patrol after engaging D.F.W., I noticed a hostile machine [Aviatik] being fired at towards Bethune. I turned from SW to NW to try and head him off. He then opened fire on us, and the observer replied with the gun, which finally jammed, whereupon I came down to 5,000ft and made towards Bethune, thereby shaking him off. The whole time he was being engaged by our anti-aircraft guns.

FL Mond 2nd Lt

In the top right-hand column of Francis Mond's logbook, under 'Remarks', there are four hand-drawn symbols. They provide an additional visual guide to his sorties over the Western Front. One symbol is a thick black dot, signifying that he had been assailed by anti-aircraft fire (or archies); a black dot in a circle denoted that he had been hit, probably by the same shell bursts. Crossed swords indicated aerial combat and, finally, the black shape of a bomb and a figure signified the number of munitions dropped over enemy lines. He wrote to his little sister May on 26 July:

I have been aloft nearly every day so far and the life out here is very exciting as you can guess. I will try and bring you home some interesting souvenir when I come back on leave. I expect to get about five days in another couple of months or so! I enclose a cutting from the 'Weekly Despatch', which you might give to Mother for me? It is a brief mention of my two fights with the Huns on the 16th. From the two places mentioned you can glean my <u>partial</u> whereabouts when I say they are on the lines facing us, and are the northern half of our own particular area. ... We are no longer in the chateau, but have moved [to Merville], and I am sleeping on straw in a loft! *'A la guerre comme a la guerre!'* which means, as you know, 'I <u>should</u> worry!'

Your loving brother
Francis

On every mission, Francis flew with either an officer observer, or, occasionally, with a member of the ground crew engineers. Taking an engineer 'up' ensured these skilled men worked to the best of their ability on the aircraft, in the knowledge that they themselves might be 'invited' for a ride.

After each sortie, Francis noted the nature of the mission – reconnaissance, photography, artillery registration – sometimes returning early owing to poor visibility or stormy weather, landing in a rainstorm. On his second flight he was 'After a Hun', and four days later, on patrol his 'First experience of "Archie"'. There were engine troubles, the 'hurried descent!' owing to an 'oil leak' and fire, a 'broken wire', a forced landing in French lines because of a 'vibrating engine', an unfortunate descent into a ditch. Spindles broke, bearings 'seized'. And then the missions: the artillery registration for the Meerut [Indian] Division; the attack on the 'supposed air-ship shed' at Haubourdin, the two bombs that missed and the third that 'did not come off' from the underside of the fuselage. An unreleased and primed bomb presented a very real danger when returning to the aerodrome: never was a smooth landing more required.

The pressure on these pilots was unrelenting. Very poor weather, with low, heavy cloud, would ground operations, but otherwise, Francis flew practically every day for a week or more and sometimes multiple sorties during one day. On 23 August, he records that he flew at 6.5 am, 11.40 am, 3.25 pm and again at 5.30 pm.

Francis was undoubtedly a brave and skilled pilot. By September 1915, he had clocked up ninety hours' flying experience, nearly sixty hours since joining his squadron. There is no indication of 'battle fatigue' or of frayed nerves.

6 September 1915, 16 Squadron Aerodrome

Francis Mond was up early. He was scheduled for a dawn reconnaissance flight over the French town of Hazebrouck with his observer, Lieutenant William Day. The morning was cloudy, not good for observation, but they took off anyway, climbing to 8,000 feet and headed east. The flight was not long: they returned after sixty-five minutes, the cloud too dense for photography. They would try again at 9.30 am.

The second flight was not successful either, but for different reasons. Their BE2c had climbed without a problem, but at 8,500 feet they suffered a technical hitch, a pressure pump failure that forced a return to the aerodrome and some hasty repairs before setting off again for the third time that morning. Now, at 11.30 am, shortly after takeoff, a magneto failure caused his BE2c to side-slip and then nosedive a hundred feet to the ground: both Mond and Day were extremely lucky to survive. The officers were bloodied and bruised but the machine was entirely wrecked: 'Exit BE2c 1731', Mond noted in his logbook – a jocular remark, though both men were severely shaken by the experience.

Ten days after the crash, Francis was sent to the 2nd London Clearing Hospital at Merville and then to the 14th General Hospital at Boulogne, where he stayed for a couple of days. On 19 September, he boarded a hospital ship, the *St Patrick*, bound for Southampton, from where he was taken to 10 Palace Green, Kensington, the Special Neurological Hospital for Officers. The hospital, a former private home, was opened in January 1915 for officers suffering from functional neurosis, traumatic neurasthenia and other psychoses.

Francis would not fly again for two years and he would not return to active service over the Western Front until March 1918.

Chapter Two

'One Hun came round from somewhere and started coming up under my tail – but he didn't get very far, as my observer, who regards this position of the machine as very private property, opened fire over the back at long range, and the Hun soon discontinued his attentions.'

Francis Mond, 57 Squadron, Royal Air Force,
letter 10 May 1918

27 March 1918
Hotel Folkestone, Boulogne-sur-Mer
Dear Mother
Here I am back in Boulogne again after over two years.

We lost no time getting over – train left at 7.40, and boat at 9.50.

We were escorted over, but three quarters of the way over, something went wrong with the steering gear of our ship, and we did a kind of crab crawl into harbour, being towed in at the finish by a tug!

There are several fellows I know very well – two from Marske [Auxiliary School of Aerial Gunnery in Yorkshire] – we three were all in Saltburn last Saturday and we are a very cheery crowd.

Of course, as yet we have no idea where we are going. We have just had a most <u>excellent</u> lunch here – white bread and meat (no capers!) and report again at 4.0 this afternoon, and I suppose we shall move up tonight.

It was so nice to have been able to see you last night, I'm afraid many people never even had a glimpse of their people!
Ever
Francis

With terribly conflicted emotions, Angela Mond had travelled to the coast to see her son one last time as he returned to active service and the Western Front. She would have grown used to his being back home, and grateful that he was spared the worst horrors of the fighting in the years since he returned to England with shell shock. The Battles of the Somme, Arras, Third Ypres, better known to posterity as the Battle of Passchendaele, had all come and gone, leaving their trail of misery for families at home.

Francis, for the most part, had been working in London, with a job at the Air Ministry, first at Adastral House and then in the requisitioned Cecil Hotel: a nice, secure living, albeit with long, hard days of paperwork. 'We get more and more work to do every day, and I don't finish until eight or even sometimes nearly nine o'clock at night now, and put in half Sundays as well!' he wrote to his sister in July 1917. This was a world away from the life-on-the-line living he had known. Such an existence probably appealed to some, grateful for the security, but the passivity grated on him.

It is hard to reconcile Francis's chatty, jovial letters to his family with the medical reports that he was suffering from neurasthenia. Francis appears to have returned to some of his pre-war exploits with ease, even making a reappearance in court on 30 October 1915 to answer a charge that he was not only speeding on the Epsom Road while on a motorbike, but, when stopped by the police, failing to produce a valid licence when asked. His desire for excitement was not altogether curtailed by a vertical drop from 100 feet.

His mental and physical condition was the subject of further medical board examinations in October and November 1915. In early December, he was sent to Norwich and 9 RAS where he undertook a week of short instructional flights. The first, just nine minutes in duration, he described as 'Very bumpy and unpleasant'. In all, he made fourteen flights, taking the controls in the old Maurice Farnham aircraft of his initial training days. Most of the flights were ten to fifteen minutes' duration, with only one trip lasting half an hour. This was a man with sixty hours' flying time, experience of aerial combat and bombing runs on the Western Front, yet it was like returning to cadet status. During these brief flights he would have been under close observation and may not have fared well, for on 3 January, the assembled medical experts agreed that 'He [was] not yet in a fit state for flying' but he was, they felt, fit for the 'duties of superintending the laying out of camps for aeronautical purposes'. On 6 January, he was ordered again to appear before a medical board. The notes of the meeting revealed that he was even now suffering 'considerably' from September's crash. While no bones had been broken at the time, he had 'suffered some contusions', the report noted. Francis was experiencing 'insomnia, headaches, restless[ness], depression, lack of confidence', though these symptoms were 'lessening'. Interestingly, the report ends noting that Francis was 'still under the influence of the shock and requires rest'.

The next day, and with this limited recommendation as to his working capabilities, Francis took charge of a draft of fifty air mechanics embarking for the Western Front and the RFC General Headquarters at St Omer. His orders were to hand over the draft and return on 'completion of duty'. This, as it turned out, did not include an immediate return to England. Instead he was given the menial but nonetheless important job of supervising road building, as he explained to his 11-year-old sister, May, in a letter.

Yes, road making does seem funny after flying … but you see, to strafe the Germans you want bombs; now bombs have to be kept in a safe place, because they make a nasty mess if they go off this side of the lines. So you have to select a good sheltered place for them [St Omer]. As this happened to be off the road, we have to join it up by building a new road.

At the end of January, Francis took two flights as a passenger in a BE2c accompanying a Second Lieutenant Patrick who took the plane to 3,000 feet, looping the loop three times. Francis, a man who was so thrilled by speed, is likely to have found this both exhilarating and a test of his still unstable nerves. He remained in France, overseeing improvements to 12 Squadron aircraft hangers. But by mid-February, he was on his way home and to a job at the Air Ministry in the Department of Aeronautical Supplies (a department later taken over by the Ministry of Munitions), where he remained for eighteen months. He flew just twice in that time, and on both occasions as a passenger.

Francis could have seen out the war in the Hotel Cecil, and there is some evidence that his parents encouraged him to do so. No one could accuse him of having shirked his responsibilities or having not done his 'bit' for King and Country. On 24 September, owing to a reorganisation in his department, Francis Mond left the Ministry and was 'placed at the Disposal of the Army council' and ordered to return to duty with the RFC. Even then, after vacating his Staff appointment, he was offered another job that would have kept him at home for the rest of the war, but turned it down. What courage, then, did it take for Francis to return to active service, submitting himself to the critical eye of instructors who would have to be certain of his recovery? He would need to learn new skills with aircraft considerably in advance of anything he had flown just two years before. He would also have to refresh his memory of aerial photography and absorb the technical improvements in the art of signalling from air to ground.

In mid-October, he arrived at Wyton aerodrome, 83 Squadron, to begin again. His time in the air varied – four minutes, ten minutes, five minutes, seventy-five minutes, rarely venturing above 3,000 feet – but as self-belief grew, he flew longer and higher, practising aerial photography once more. On 20 October, he added a personal note in the margin of his logbook: 'First Solo since 30.12.15'. Two days later, he was flying at 6,000 feet and for over two hours' duration.

By the time his squadron moved to Narborough in Norfolk, much of his old élan was returning, as a friend and fellow pilot noticed: 'Though he had been out of flying so long, he was not only a very good pilot but a very plucky one too, and was always looping and doing other stunts ...'

In all, he undertook over sixty-two hours of further training before being permitted to return to the Western Front. His last flight, at 9.35 am on 21 March at the School of Aerial Gunnery, was duly noted in his log. It was a twenty-minute flight at 2,000 feet, perfecting his camera skills between Marske and Saltburn on the Yorkshire coast.

This flight was taken just a few hours after the Germans had launched their great Spring Offensive. The Western Front dissolved that morning into chaos and crisis and, within days, it became clear to the Allies that the outcome of the entire conflict was now, seemingly, in the balance.

For the entirety of the war, the Germans had been fighting on two fronts, Eastern and Western. This divided campaign had proved militarily and politically exacting, so, since mid-1916, the Germans had fought on the defensive in the West while conducting a more aggressive offensive war against the Russians in the East. But with the Russian Revolution and the withdrawal of Russia from the war, the Germans had been able to move to the west vast numbers of battle-hardened troops. Spring was chosen by the Germans as their opportunity to break the deadlock of the Western Front, to use their numerical superiority to their advantage before America, an ally of the Allied powers since 6 April 1917, brought enough soldiers to the trenches to tip the balance irretrievably against Germany and her allies.

The German offensive had overwhelmed forward positions, smashing through British trench lines. Vast numbers of men and huge quantities of guns and ammunition were captured; some airfields were overrun within days, a number of Germans witnessing with evident surprise one plucky pilot making a dash for his aircraft just as enemy troops stormed the aerodrome. The British press placed the most advantageous spin on events but the journalists did not disguise the extent of the breakthrough, the public being seized by anxiety and foreboding. It was as the full scale of the crisis became apparent that Francis Mond was given immediate orders to return to France. It was in this sudden state of high apprehension that he said goodbye to his mother on 26 March, sailing for Boulogne. On 1 April, the Royal Flying Corps changed its name to the Royal Air Force, a matter of historical significance; at the time, a matter of minor interest in the light of prevailing battlefield traumas.

30 March: The Western Front
Dear Mother
Since my last letter from Boulogne, there has been nothing of interest to say.

Of course it is raining, and so rather miserable, but we are very cheery. I did not expect I should have to leave at such ridiculously short notice as I did, but I suppose they want all the pilots over here they can get hold of.

All the same, I have now been two days in the 'pool', waiting to be posted to a squadron, and as yet have no idea where I am going. Orders may come through any moment, however, and being only in a temporary camp – a very temporary one as regards arrangements for food and sleeping when we arrived! – I've not had my clothes off since Thursday morning, – being afraid to unpack all my valise – and it being very cold still all night …

Francis Mond would hear soon enough. In the week since the German offensive had begun, the RFC, in France alone, had lost seventy-six officer pilots killed and many more wounded or taken prisoner of war. In a twenty-four-hour period between 31 March and 1 April, one squadron, 57 Squadron, lost eight flying officers;

seven killed in action, and one taken prisoner of war. These were
grievous losses as even a full strength squadron had just eighteen
flying officers; excluding its commander. Over 40 per cent of his
pilots had been wiped out and would have to be made up quickly
from the 'pool' waiting at St Omer, and at least four aircraft were
lost too. Francis was ordered to leave immediately for the squadron.
Of the replacement officers sent to 57 Squadron in the first days
of April, four would be killed before Francis and a sixth killed five
days later; at least one other was wounded. Only one of the pilots
was aged over twenty-five.

4 April: Le Quesnoy. 'C' Flight, 57 Squadron, Royal Air Force
Dear Mother

Have arrived at last, or to be exact, yesterday evening, having
motored some 30 miles from the pool.

During the last week or so, I have done literally nothing, a
nothing with a big 'N', except eat, drink and sleep, and chafe
inwardly and outwardly at being sent over at twelve hours'
notice and then kept kicking my heels for a whole week doing
nothing – but I suppose it could not be helped.

Anyway, I am at last with a squadron – 57 – flying DH4s
with Rolls-Royce [engines] – quite one of the best machines
we have.

Our job is bombing, plus a little photography – but the
former is our *raison d'être*.

The aerodrome is terribly small and none too good, and we
are under canvas; it having rained pretty consistently for the
last three days, the camp is rapidly degenerating into a sea of
mud!

I can't, of course, say where we are [Le Quesnoy], but we are
a good way back from the lines in the open, somewhere north
of the Somme.

Today is completely 'dud', and Bridge is in full swing.

I spent the morning cutting up maps and pasting the strips required on boards for future use, and in going over the machine – the engine of which is new to me.

10 April

Dear Mother

I was so pleased to get your letter this morning – nearly a fortnight without any letters seems, and is, an age out here!

I have not been over the lines yet, as every day so far has been 'dud', although the last few days I have been detailed for a raid.

I have had a practice flight of just over an hour, during which we went to the coast, and passed over Berck! How many years is it since we were there, 15 – 20?! We also passed over Paris-Plage.

The machines and particularly the engines, are priceless, of course Rolls-Royces speak for themselves!

As I mentioned in my last letter, I am now installed in a billet, my own arrangements, however, as we are officially under canvas, and have quite a nice room with a bed, which is the great thing.

The family consists of Madame, who works on the farm, and always wears rather a preoccupied look – her husband is a prisoner in Germany, captured during the Battle of the Somme, her little five-year old son, Louis, and two old ladies – and lastly an uncle who is infirm – slightly paralysed down one side – and who sits all day in a chair and pulls at his moustache or smokes a somewhat battered pipe.

I have been showing Louis this afternoon – for it's dud again today, – how to tie a piece of card round a stone and twirl it up into the air – so far no broken windows!

They sell us eggs and vegetables, and are allowed to collect the swill from the camp for the pigs, one of which was killed the other day amid much hideous squealing.

The old ladies have been very upset the last day or two, because they are expecting the old cow to have a 'picaninni' every hour as far as I can make out, and pay numerous nocturnal visits to the said animal.

The spring is very late here – the trees are only just beginning to look feathery. However, a pair of chaffinches – or rather Mrs Chaffinch – are busily engaged in nesting operations in a place just outside my window.

By-the-way, one of our fellows out alone (with observer) the other day on photography fought five Huns, and brought down one, his machine being rather shot about – in fact he had to land on an aerodrome near the lines somewhere and have a few repairs made before continuing, and his observer was just grazed by a bullet. A good show, what?

The guns have been going very hard this morning in the distance, and as you see by the communiqué of last night, the centre of pressure has gravitated more to the north. In fact, I see that the Huns have been attacking exactly where I was with 16 Squadron in '15 – Neuve Chapelle, Fauquissant, Laventie and even Estaires is mentioned.

But as the French say – *'ils ne passeront pas'* ['they shall not pass'] – that's also what the old man in my billet asks me every day, and also when it's dud – *'pas partir aujourd hui?'* ['not going out today?']

I wonder if you would ask Philip [Francis's brother] to get me the following things?

1. A fountain pen. Swan – medium – thin nib – (not too thin!).
2. Packet of 'Browns' toilet paper.
3. 3 or 4 new 6/- novels – (not sea or historical stories).
4. A bottle of Uncle Carlo hair oil (with grease!) from Hill's, in Bond Street.

That's all for the moment I think.

So goodbye … My best love to everyone.

Ever Francis
P.S. I'm as fit as a fiddle.

LOG BOOK
11/4/18 3.25 pm DH4 A7645. Observer: Lt [George] Eastwood. 135 [minutes]. Height 15,000.
1st Bomb Raid. Objective – Billets at Favreuil, Beugnâtre, & Sapingnies, nr B. 12–25lbs bombs

12/4/18 6.50 am DH4 A7645. Observer Lt [William] Winter. 130 [minutes] Height 15,000.
2nd Bomb Raid. Roads round Bapaume. 1–112lbs bombs.
11.45 am DH4 A7645. Observer Lt Winter. 100 [minutes] Height 15,000.
3rd Bomb Raid. Roads round Bapaume 2 -112lbs bombs.
3.40 pm DH4 A7645. Observer Lt Winter. 150 [minutes]. Height 15,000.
4th Bomb Raid. Roads around Bapaume 2–112lbs bombs.

13/4/18 7.0 am. DH4 A7645. Observer Lt Winter. 115 [minutes]. Height 15,000.
5th Bomb Raid. Half formation crossed lines over clouds (4 mc/s). Between Bapaume & Cambrai 2–112lbs bombs. Landed empty aerodrome nr Fruyelles (mist) nr Abbeville.

13/4/18
Dear Mother …
We've been more than usually busy during this short spell of fine weather.
I've not had a shave even for three days!!
Unfortunately, I can't give you all the details I should like to.
I've done 5 bomb raids since the afternoon of the day before yesterday – one Thursday afternoon, three yesterday (I think this must be somewhere near a record for the squadron) – one of

which was before breakfast, one before lunch, and one in the afternoon – and another raid this morning.

In the five raids, I have dropped over a thousand pounds of bombs, flying at 15,000ft each time over the lines.

Archie was normal to very poor in four of the raids and we weren't attacked by Huns at all – in fact only saw about 5 a long way below us.

This morning the weather was none too good when we started, and when we got well up, there was an impenetrable blanket of clouds stretching from this side of the lines back East.

Half the formation washed out and went down, but four of us went over – a good long way over to ensure our bombs dropping behind the Hun's lines – and laid our eggs through the clouds. Of course we didn't know what we hit, the ground being completely hidden from view. I think it must be rather unpleasant though, to have bombs suddenly come down through the clouds from nowhere, no machines visible or possibly even audible!!!

So far, so good. But on the way back, we found the weather had become absolutely hopeless. The machines lost touch with each other – I hung on to the leader, having no notion where I was, except that I <u>was</u> <u>W</u> of the lines! – until we came to a main road I know very well.

The leader went a bit off the track home, so I left him and started flying along this road, until I found myself getting into a thick mist at 200 feet from the ground.

I didn't think it good enough to risk going on, as if it developed into a ground mist further on – as it did in parts – it meant a crash in the end for a certainty! So I turned back and landed on an aerodrome we had just passed alongside the road, to find it was empty of all life except a couple of carpenters who were acting as caretakers – although there were a number of tents up (for ncos and personnel)!!!

The next thing to do was to try and telephone the squadron that we were down safely – I had dropped our bombs – but of course there was no telephone anywhere near.

So I stopped a staff car, and got a lift to the nearest town to our aerodrome here – some 20km from where I landed, and got a side-car from there to here.

The C.O. was very relieved, I think, to see us back – two of the other machines landed as I arrived, having been flying round completely lost all the time I'd been down – about an hour and half – I believe they did land somewhere else too.

Anyhow we all got down, and they seemed quite pleased we dropped our bombs.

I then went back in a tender to fetch my wretched observer, who had remained with the machine – and took my rigger and fitter and petrol etc, shoved the machine in one of the empty tents, came back – lunch, a shave, and here I am writing to you!!!

Some morning, though! Formation flying is not too easy, it depends to a great extent on how good your engine is – but practice makes a lot of difference. It is, of course, most important to keep formation, for stragglers are often picked off by eager and hungry Huns hovering in the rear waiting their opportunity.

The only trouble is that coming down – even slowly – the change of pressure makes itself felt, and your ears buzz most annoyingly – in fact mine have been so doing continuously since Thursday evening! The gramophone sounds like nothing on earth! (of course it goes nearly all day and at every meal, – from the Bing Boys to Price Tsar!)

All the same, the C.O. told us yesterday we should have to work extra hard for a few days, and that the work we were doing was important and good. And naturally, one would do ten raids a day if it were humanly possible.

In the close-knit community of the squadron, every new officer filled the seat of another departed, transferred to another squadron, perhaps, wounded maybe, but just as likely dead, shot down in action. An uncontrolled descent was highly likely the end for both pilot and observer when there was no parachute to turn to. If the engine caught fire, then death would be grizzly save for a sudden leap from the aircraft or a self-inflicted revolver shot: an enemy machine-gun bullet was by far the most preferable end. The pilots and observers of the Royal Air Force returned after each sortie to a strange normality, to beds, sit-down dinners, and coffee served in the mess. And then at short notice a return to the air, life once more placed in the balance, and new empty chairs.

As officers departed, so new ones arrived. On 21 April, Lieutenant Edgar Martyn turned up, twenty-five years old, a one-time railway contractor from Ontario, Canada, and a former infantry officer of the 19th Canadian Battalion. He was officially an 'Observer on Probation', perhaps a slightly disconcerting title for such a vital job, but with Francis Mond he would find an excellent pilot with whom he could work when the time came.

In the pressure cooker world of the squadron, when friends, most in their late teens or early twenties, could be dead the next day, life was lived to the full, enjoyment and frivolity grabbed with both hands.

On 24 and 25 April, the squadron made the most of the officers' homespun entertainment, as Francis described with obvious glee in a letter. The weather had turned, low clouds were accompanied by thunder and rain and all flying was suspended.

The frivolity came two nights after the weather had turned for the worse and the last flight for two or three days had been made by 57 Squadron, though it was hard to accurately predict the weather. It had been an evening raid, made from 11,000 feet, with a number of bombs dropped on the Somme town of Bapaume, seeking out, amongst other things, ammunition dumps. There had been a great deal of anti-aircraft fire and the squadron's planes had been chased over the lines by a number of enemy aircraft. Francis wrote in his logbook, 'One machine badly hit in [the] sump, and burst into flames while landing. Observer burnt, pilot died.' The dead were dead, the living carried on with new mess seats to fill. The fate of short-lived comrades was a matter of a passing note in letters home, though the emotional turmoil felt by these young pilots, suppressed at the time, affected their lives for years, if they themselves were fortunate enough to survive. In Francis's logbook, the intensity of the fighting can be seen in his notations: in almost every flight he was assailed by anti-aircraft fire and on at least two occasions, his plane was hit by shell bursts.

25/4/1918

Dear Mother

I was delighted to get your long letter, and very glad you are as cheerful as you can be under the circumstances – it is perhaps hard to be so – but is, after all, the only thing to be.

I know you must be anxious too, but I have absolute faith in my safe return to you all, and I know you would not have things otherwise, particularly during the present crises. It is, I think, an honour to be able to take an active part in the show at the present moment. I have never regretted that I elected to return to flying again, although there have been moments when I have thought it rather a foolish decision from a personal point of view!!! However, no mock heroics! ...

I must here tell you that we have sometimes at meals – prompted by the gramophone – the bitterest arguments about music – Puccini vs Wagner and the rest – and Chin-Chin-Chow versus everything else etc etc.

The Puccini enthusiast is very far gone, and quite unconvertible to Wagner or the Russian operas, with the late Debussy being my choice, in which I am gallantly upheld by a most worthy Anglo-Australian.

Last night, after an impromptu accompaniment (Beware of Chin-Chin-Chow) on all available tin plates and glasses, everyone made themselves up with burnt cork, much to the general amusement – I looked very fierce with a Brigand Moustachio, applied by the above means and the aid of a silver cigarette case! Tonight, the weather having turned dud (it's thundering now) we are having a fancy dress dinner – most people only seem able to make up a pair of silk stockings – but personally, I shall stick to my brigand-chief – perhaps 'Captain Hook'.

By the way, I have now dropped over a ton of bombs on Hunland, and done about twenty-two hours in the air in this Squadron – comprising eleven bomb raids (in 3 weeks, of which about 10 days have been flyable). For the second time I did three raids in one day – last Sunday, the 21st.

In a raid the day before [20th] we caused an enormous explosion, and numerous fires, and on Sunday on one of the raids, two were very big explosions, visible long after we had re-crossed the lines.

On one of those three, I was trying to clear a blockage on my Vickers gun, which I had been testing (by firing into space over the lines) – this was just on the turnback – when two archies burst very uncomfortably near – rather unexpected!

On another [over Bapaume], my engine cut out completely, picked up a bit, spluttered, and finally stopped dead! I immediately turned west, and started gliding down, with visions of scraping over front line trenches and crashing in a shell hole – as we would, I think, have been able to make the lines.

Then it suddenly dawned on me that I had not changed over petrol tanks (we have two main ones on these machines), and that we had run dry on the one tank! – entirely my own fault, and she picked up again ok as soon as I turned on the other tank, and I dived and caught up the formation again.

But it put the breeze up my observer [Lt Winter] and self for the moment!!

The evening before last, about six o'clock, it was decided to have a raid [over Bapaume] (it had been a dud all day).

As there was hardly sufficient time to get up to our usual height [15,000 feet] before going over, we crossed at four thousand feet below the usual one and got archied like stink all the time.

There were clouds just above us, on which Archie could range to perfection.

You never saw such dodging, – side-slipping, diving, banking, climbing – but always keeping formation.

It was very exhilarating, and at times, when archie burst so close, in addition to the 'woof, woof' of the explosion, you could hear the s-s-ss-sss-s of bits scattering through the air above the roar of your engine – well, rather <u>too</u> exhilarating!!

However, we all laid our eggs and got back to the aerodrome, when we had rather a distressing accident.

One machine suddenly burst into flames at about 50 feet from the ground and dived head foremost into it. The observer [2nd Lt Charles Souchotte] was apparently knocked unconscious by his gun, and unable to get out – and burnt to death. The pilot [Lt William Townsend], pluckily extricated by our RAMC orderly and a mechanic, was apparently dead when pulled out, but regained breathing on artificial respiration being applied, only to die on admission to hospital a quarter of an hour later.

Poor devils, it appears they had a huge chunk of archie through the engine sump, and that consequently all the oil had come out – the pilot had apparently been trying to get home with what must have finally been a seized-up engine, – only to crash right over the aerodrome. (Also, we – six machines – were followed back to the lines by about 20 Huns on this raid – but they were too far behind us to do any real fighting – although our observers were shooting back at them to show we were awake!)

We had a bit of archie clean through one of our planes – but nothing to hurt at all – (it was my flight commander's machine too!!) – borrowed for the occasion, mine having its oil changed at the time, as it had been dud all day up to then).

All these things are in the day's work, though, and I beg of you not to take too much notice of them – crashes, archie and the like. I only tell you of them in order to give you as true and as comprehensive an account of my time out here as I can.

And on the other hand, you will have seen by now that we have downed old man Richthofen at last. In fact, from all accounts, experience, and captured evidence, we have certainly got one up on the Hun in the air, and he is a bit demoralised.

Exactly how far air supremacy will affect the ultimate general issue of the war remains to be seen, however.

28/4/18

Dear Mother

Nothing of any interest or importance has occurred here since last I wrote you. The weather has been quite hopeless from a flying standpoint – low clouds, thunder and rain and I have not left the ground at all.

We had our fancy dress dinner that night. I went as 'Captain Hook', from 'Peter Pan' – all moustache and bloody knife. A red jersey (football), bandana handkerchief, fisherman's cap (red and blue rings), flying boots turned over at the top, eye-patch and revolver, not to mention a fearsome carving knife obtained from the kitchen, formed my costume – and last a hook, manufactured in the workshop in a quarter of an hour – bit of a bully-beef tin and a bit of iron. You put your hand inside the tin, having pulled your sleeve over the top of it, grip the projecting end of the hook inside the tin, et voila!!

It was quite a success!

The company which sat down to dinner in our marquee, to the strains of music produced by a violin and <u>the</u> most appalling piano you ever did hear – but none the less enjoyable, – be it said – consisted of d'Artagnan, the doughty Musketeer (my flight commander – who is very short – and who had raked out a wonderful hat and feathers and a sword twice as long as himself from the chateau he is billeted in, – Chin-Chin-Chow of China, – an Indian squaw – a Graeco-Roman complete with toga, two utterly impossible females, and the inevitable assortment of minstrels (and a heterogeneous collection of lord-only-knows-what).

And after the repast, we journeyed in sundry conveyances to a neighbouring squadron, where high revels were held – including national and irrational dances, and much 'for he's a jolly good fellow'-ing, until we took our departure amid volleys of Very lights!

[Today] nearly everyone has gone to the same squadron to play rugger. I was going, but am taking the opportunity to write and attend to various things I have to do.

Have just been having coffee (tea-time) with the French people in the farm next to mine. (We all go there for breakfast when we are too late to get any in the Mess, and use it for writing and cards.) We have been having a most amusing, and for me, a highly instructive argument about everything imaginable. It certainly pays to be able to talk the language – in fact it makes all the difference.

Well so long for the present.

Francis

The fancy dress party came just twenty-four hours after the sobering deaths of two of 57 Squadron's pilots. Assuming all the officers of the squadron attended the party, more than a third of the revellers would be dead within four weeks, including Francis and his observer, Edgar Martyn.

LOG BOOK

3/5/18 7.05 am. DH4 A7645. Observer Lt Martyn. 125 [minutes]. Height 14,000.

13th Bomb Raid. 2–112lbs Bapaume. Lot of Archie (fuselage [hit]).

6/5/18

Dear Mother and Father

We have had a long spell of bad weather – always low clouds, and yesterday quite a bit of rain, and thunder again.

But during the fine spells we have been busy. I did a raid on the 2nd and two more on the third, in one of which we got a bit of archie through our fuselage. …

The last two days I have been detailed for photography, which is a bit of a 'move up' as only two or three machines go out on photos a day – all the rest do bombing.

On photos you go very high, as high as you can – 18,000 feet or so, as you are entirely on your own, and don't want to be bothered too much by Huns or by 'archie'.

It is a more interesting job than bombing, and you are on your own as I said, and don't get that tedious and really rather trying climb in formation, or trying to keep formation! …

I have got the oxygen apparatus working on my machine now, and always use it over thirteen thousand. It saves a headache and coincidentally one's lungs, I suppose.

I have done away with the beautiful mask and nozzle they provide, and have just a small bit of rubber tubing in the end of the flexible wire one, which I bite on and so regulate (in addition to the pressure regulator at the side).

My machine, as you know, is a DH4 – de Havilland no 4 – built by the Aircraft Manufacturing Co., in which Father has shares – de Havilland senior is their designer. …

The engine is a 275 h.p. Rolls-Royce, and is going beautifully. Each flight in a Squadron has a distinctive marking, and each machine is numbered.

In our case one flight has had its machine numbered in Roman numerals, another in ordinary numerals, and we have ours lettered.

My machine is 'C' and is called Caesar – painted on the radiator shutters in front. 'B' is Brutus & 'A' 'Anthony'.

I thought about changing mine to 'Cleopatra' but Anthony's owner wouldn't have it at any price! – and also C-A-E-S-A-R just fits in; one letter to each shutter – (as do Brutus and Anthony) and last but not least, I wouldn't change the name of my machine at all – 'Caesar' is doing very well!

'E' & 'F'' [flight], by the way, are nameless (and always being crashed) but 'D', Lord only knows why, is called 'Dean Swift'!!!

Spring has come here at last, very late. The fruit trees in the orchards are only just beginning to blossom. There are lots of birds here – more than I would have believed for France, – all in the little oases of trees and villages which dot an otherwise undulating agricultural district.

And don't laugh! I have taken to bird-watching and find my old interest has not evaporated one iota. Three of us are having a competition as to who can get the most species. At present I am four up with Magpie, Carrion Crow, Blackbird, Hedge Sparrow, Yellow Hammer and Chaffinch. Of course the Swallows have arrived – and the Cuckoo – about ten days ago.

This pastime keeps one very fit with the long walks it entails, and provides a welcome change from the eternal poker.

This afternoon is still dud – and no chance of getting up for photos and another squadron is coming over to play us at footer.

So cheerio for the present. My very best love to each and every one of you. Ever, Francis

LOG BOOK

8/5/18 10.50 am DH4 A/7645. Observer Lt Martyn. 195 [minutes].

Height 15,000. Photography. Too cloudy. landed at Arienne (French aerodrome).

8/5/18 3.45 pm DH4 A/7645. Observer Lt Martyn. 150 [minutes]. Height 16,200. Photography. Camera not ok. Crossed lines as far as Bapaume. Observation Patrol round Arras for ½ hour.

Joined SE5 formation for a bit – crashed on landing – (not bad).

9/5/18 2.0 pm DH4 A/8070. Observer Lt Martyn. 110 [minutes]. Height 14,000.

15th Bomb Raid 12–25lbs on Bapaume, and hit a dump – 3 explosions.

[No time given] DH4 D/8377 Observer Lt Martyn. 150 [minutes]. Height 13,000. 16th Bomb Raid. 12–25lbs on Bapaume. Observer engaged one E[nemy] A[ircraft] at about 800 yards, which turned off. 8 EA attacked formation.

10th May

Dear Mother …

Today is going to be dud, I think. We were up at 5.30 am for a raid – quite nice then – but it came over bad almost immediately – that's the worst part – getting up early and then no show!

The day before yesterday I went up for photos – and did nearly six hours continual flying – a break for a late and very cold lunch half way through – but the first time it was too cloudy to take any, and the second time, although we had started to take, the camera was against us.

As we had climbed all the way up, it seemed a pity to come down at once, so I pottered about over the lines for a bit looking for Huns, and joined some scouts looking for trouble for a short while.

There was nothing doing, however!

Perhaps as well, as yesterday two of our machines up on photos were attacked – separately – by about a dozen Huns – and well strafed.

Both crashed on arriving back here, one not badly [Lt Conrad Powell], but the other, the pilot of which had apparently been wounded, and fainted 50 feet from the ground, with some of his controls shot away – crashed badly and the airman observer [Lt Richard Rumsby], died almost at once from a knock on the head from his gun-mounting – very bad luck indeed. The pilot [2/Lt Louis Weiner], however, though a bit smashed up, is very cheery and will be all right in time. [Second Lieutenant Weiner was killed in action one week before the Armistice.]

I took part yesterday in two bombs raids, both between lunch and dinner, in which we caused three large explosions, and I have reason to believe, from what my observer tells me, our machine was responsible for one of them!

On the way back from the other one, we were attacked by some Huns – but our machine was not in the part of the formation they went for – (I was flying another machine, whose engine was not too satisfactory, and was a bit low, under the front of the formation (and so completely safe).

However, one Hun came round from somewhere and started coming up under my tail – but he didn't get very far, as my observer, who regards this position of the machine as very private property, opened fire over the back at long range, and the Hun soon discontinued his attentions – without firing at us at all, as far as I could see. (He was too far off to do any damage – about 800 yards or so.)

Altogether, yesterday was a fairly exciting one!

My work to date is nearly 40 hours flying (37 hrs 42 mins), and over 1½ tons of bombs delivered in sixteen raids.

'Caesar' met with a slight mishap the day before yesterday on landing after the second photo show – undercarriage, radiator, and the two bottom panels went west – but she will be ok again tomorrow I hope. This was due to a very slight misjudgement when just about to touch the ground – due,

I believe, to one's sense of distance and judgement generally being a bit affected by being up at 16,000 feet for a long time – as I generally make quite decent landings.

Anyhow, it was nothing to worry about, except that it meant extra work for the flight – which is always to be deplored.

I had to 'borrow' machines yesterday – but tomorrow should see 'Caesar' flying again.

Well, I think that's all the news for today.

My best love to all of you. Ever, Francis.

LOG BOOK

10/5/18 3.55 pm DH4 D/8377. Observer Lt Martyn. 120 [minutes]. Height 12,500.

17th Bomb Raid. 12–25lbs on Bapaume with camera. Engine very dud. Spun down 500 ft over Bapaume avoiding another m/c's bombs. 13 explosions.

11/5/18 2.40 pm. DH4 A/7645. Passenger Air Mechanic Lockead. 10 [minutes]. Height 900. Rigging test. Aerodrome. OK.

The weather had cleared just enough on the afternoon of 10 May and Francis flew, dropping twelve bombs while also taking a number of reconnaissance photographs. The next day, *Caesar* (A7645) was returned, fixed, and Francis spent the day testing the rigging before flying for ten minutes around the aerodrome. The weather remained poor and his next flight was postponed until 15 May. It was to be Francis's eighteenth 'Bomb Raid'.

14 May, Grey Friars, Storrington

My dear Francis

Your letter of the 10th arrived already yesterday, together with your letter to Mother. We were very pleased to receive good news from you and they contributed largely to make my [53rd] birthday a happy one. Mother gave me a magnificent fountain pen, which I am trying on you now. ...

I am glad that you manage to keep fit, notwithstanding your very strenuous work and hope that you are not overdoing it. But I quite imagine that they work you fellows for all you are worth. Everybody realises what significant work the R.A.F. is doing and the results are really most satisfactory.

[It's] a good thing they supply you with an oxygen apparatus nowadays. It must make all the difference. I was most interested in your description of Caesar and hope he has by now completely recovered from his little mishap and that he will behave well in future. I have sent you a case of port wine about a fortnight ago and when you get it I want you to drink Caesar's health. …

Mother got a cold about a week ago but she seems to be getting over it all right. I must say the weather is very trying. The Spring seems to have come most reluctantly this year and it is mostly cold and windy. Still the countryside begins to look beautiful. The young green is out and the swallows in my porch are chirping most noisily whilst I write in my study. I was so amused to hear about your old interest in birds nesting. Keep it up, old man. The more hobbies one has in life, the better. …

Well, *ave Caesar*. All send you their very best love.

Your affectionate father.

* * *

Shortly after 9.00 am on 15 May 1918, twelve aircraft belonging to 57 Squadron, Royal Air Force, took off from Le Quesnoy aerodrome. Their objective: a raid on supply dumps near Bapaume. Over a hundred bombs were dropped and photographs taken, but on the return journey, two planes were destroyed. The first, a DH4, flown by 20-year-old 2nd Lieutenant Hubert Crabbe, came down behind German lines, killing both Crabbe and his 19-year-old observer, Lieutenant Edward Piper. The second, also a DH4, became involved in a dogfight near the enemy-held village of Le Hamel and was seen to crash between the opposing front lines.

It was *Caesar*, flown by Captain Francis Mond. Both Francis and his observer, Edgar Martyn, were killed instantly. The wreckage and the bodies lay close to trenches held by the men of 31st Battalion, Australian Imperial Force (AIF), and its commanding officer, Lieutenant Colonel Neil Freeman.

Chapter Three

'It should be borne in mind that on the termination of hostilities the nation will demand an account from the Government as to the steps which have been taken to mark and classify the burial places of the dead, steps which can only be effectively taken at, or soon after, burial.'

General Douglas Haig, Commander-in-Chief, First Army, letter to the War Office, March 1915.

The dead would be fêted after the Great War. As distinct from conflicts in the past, it was impossible to ignore either their vast numbers or the world from which they were drawn. The majority of those who fought and died were civilians in spirit – volunteers or soldiers conscripted through national emergency. They were conveyed from all corners of the country and the empire, recruited from every conceivable occupation and every social class. General Douglas Haig's appreciation of the requirement for proper burial and classification was prescient; he understood that the nation would 'demand an account' because the bill so many families had paid, and would continue to pay, could not be reconciled by the pageant of ultimate success, emotional devastation assuaged through the warm afterglow of victory.

The professional, regular troops who marched to war in 1914 thought or cared little themselves of how they might be commemorated, let alone had any anticipation that in the fullness of time, a grateful nation might design beautiful cemeteries with dedicated, individual graves for the fallen. For the generations who had marched before, death was an occupational hazard, feared less than its manner. When a soldier fell on the battlefield, his name was noted without ceremony by the regimental sergeant major in the unit muster roll, and that pretty much was that.

If a son or husband failed to return from the Battle of Waterloo, there was no grave to visit. The news of death was passed on by the regiment or by word of mouth, not circulated from a consolidated roll or centralised army list. The dead were disposed of anonymously and battlefield clearance after combat was rudimentary: thirty or forty bodies at a time rolled into pits by paid civilians, their work overseen by an army officer who made a cursory attempt at identification. When the work proved overwhelming, funeral pyres were built to help clear the corpses and avoid the spread of disease, a genuine risk under a hot June sun in 1815. There was little sentiment for the dead, some of whose bones were later ground down for fertiliser, teeth extracted from skulls to make dentures.

Waterloo did prove to be something of a watershed event in the public's attitude towards the army. Napoleon, Europe's greatest threat to peace and stability, had been removed in a single cataclysmic feat of arms. The stoic, patriotic courage shown by British soldiers elevated their collective status, even if individually they remained the 'scum of the earth' (Wellington's words). Forty years later, the Crimean War witnessed a further change, with 139 cemeteries established, though the graves were marked in the main only by individual family payment. Even so, the government's belief was that a soldier's death remained the responsibility of the army, while the army viewed it not as their issue but that of the dead soldier's family. Those dead whose graves were not purchased by the family were still rolled into common burial places; effectively a pauper's grave, and hardly different from how bodies were treated in civilian life.

The care for these Crimean cemeteries was placed under a newly created government department, the Office of Works, though there was no proper long-term preservation of them, a point made during consideration of cemetery maintenance after the Great

War. Towards the end of the war in 1855, the Turkish government, then an ally of Britain's, gave a cemetery for the burial of almost 6,000 British troops, the majority of whom died during a cholera epidemic. In this, the Haidar Pasha Cemetery, there is only a granite obelisk to mark their collective resting place, though at least this was paid for by the British government.

While a soldier's burial place remained problematic, there had been a discernible shift to civic pride in the army's exploits, reflected in the growth of public memorials to the fallen in the second half of the nineteenth century. The Maiwand Lion in Reading, erected in 1884, is one such example: it commemorates by name all 329 men of the 66th (Berkshire) Regiment of Foot who died in the Second Afghan War, 1879–81. More memorials appeared after the Second Boer War, 1899–1902, when once again, ordinary rank and file soldiers were remembered on plinths in towns such as Bristol, Manchester and Hull, this last tribute paid for by local public subscription. These memorials offered the families of the fallen a place of mourning when the dead – and 24,000 had died in South Africa – were so far from home.

For the first time, the British Army took a greater roll in the administration of the dead. In the last year of the Boer War, the Royal Engineers were asked to record the individual burial places of those who fell in battle or who succumbed to disease, though the army steered clear of any formal responsibility for tending the graves. To help fill the void, the Guild of Loyal Women was formed in South Africa, a voluntary non-political organisation, though loyal to the British Crown, which took up the work of compiling registers of soldiers' names and the places where they were buried. This organisation would oversee the erection of simple cast iron grave markers over soldiers' graves for those families that could not afford a private memorial. 'For Queen [or King] and Empire' were the words on plaques attached to each cemetery cross, with the name of the casualty and a date of death. Upkeep of cemeteries that were dispersed over a wide area was well beyond the care of this organisation, though it had over 3,000 members at its height, and in time, many cemeteries, like those of the Crimea, became neglected.

The idea that a body should have a recognised resting place had been established, however rudimentary the burial plot and subsequent care. The Great War would push the work of caring for the dead much further down the track, not only with named graves for individual soldiers, but graves that established the concept of equality of treatment, graves cared for by public funds and in posterity. Much of the groundwork for this advance was owed to the clear-sighted determination of one man, Fabian Ware, though his ideas were hardly derived from the ether. Between 1901 and 1905, Ware and his wife had lived in South Africa, where he was undoubtedly aware of and influenced by the dedicated work of the Guild of Loyal Women.

Aged forty-five in August 1914, Fabian Ware, the dynamic former editor of the imperialist *Morning Post*, was too old to enlist. Instead, with a number of other members of London's Royal Automobile Club, he responded to an appeal made by the War Office to travel to France in their private cars in order to look for British soldiers, stragglers – often wounded stragglers – separated from their units during the army's epic retreat from the Belgian town of Mons. This motley civilian cavalcade, which included Clement Cazalet, a tennis medal winner from the 1908 Olympics, drove to the continent and began their search in September. It soon became clear that stragglers, if they existed, were inaccessible behind enemy lines, hiding in barns, villages and woods. Rather than simply going home, Fabian Ware and his friends offered their services to the British Red Cross Society in Amiens and Paris, successfully ferrying the wounded to Dressing Stations.

In October, Ware and his autonomous group were officially recognised as Ware's Mobile Unit of the British Red Cross Society, and an additional number of touring cars and motor ambulances were assigned to it. It was while ferrying the wounded for medical treatment that the unit began to identify and make note of isolated

British graves, Cazalet writing the unit's first report (10–14 October) describing what he had seen as he drove from Amiens to Compiègne and onwards to Soissons. Ware would write:

> The experience gained in the search for British wounded, [had] helped the Unit in taking up another most useful piece of work viz the identification of places in which British killed have been hastily buried, and the placing of crosses on the spots thus identified, with inscriptions designed [details painted on the reverse of the cross] to preserve the rough [pencilled] records which in many cases are already in danger of being obliterated.

Ware's Mobile Unit grew: by Christmas it had around thirty vehicles and fifty to sixty personnel. Grave registration was expanded and as cemeteries proliferated, so a process began whereby the particulars of the dead were at first stenciled then later stamped onto aluminium tags and fixed to each soldier's wooden cross. In addition, an attached brass plate bore the information that the crosses had been erected by the Mobile Unit of the British Red Cross Society, to protect and preserve the details found at each spot. One of the earliest cemeteries, begun near the old prison in Ypres, was named 'Broadley's Cemetery', after the sterling work undertaken there by one of the unit's civilian volunteers.

The public at home was already flagging up its concern that graves should not be neglected. On 9 January 1915, in a letter to *The Times*, an unnamed lady was reported to have visited France in order to find the grave of her brother.

> Comrades in his regiment had given her particulars of the exact locality and even described the temporary wooden cross and its inscription, erected over the grave. She found the place, where quite a number of victims had been interred, but every trace of the identifying crosses or other marks had disappeared. I will not dwell on the distress of our friend.

The unit's diligent work came to the attention of General Nevil Macready, the BEF's adjutant general. On 2 March 1915, he gave it a more permanent standing and a new title: the Graves Registration Commission (GRC), with Ware given the rank of honorary major, and Cazalet the rank of honorary captain. On 9 March, the first Graves Registration Unit (GRU) was established in the French town of Béthune, with clerks and drivers. A second unit was begun at the end of March and work was started on systematically combing the conflict's early battlefields of the Aisne and Marne for the dead. Another unit was created in June to scour the Lines of Communication, and additional GRUs were gradually established, including on the Somme in the summer of 1915, when the British in widening their commitment to the war effort took over ground relinquished by the French. As part of the GRC's expanding role, a Photographic Branch was formed, allowing grieving families to apply for an image of a grave.

In October 1915, the GRC was formally taken over by the army. Most of the existing personnel were enlisted and further recruits to the units were obtained from army sources and vehicles provided from the Mechanical Transport Section of the Army Service Corps. In March 1916, the GRC developed into the DGR&E (Directorate of Graves Registration and Enquiries). The army would continue to bury the dead, but the DGR&E was now made fully responsible for recording burial details and locations.

The work of the DGR&E was extremely important for morale, as Douglas Haig, the Commander-in-Chief, made clear in March 1916:

> It is fully recognised that the work of this organisation is of a purely sentimental value, and that it does not directly contribute to the successful termination of the war. It has, however, an extraordinary moral value to the Troops in the Field as well as to the relatives and friends of the dead, at home. The mere fact that these officers visit day after day, the

cemeteries close behind the trenches, fully exposed to shell and rifle fire, accurately to record not only the names of the dead but also the exact place of burial, has a symbolical value to the men that it would be difficult to exaggerate.

Although bodies were buried by the army, there was no formal oversight of the committal practice. There were rules as to where the dead could be buried: no nearer than X from a village, no closer than Y to fresh water. Nevertheless, it was felt that a formal supervisory role was needed and so both Corps and Divisional Burial Officers were appointed to oversee army burials and to liaise with the DGR&E. Divisional Burial Officers worked in conjunction with officers from infantry battalions appointed to manage the burial of the dead and a high degree of co-operation and standardised practice was developed. As one officer, Lieutenant Knee, wrote in August 1916:

Orders had been given that we were to take from their pockets pay books and personal effects, such as money, watches, rings, photos, letters and so on, one identification disk had also to be removed, the other being left on the body. Boots were supposed to be removed, if possible, as salvage was the order of the day. A small white bag was provided for each man's effects, the neck of which was to be securely tied and his identity disc attached thereto.

From the war's earliest days, Ware had been struck by the care local people had given to isolated graves. 'With very few exceptions the graves which we have seen up to the present are beautifully made and kept,' he wrote. 'The personal interest will cause many relatives to hesitate after the war before removing them.' This may have been Ware's fervent hope, though it was not always the case.

In early 1915, the army became aware that a small number of families had not hesitated at all; quite the contrary. Around forty sets of remains had been privately removed from the Western Front by grieving wealthy families. One, the body of the grandson of four times Prime Minister William Ewart Gladstone, had been returned to Wales and the family vault, accompanied by considerable newspaper and newsreel attention. It was clear that such a privilege could not be permitted for a minority when everyone else remained overseas, at least for now, so the army prohibited the wartime removal of any further remains from the Western Front. It left a final decision over whether to repatriate bodies to another day, although behind the scenes it would be apparent to those who looked carefully that there was little appetite for what would be a costly and complex enterprise. Three years later, after the Armistice, the decision to forbid exhumations was extended into eternity, much to the anger of some.

If the dead were to remain overseas, it was evident an accommodation must be made with the French. From the spring of 1915, and at the army's behest, Ware was in regular contact with the French government, talking over the long-term status of British graves in France. A fluent French speaker, Ware was able to advance the prospect that graves might be given permanent status in France. No one could have foreseen just how much land might one day be required when the great battles of the Somme and Third Ypres lay ahead. Casualty figures were spiralling in 1915 and the Germans were showing no signs of weakening when the French government, after much discussion and debate, passed into law (29 December 1915) that land would be given in perpetuity for Allied dead. The cost of the land would be borne by the French, the maintenance and upkeep by the British through a 'properly constituted' authority. The law set in stone a great act of French generosity, explained Ware:

> The [British] Army Council finds it difficult to express in adequate terms its appreciation of the noble and generous impulse which led the French Nation to provide, at its own cost,

permanent resting places for the British soldiers who fall on French soil. The British Army and Nation have been deeply touched by the eloquent references to these soldiers made in both the French Chambers during the debates on the Law and by the statement that France desires to treat as her own children those who cannot be buried in their native land.

The work of the DGR&E would suffice for war, but not for peace. In London, the government's Office of Works remained responsible for the small handful of British graves overseas, most from the Crimean War. Heading this office was the First Commissioner of Works, Sir Alfred Mond, Managing Director of Brunner Mond, Liberal Member of Parliament and a Minister in Lloyd George's coalition government. He was also Francis's uncle. The blurring of roles between his government office and that created by Ware and the DGR&E would not always make for an easy co-existence.

As far as Ware was concerned, the care for soldiers' graves on the Western Front was his domain, a function he carefully nurtured and guarded. To his mind, the vast number of graves on the Western Front, and elsewhere such as on the Gallipoli Peninsula, required concentrated supervision by one dedicated organisation, the DGR&E, and could not become the sub-work of a government department, with half an eye on other unrelated but equally demanding tasks.

It was clear that the cemeteries required long-term guardianship and the army turned its mind to a post-war world, proposing the creation of a National Committee for the Care of Soldiers' Graves. In the end, this short-lived committee achieved little except to cement the idea of a permanent dedicated authority for the care of cemeteries. This committee eventually gave rise, in May 1917, to the founding by Royal Charter of the Imperial War Graves Commission (IWGC) to carry on and complete the work of the Directorate in peacetime. It was everything Ware could have wished for.

The French gift of authority over the cemeteries allowed Britain to control how they would appear, free from interference. Even before the generous French gesture, Red Cross funds had been made available to embark upon a scheme of planting to make the cemeteries appear 'less miserable and unsightly'. Once control was ceded, Kew Gardens sent its senior director, Arthur Hills, to advise on flowers and foliage. Nurseries were established, and in the spring of 1917, a full-time Horticultural Officer was appointed to supervise the work of a growing number of gardeners. Care for the dead had come a fair way in a short time.

Rules were laid down as to how graves were to be prepared, with set dimensions and spacing. There were guidelines for marking graves, with Chaplains charged with ensuring the work was done properly with pegs and labels and an individual's particulars written in hard black pencil. In established cemeteries, numbered pegs were pre-placed to indicate where graves should be dug, numbers that were to be shown on burial returns.

Collecting individual particulars and achieving cemetery symmetry could not be maintained at all times, especially during the battles of the Somme, Arras and Third Ypres when corpses littered the ground and, close to the fighting, Casualty Clearing Stations were overwhelmed with the mortally wounded. Respecting the dead outstripped the capacity of anyone to properly bury and register all – as 72,335 names recorded on the Thiepval Memorial to the Missing on the Somme testify. Nevertheless, such rules could be applied well behind the lines or, as the fighting moved on, in the cemeteries that grew up on former battlefields.

The DGR&E would continue its work with Ware at its head, but Ware would also wear another hat, sitting as a commissioner on the board of the IWGC, with the Prince of Wales as president. Other members included the Secretary of State for War, and Sir Alfred Mond, as First Commissioner of Works, as well as three other government ministers. Representatives from the empire were also included in a clear indication that this new organisation was determined to see the valued input of all in an equal partnership. In another sign of its admirable long-term ambitions, men such as the author Rudyard Kipling were brought into the fold as unofficial members. In time, Kipling served as the commission's literary adviser, and would write the commission's most important cemetery inscriptions.

The IWGC was bestowed with all the legal authority it would need to care for cemeteries. It would also be the keeper of records and the provider of cemetery registers. Crucially, it would decide how remembrance and commemoration were framed.

Despite there being no end to the war in sight, the IWGC began to plan, bringing into an advisory committee the world-renowned architects Edwin Lutyens and Herbert Baker – two highly talented individuals, but men who had not always seen eye to eye. A third architect of equal standing would join them later that year. He was the former head of the Royal Institute of British Architects, Reginald Blomfield, a man as different from Baker and Lutyens as they were from each other. In the meantime, Lutyens and Baker, along with Charles Aitkens, the Director of the National Gallery, would travel between the IWGC in London and the DGR&E in France.

All three men could not help but be moved – even depressed – by what they saw. Lutyens wrote to his wife:

What humanity can endure, suffer, is beyond belief. The battle-fields – the obliteration of human endeavour, achievement, and the human achievement of destruction, is bettered by the poppies and the wild flowers. … The graveyards, haphazard from the needs of much to do and little time for thought – and then a ribbon of isolated graves like a milky way across miles of country, where men were tucked in where they fell.

Surrounded by the detritus of war, the men mulled over ideas, discussing the complex questions of cemetery planning and the erection of permanent memorials. Lutyens's architectural style gravitated towards the grandiose, Baker's towards smaller and simpler concepts, though full of 'English' symbolism. Lutyens urged that the appearance of cemeteries should be uniform: that a continuous idea would flow seamlessly from cemetery to cemetery. Inevitably there were differences of opinion. A cross was needed in each cemetery, believed Baker, one that would be in the style of those found in an 'English village churchyard'. In preference, Lutyens wanted a great stone, a monolithic altar. For religious reasons, Baker felt uneasy about the idea of an altar and also suggested that such a great stone might be impracticable for all cemeteries. They agreed that each cemetery required a covered building without religious trappings where civilians could shelter and pray, and that all cemeteries would have a boundary wall. The vacated Somme after the German tactical retreat from the region in the spring of 1918 gave the men unhindered access to the ground, and a place to consider the practicalities of laying out cemeteries. All three were awed by the destruction, visiting key landmarks: the Butte de Warlencourt, an ancient and distinct burial mound in the centre of the battlefield; the Thiepval ridge, a once-strategic point in the German first line of defence; and Delville and High Wood, where the trees had been ripped and splintered to stumps. All were considered sites for future monuments. Lutyens speculated that High Wood might have a 'broad terrace walk bounding its edges', a mine crater in one corner preserved with an adjacent tower with a chapel affording views over the battlefield.

> there must be nothing trivial or petty where our valiant dead lie in oneness of sacrifice and in glorious community of Brotherhood of Arms. All that is done of structure should be for endurance for all time and for equality of honour, for besides Christians of all denominations, there will be Jews, Mussulmens [Muslims], Hindus and men of other creeds; their glorious names and their mortal bodies all equally deserving enduring record and seemly sepulture.

But though it will be important to secure the qualities of repose and dignity there is no need for the cemeteries to be gloomy or even sad looking places. Good use should be made of the best and most beautiful flowering plants and shrubs; indeed it is much to be desired that the Roses of England and the Lilies of France should meet and blossom together in the places where the fighting men of both countries fell side by side.

On this point Baker was in agreement. Later that year and with an obvious nod towards his idea of a British setting on foreign soil, Baker wrote:

I would especially keep the home of indigenous British trees or trees of the Dominions where possible, avoiding all exotics and freaks, and giving preference to such trees as the yew and Kipling's trinity of 'the oak, the ash and the (white) thorn' – the forest rather than the garden tree, and the trees of the English poets. The yew in itself would stamp a British character on the cemeteries for centuries.

Of paramount importance was the men's expressed desire for the cemeteries to execute equality in death. All graves would look the same, which meant the wishes of the individual to commemorate the dead with personal memorials would be forbidden.

In formulating their thoughts, there was no sense of fiscal restraint. As far as Lutyens was concerned, the dead deserved the best and the best built to last in perpetuity, and Baker did not demur. In the theatre of war and communal loss, talk of economy might appear to dishonour the collective sacrifice, especially before any final decisions had been taken. These were men of ideas, not accountants. In the years to come, cost would prove to be a thorny issue. Charles Aitken was hardly an accountant either but he was socially aware and, to an extent, an administrator in his civil work at the National Gallery. He believed some financial modesty should be part and parcel of the IWGC's plans. Soon after returning from France, he sent a letter to Ware setting out his stall.

One would naturally <u>like</u> to lay out all these graveyards perfectly, but I scarcely think the enormous cost has been reckoned up in view of the fact that there will be great shortage of money after the war and imperative demands for reconstruction, housing, education, the wounded, and the fatherless children, it seems to me quite improper and indeed unjustifiable that <u>much</u> money should be spent on most of these graveyards. To spend £500 on a chapel or shelter for a few relatives visiting a remote grave is indefensible, considering the crying needs for housing in England. It is a delightful idea but I do not think it is practicable and no real tribute to the dead hero, if his children are sacrificed to provide it and this I think does and will in practice defeat all ambitious plans. Personally I think it is quite useless to contemplate them seriously or spend money on clerical work on these plans which are so unlikely to be executed.

It is very difficult to work out expenses at all closely, but I have jotted down on the next sheet a few items only on such basis as I can get without close inquiries. The tombstones alone it seems to me will cost either £1,250,000 (at £5 each) or £2,500,000 (at £10 each). I imagine the well-lettered stone or bronze tombstones with regimental badges, such as we contemplate, will cost at least £5 each, and probably £10.

He estimated that Lutyens's great altar stones would cost £500 each and across 500 cemeteries, this would prove to be prohibitively expensive. Better to concentrate such stones in 'a few monumental graveyards'. Aitken suggested hedges and not walls in 90 per cent of cemeteries to cut costs, with 100 gardeners costing £100 each per annum to care for the cemeteries that would contain, he estimated, 250,000 separate graves (100,000 being without identified bodies). Aitken had done the rudimentary maths but his calculations fell far short of the mark when, unbeknown to anyone, the conflict still had fifteen months to run.

As the British government and overseas Dominions had committed to paying for individual gravestones and the maintenance
of cemeteries, there seemed little chance that there would be any
repatriation of bodies at the end of the war. Paying for the dead
meant ownership of the dead. Cemetery design ran concurrently
with design options for individual gravestones, ideas advanced to
Ware by November 1917. How these graves would be marked was
still up for discussion and argument: would there be a headstone or
a physical cross; this would prove a particularly contentious issue
with the established Church, which sought the latter. The IWGC
would press for what it wanted, but in doing so, it would seek
through consultation to garner support and to reduce the potential
for future controversy.

Those whose voices would have greatest resonance were the
soldiers themselves. In a letter written to *The Times* newspaper
shortly after the war, Henry Lewin, a colonel with four years' service
in France in the Royal Field Artillery, described how those under
his command had been asked for their opinions right from the start:

At the conclusion of the long Passchendaele offensive
[November 1917], the proposals of the War Graves Committee
were submitted to units to obtain their views. Drawings of
the proposed gravestones and sketches indicating how it was
proposed to lay out the cemeteries were sent out on such a scale
that it was possible for all ranks to see and study their effect.
In order to obtain a detailed opinion of how the proposals
were viewed, I assembled a small committee of all ranks in
each unit, whose duty it was to draw attention to the proposals
of the Graves Committee, explain them fully, and obtain
individual expressions of opinion from every man serving.
The replies I received from these committees were remarkable
in their unanimity. The uniformity of design was what appealed
most strongly to all. That the fellowship of the War should
be perpetuated in death by a true fellowship in memorial was

the unanimous and emphatic desire of everyone, officer and man. Death, the great leveller of all rank, was very near to those men at the time, and their deliberate and expressed wish was that, as they fell, so they should lie, and their memory be perpetuated in like form throughout. Since the taking of that census of opinion many of those who voted have been laid to rest in France. They lie buried now on the fields where they sealed their royal fellowship of death and sacrifice.

A little over a year later, Lewin's opinions were read out during a House of Commons debate on the proposed standardisation of headstone design. The letter was being used to bolster the Commission's position, though not everyone accepted the results of the unofficial 'trench line' poll. Lord Robert Cecil was sceptical:

> That does not prove anything. I am afraid I do not really attach any great importance to this kind of consultation, unless I know how it was carried through. … Assuming it really represented their [the soldiers'] wishes, even then they can only speak for themselves: they cannot speak for the dead.

In the same debate, Viscount Wolmer, rising in support of Lord Cecil, directly questioned the reported unanimity amongst soldiers. 'I know a case where a boy, who was subsequently killed, expressed the greatest disgust at the conception of the Imperial War Graves Commission. He had seen the pamphlet which they [The Commission] circulated.'

It is futile to speculate whether soldiers' views, had enough of them run counter to the IWGC's stated plans, might have derailed them. It is certainly less speculative to imagine that the 'unanimous and emphatic' support as recalled by Lewin must have emboldened the IWGC and confirmed that it was on the right track.

Inevitably, conflicting ideas could not all be reconciled amongst those in the Church and politics whose opinions were also sought. To reach a considered and broadly coherent position, Ware approached Sir Frederick Kenyon, Director of the British Museum, a highly respected man who had served in France. He would assess the various architectural ideas, reconciling where possible the differences and writing a report outlining his proposals to the IWGC. In the meantime, in the short hiatus, Ware issued a statement outlining the IWGC's views and the direction of travel.

all those who died for the Empire's cause are members of one great family, children of a common mother, who owes to them all alike an equal tribute of gratitude and affection. Men of all ranks from General to Private fought and fell side by side, and it seems proper that in death all should receive equal honour and that their last resting places should be adorned with a common memorial, the symbol of their comradeship and of the cause which they died to maintain. ...

The rows of headstones in each cemetery would suggest the ordered regularity of a battalion on parade. The graves, wherever possible, face to east towards the enemy, as the Army faces now. ... The Commissioners are convinced as the result of careful enquiry that their proposals in this matter would be entirely acceptable to the men at present fighting at the front. ... Their wish would undoubtedly be that if they themselves were killed their graves should be treated alike, without distinction of rank or class.

While the Commissioners have thus decided that in the cemeteries abroad the memorials should be of a corporate character, their view is that memorials of a more personal and individual nature have their proper place at home, where they would stand as an example for all time to the kinsmen and descendants of those who fell in the war and as a visible witness to the great cause for which they gave their lives.

Kenyon worked thoroughly and quickly. He visited the Western Front in the depths of winter, viewing the great Base cemeteries on the coast as well as the small, 'squalid' cemeteries at the front. He consulted the 'representatives of the principal interests involved', albeit in line with the paternalistic times, not the public at large. Within two months he had written his report, reiterating the widespread belief that all should be treated equally in death. Private memorials would only give an impression of individuality and disorder (and if private memorials were poorly conceived, then bad taste too). What was needed was conformity; the graves would be symbols, of 'common life, common death, the common sacrifice'. Kenyon's observations were a careful, intelligent synthesis of Ware's own views and broadly the views of the three principal architects too. The graves would be Lutyens's vision of headstones, rank upon rank, with regimental details, name and date of death. Space would be given at the foot of the grave for families to inscribe their own epitaphs. Certain headstone designs, in particular Baker's more intricate stone carving (Baker was interested in Heraldry) were quietly dismissed. As a compromise, Kenyon adopted both Lutyens's 'altar' and Baker's cross, a cross Blomfield would fashion and to which he attached his own artistic touch, a sword of bronze. Ware recalls that Kenyon's report was presented to the IWGC on 18 February and adopted, though the contents were kept secret until publication in November 1918. It was no coincidence that the decision to leave overseas all who fell was announced at almost the same time: the dead were always going to remain overseas.

Since joining as one of the IWGC's three chief architects, Blomfield's relations with Baker and Lutyens, though at times strained, were productive because of their adherence to visions of simplicity and of good design. As Ware and the IWGC read

Kenyon's report, Blomfield paid a week-long visit to the Western Front. He identified four distinct cemetery types, defined largely by how they were established: directly on the battlefield after fighting; adjacent to civil communal cemeteries; next to a battlefield hospital; or at the Base hospitals near the coast. In all cases, he was keen that the cemeteries were allowed to maintain individual idiosyncrasies that reflected their origins. 'In the designs for all these cemeteries the dominant motive will be the permanent record of the sacrifice of those who lie there and of the pathos of their death, and from this will follow certain guiding principles of design.'

He was keen that the stamp of the architect should be as little in evidence, that the design should be abstract and impersonal. It should not tell the story of some particular trait or taste of the designer, nor the time period in which he was working. 'The utmost simplicity and austere restraint' was what was required. The dead should be left as far as possible to tell their own story, 'The circumstance of their death and burial should be kept steadily in view,' he wrote. 'In certain cemeteries where hasty burials were inevitable after some great action, the rows of graves are not always symmetrical or laid out of the same axis line. I think as a general rule, this arrangement should as far as possible be preserved even at the cost of design, because it is part of the history of the cemetery.'

The fabric of the cemeteries did not have to be uniform, with symmetrical perimeter walls. 'At Sailly Sur Lys, for example, one of the cemeteries has been formed in an old strong point in an orchard surrounded on three sides by the old trenches. In such a case this characteristic piece of history should be preserved in preference to a formal and symmetrical design.'

Bloomfield spoke of Lutyens's altar and Baker's cross, though the former was now described less controversially as a 'Memorial Stone' and would eventually be known as the 'Stone of Remembrance'. Both stone and cross would be incorporated into the design for each cemetery and placed in such a way that no part of the cemetery felt isolated or forgotten. 'One does not want relations visiting these cemeteries after the war to feel that their boy is out in the cold.' The cross, as well as its obvious symbolic aspect, would also prove useful as a guiding landmark for those cemeteries tucked away or hidden in a fold of the ground.

Bloomfield recommended that the three architects would oversee the drawings made by junior architects, 'the designing staff', army officers who were also trained architects. These men were based at General Headquarters (GHQ) working 'under the same broad inspiration', Bloomfield, Lutyens and Baker making alterations where necessary and visiting France to keep in close touch with the work.

The simplicity of design and the broad replication of cemetery styles served another useful purpose: it would save money. In Kenyon's report, he addressed the awkward question of finance: 'The country needs dignity and refined taste, not ostentation, and then it will not grudge the cost. It surely will not refuse the cost of one day of war in order to honour for centuries the memory of those who fell.' His blueprint for the Western Front anticipated restraint and modesty. The cemeteries were simple statements of fact, neither triumphalist nor apologetic. That in their vast number they would stand as a warning against war was an idea yet to dawn on anyone.

Three experimental cemeteries were chosen for design and construction, testing ideas and helping to make assessments as to costs. Each of the three architects was given a cemetery, all well behind the lines and a Treasury-sanctioned £15,000 budget. No one could precisely assess what the final bill would be: a grave in France was unlikely to cost the same as a grave in Mesopotamia or Gallipoli or Africa or Salonika, where variables in land prices, in distance and of terrain would present different challenges and costs. Likewise a grave in a large, easily accessible cemetery on the

Western Front was unlikely to cost as much as a grave in a remote, difficult to reach part of the battlefield with challenging geology.

It seems strange in retrospect that cemeteries designed to last for hundreds of years were being envisaged – three already under construction – while the war was yet to be won. Indeed, building was under way just as the Allies were preparing to receive the anticipated all-out German offensive, the offensive that had propelled Francis Mond back to front-line service and death.

Chapter Four

'As a man one could hardly help getting very fond of Francis, for a more open-hearted fellow, or one less given to backbiting, I have never met. I can honestly say I never heard him speak an unkind word of anyone. Though he had been out of flying so long, he was not only a very good Pilot, but a very plucky one too …'

Maurice Blake, Instructor 83 Squadron, December 1917
Letter of sympathy, 12 June 1918

The letter written by Emile to Francis on 14 May, the eve of his son's death, had concluded with a few lines that spoke of another world than the Western Front and interests from another time:

the swallows in my porch are chirping most noisily whilst I write in my study. I was so amused to hear about your old interest in birds nesting. Keep it up, old man. The more hobbies one has in life, the better. …
Well, *ave Caesar*. All send you their very best love.
Your affectionate father.

Next day, 15 May, the letter was taken to Pulborough village post office, 5 miles from Greyfriars. It was franked by the postmistress at precisely **11.30 am**. A day or two later, the letter reached France and 57 Squadron but was returned to Emile: 'Deceased 15/5/18' handwritten on the envelope.

* * *

15 May. 'In the Field' France, 31st Battalion AIF [Australian Imperial Force]

Dear Mr Mond

It is with the greatest regret that I have to inform you of the circumstances attached to the death of your son, Lt Mond. I am Commanding the 31st Battalion A.I.F. and am at present in the line. This morning your son was flying in a bombing machine over the German lines at about **11.30 am**, when he was attacked by several German scouting machines. I saw him crash from a great height. He fell with his machine in No Man's Land, about 100 yards from my front line. One of my officers, Lieut. Hill, crept out and brought in his body with that of his companion, Lieut. Martyn, a Canadian.

Death had been of course instantaneous, in fact, I think that your son was probably killed in the air. Both bodies have been sent to the rear, where they will be buried in a military cemetery. I thought it best to let you know that absolute fact, in case you might be left in ignorance of same.

Please accept my sincerest sympathy in your time of sorrow. I know you will feel your son's loss keenly, but you will have the satisfaction of knowing that he died in action, doing his splendid work.

Neil Freeman

Lt Colonel

Just outside the small hamlet of Bouzencourt, Francis Mond's plane had crashed in a field close to the bank of an un-metalled and sunken road.

22 May. Greyfriars, Storrington

'I do not know how to thank you for your very kind letter of the 15th in which you gave me an account of the circumstances attached to the death of my dear son. It has been a real comfort to his mother and to me to receive definite news, and had it not been for you, we should have been kept in that awful state of suspension much longer. We know now that he died in action – as he would have wished to die. We know that thanks to you and to the wonderful devotion and care of Lt Hill his body now rests in a proper grave in our lines. These facts are a great solace to us in our sorrow and we are deeply grateful.

Sincerely yours

EM [Emile Mond]

During the Great War, the British Expeditionary Force had kept to Greenwich Mean Time, rather than altering their clocks to French time. In their grief, did Francis's parents notice then or later the significance of the franked time on the envelope returned by the squadron, and the time Lieutenant Colonel Freeman noted as Francis's death?

*   *   *

What steel did it take Emile Mond to reply to Lieutenant Colonel Freeman's letter of fact and consolation? Did he already know that his son was missing? Had he received a telegram from the War Office officially informing him of the King's sympathy, and with it the terrible fear that 'missing' must, on the balance of probabilities, mean 'dead'? The Forces' postal system was extremely efficient and quick, so was Freeman's letter the first news the family received, opened, perhaps, at the breakfast table? Was it really, as it appeared, some cold comfort that his son had died in a good cause, fighting for his country? In replying to the 28-year-old commanding officer, Emile expressed his gratitude for the kindness of a stranger.

Francis had died instantly, it seemed, and his body recovered by a comrade's act of selfless courage. By 22 May, he would be buried in an established military cemetery behind the lines, his grave noted in a burial return. The Mond family would be saved the misery that haunted so many others, that of a missing son, last seen going into action but not seen since. Saved, too, from the fear, common to so many others, that a son had suffered a lonely, agonising death in a shell hole, with no known resting place, no personal possessions to be retrieved and sent home. There was some crumb of consolation to be taken from Freeman's letter with the knowledge that they could visit a grave after the war.

The family was undoubtedly grateful to Lieutenant Colonel Freeman, but they were also indebted to the man who had risked his own life in recovering the bodies of Mond and Martyn. At the same time as Emile had written to Freeman, he also wrote to Lieutenant Hill.

May 22nd

My dear Lt Hill

I have received Col Freeman's letter of the 15th in which he informs me of the circumstances attached to the death of my dear son Lt Francis Mond, R.A.F. He mentions the wonderful act of courage and devotion which you performed in creeping out into no man's land to secure my son's mortal remains and those of his observer – we know well at what risk. I cannot attempt to express his mother's feelings of gratitude, nor mine for what you have done. If anything can alleviate our grief it is to know that our dear boy lies now buried within our lines – and this we owe to you. We sincerely hope we may have the opportunity of thanking you personally one day.

Most gratefully yours

EM

On 8 June, Hill expressed his appreciation for Emile's letter, adding his own words of sympathy: 'I knew him not, but I look upon his death in the most sacred light, knowing so well that they are the bravest of our men who make these daily flights. ... The circumstances concerning your son's death, and the removal of his body behind our lines, I will not touch on here ...' The next day he wrote to Angela Mond.

France
9.6.18

Dear Mrs Mond

What can I write that will convey to you some idea how deep and tender is my sympathy in the loss of your beloved son, Francis.

Will you accept the sacred respect from a stranger? We all have to depart sooner or later, but I cannot conceive a nobler ending to a brave man's life than that of Lieut Mond who was facing, and fighting, two enemy aeroplanes twelve thousand feet above when he made the supreme sacrifice.

I am indeed grateful to you for this letter, also [your] kind invitation to meet you when on leave. I assure you it is an honour which I will avail myself of at the first opportunity.

Yours very sincerely

Harold Hill

Lieutenant Harold Hill's 'wonderful act of courage' was not the first time this rugged, 29-year-old sheepshearer from Victoria, Western Australia, had risked his life for others.

The son of a British naval officer, Albert Harold Hill was born in England but grew up in Australia. He had enlisted into the Light Horse in June 1915, working his way up to the rank of sergeant before embarking on overseas service. After a year on the Western Front he was commissioned in September 1917, and by May the following year, he was serving with the Australian Army Medical Corps attached to the 31st AIF. His bravery was without question. He won the Military Cross on 21 March 1918 when, from an exposed position in front of Allied lines, he fought off a German assault party. On 2 May, Hill captured a German lance corporal while in no man's land and three days later, he was wounded but remained on duty. Then, days before he recovered the bodies of Mond and Martyn, he was recommended for the Military Cross once more for 'conspicuous gallantry and bravery in the field'.

Hill had witnessed a British aircraft, a Sopwith Camel, land out of control just 37 metres from the German outpost line near Bouzencourt. The plane had capsized and the pilot was seen to wriggle out from under the debris before attempting to reach Allied lines. He was fired upon and dropped to the ground. Believing the pilot might still be alive, and despite the fact that the Germans were targeting the aircraft, Hill went with a stretcher and a volunteer, Private Harry Broughton, and 'with the greatest coolness' crossed 450–550 metres of no man's land to reach the pilot, Lieutenant Herbert Barker, 80th Squadron, who was dazed but unwounded. Placing Barker on the stretcher, Hill carried him back to safety, preventing his almost certain capture.

After venturing out to retrieve the bodies of Mond and Martyn, Hill returned to the trenches using the cover of the sunken road. From the trenches, the bodies were carried into Bouzencourt village and a partially ruined farmhouse. Amongst the dust and debris, the men were identified from their personal belongings, Hill bagging and labelling their effects. At nightfall both bodies were taken from the farmhouse, Hill supervising their evacuation by a small boat that had been used earlier that day to bring food to the trenches. This boat passed down the Somme canal to the village of Vaire-sous-Corbie, where the bodies of Mond and Martyn were unloaded.

Lieutenant Hill was relieved of his responsibility to the dead men from the moment the boat slipped off down the Somme canal, but not, he felt, of that to the Mond family. His nascent relationship with them would alter significantly in the months to come.

Although Emile and Angela were acquainted with the essential facts, further, more personal, details emerged. On 1 June, Angela wrote to a fellow squadron officer, Lieutenant William Eastwood. In answer to a request from Angela, Eastwood passed on the Canadian address of Lieutenant Martyn's mother before adopting the normal respectful platitudes: Francis's willing death in a just cause; their son was 'an expert pilot'; and that there was 'every reason to believe that the Hun paid dearly before they were brought down'. Both men died painlessly, he assured the Monds: 'I don't think they would feel anything owing to the rapid fall.' But this letter also gave tantalising hints of Francis's mindset that spring. Eastwood had flown with Francis just once, a bombing raid on 11 April near Bapaume, but they knew each other well in the squadron mess. 'We still miss them [Mond and Martyn]. In those days we were a happy little crowd. We used to have a little coterie at the end of the table and it was never dull.'

He then added:

Strange that you should mention ... the tone of his letters. I had noticed the same thing. After he had been here a while he was strangely happy and contented. I used to admire his coolness. He never seemed to mind taking [to] the air and indeed it was the reverse. I used to envy him this faculty. I am personally much more comfortable when the show is over.

Though I used to debate with him on musical topics, I realised then that he knew far more than I. Once we went together to a neighbouring town and I heard him play the piano [and] he probably wrote to you of his great hit as Captain Hook.

Eastwood returned to England on 9 June and visited Emile and Angela in London, before heading north to see his own family. Harold Hill arrived in England a few days later. He was granted leave on 19 June and met the Mond family within forty-eight hours. It must have been extraordinarily emotional, meeting the man who barely a month before had pulled their dead son from the wreckage of the plane.

Francis's parents asked meticulous questions and Hill was not evasive with his answers. Angela wrote that 'Hill ... described in detail the events of that day' – the trenches and the aerial battles overhead and Francis's vertical descent into no man's land. 'He did not shirk from reporting the head injuries of the bodies, amounting to severe disfigurement in the case of Captain Mond, and practically destruction of the entire head in Martyn's case.' A catastrophic fall from several thousand feet rarely left the bodies anything other than severely broken; in many cases, pilots were also burned to death on their descent and their charred remains made identification problematic at best. At least Mond and Martyn did not suffer this fate.

The circumstances of their son's death in action were explicitly and painfully understood and the crash site could be located accurately on any map. But where had the two bodies been buried? Which cemetery would the family visit after the war?

Unaware of how quickly burial details were processed by the IWGC, Emile and Angela waited patiently for news. They would have been anxious to see a photograph of their son's grave. Weeks passed. By August 1918, they became sufficiently frustrated that Angela wrote to the IWGC: where was her son? It should have been a relatively straightforward question to answer, but a cursory investigation led to a more concerted one. Angela's question had flummoxed the Directorate of Graves Registration and Enquiries (DGR&E). No burial report had been processed, and they were at a loss to know why.

On 29 September, the DGR&E wrote to the man last known to have seen the two bodies, Lieutenant Harold Hill, unaware that Hill had already seen the Mond family in June.

I have an enquiry for the location of the grave of the above officer [Francis Mond], and understand that you may be able to give some information. I shall be obliged if you will send me a map reference or any details of the place where he was buried which may assist in locating the grave.

After his visit to England in June, Hill had returned to front-line service. On 29 August, he received a gunshot wound to his chest and was evacuated, first to a hospital in Rouen and then to England, and the 3rd London General Hospital. Fortunately, despite a worrying initial prognosis, the injury was not life-threatening, his health improved rapidly and he was able to read the DGR&E's letter. Hill replied that he had not seen the bodies after they were taken down the Somme canal. As he understood it, they were transported to Battalion Headquarters, to the village of Vaire-sous-Corbie, but that single additional detail was all he could offer.

Many men disappeared during the war, their final resting place unknown. Their total loss was easily explicable by the prodigious expenditure of high explosive shells. Some men, it was known, had had named graves in designated cemeteries but these too had been destroyed in later fighting. The puzzling case of Francis Mond and Edgar Martyn did not conform to either of these scenarios, or any other for that matter, and it was proving increasingly hard to explain their loss.

Given the times and the political and social circles in which the Mond family moved, Angela and Emile's questions would have received immediate attention, but there was an additional reason why the IWGC would look at this case carefully. The facts as they were known appeared to suggest that there had been a clear breakdown in the protocol established to identify and register deaths at the front.

Map 1

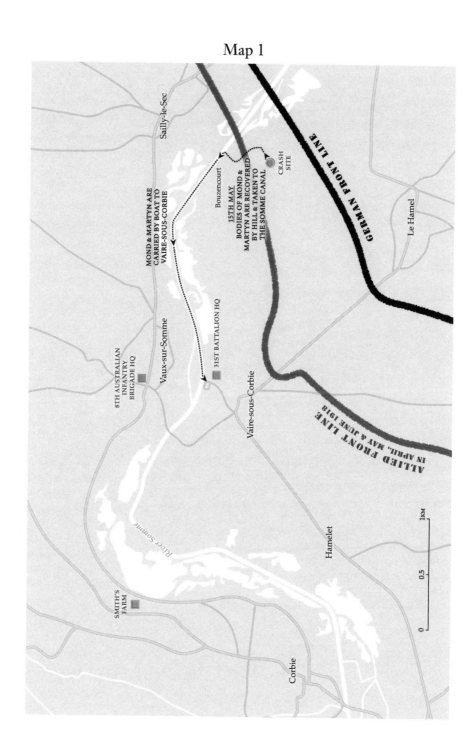

Sailly-le-Sec

MOND & MARTYN ARE
CARRIED BY BOAT TO
VAIRE-SOUS-CORBIE

Bouzencourt

15TH MAY
BODIES OF MOND &
MARTYN ARE RECOVERED
BY HILL & TAKEN TO
THE SOMME CANAL

CRASH
SITE

GERMAN FRONT LINE

Le Hamel

Vaux-sur-Somme

8TH AUSTRALIAN
INFANTRY
BRIGADE HQ

31ST BATTALION HQ

Vaire-sous-Corbie

ALLIED FRONT LINE
IN APRIL, MAY & JUNE 1918

SMITH'S
FARM

River Somme

Hamelet

Corbie

0   0.5   1KM

Chapter Five

'Lying in an old trench, behold a skull! It is clean and polished –
a soldier's head, low and broad at the brows, high at the
back. There is a frayed hole in an otherwise perfect cranium.
The simplest way to pick it up would be to put a finger in an
eye-hole and lift it. You must put both hands together and raise
it fearfully if it be the first skull you have ever found. . . Friend
or foe? Hmm – there are no identification marks on this.'

Stephen Graham, *The Challenge of the Dead*

Shortly after the Armistice, 68 Labour Company (68 LC) responded
to an urgent appeal for volunteers to undertake the deeply depressing
but necessary work of battlefield clearance, specifically, the need to
concentrate bodies into military cemeteries. The company's five
officers and 560 men were billeted in Ypres and had already been
out, clearing up abandoned trench lines and picking up debris. But
this would be an entirely new job. These men, primarily from the
City of Liverpool, were the first 'exhumation' company to begin
looking for the dead who lay in such profusion in the shell-pocked
fields outside Ypres' crumbling defensive walls.

Under the overall supervision of a 5th Army burial officer,
the men started their work in the second week of January 1919,
searching for the dead along the arterial Menin Road. Search parties
were composed of thirty-two men and eight stretchers, each under
an officer, systematically working over the ground flagged out in
230 × 230 metre squares on a map. To aid them, 'some rough notes'
were issued by GHQ as to how the bodies should be handled, but

it was hardly a detailed document: far from it, as a later DGR&E report made clear. 'No stringent orders as regards identification were issued ... they probably did not know what was required of them; their object was to clear the ground as quickly as possible.' Sanitary reasons were the primary motive for haste. Of secondary importance was the need for 'minute accuracy' in ascertaining the identities of the dead, though this was never made explicit at the time.

The job was ghastly. One private, John McCauley, serving with 2nd Border Regiment, wrote a graphic description of battle-field exhumation when bodies were still in various stages of decomposition. His experiences took place during the war, but the sense of horror his words invoke would have been all too familiar to the men of 68 LC.

We commenced our grim work in the early morning, and set out in skirmishing order to search the ground. For the first week or two, I could scarcely endure the experiences we met with, but gradually became hardened, and for three months I continued the job. ...

Often I picked up the remains of a fine brave man on a shovel. Just a little heap of bones and maggots to be carried to the common burial place. Numerous bodies were found, lying submerged in the water in shell holes and mine craters; bodies that seemed quite whole, but which became like huge masses of white, slimy chalk, when we handled them. The job had to be done; the identity disc had to be found. I shuddered as my hands, covered in soft flesh and slime, moved about in search of a disc, and I have had to pull bodies to pieces in order that they should not be buried unknown. And yet, what a large number did pass through my hands unknown. Not a clue of any kind to reveal the name by which the awful remains were known in life. It was very painful to have to bury them, be they British or German ...

Portrait of Angela Mond, circa 1910, by the English society portrait painter and sculptor Glyn Philpott RA (1884–1937). This painting has hung in the National Portrait Gallery.

Circa 1906: Francis, aged about eleven (far right), sitting on a horse with Angela holding the reins. Alfred is sitting far left, with May sitting on the knee of Sigismund Goezte (1866–1939), the Victorian artist and brother of Angela. Philip Mond is standing centre.

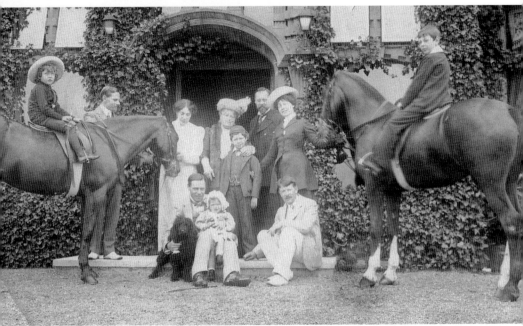

Greyfriars, near Storrington, Sussex, the countryside retreat of the Mond family, beloved by all.

May and Stephen Mond, just before the outbreak of the Great War, standing outside Greyfriars.

Emile and May Mond with Boris, the family dog, at Greyfriars, around 1916.

Angela, circa 1914.

ancis sitting in his car shortly after leaving Cambridge niversity. He was prosecuted on numerous occasions r speeding.

'No Mercy in Cambridge': just one of Francis Mond's days in court where he was fined for speeding.

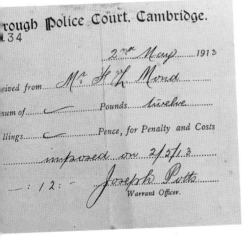

lay 1913: one of many fines issued to rancis Mond for speeding.

Emile Mond with his son Francis on the doorstep outside the family home in London, 22 Hyde Park Place. The picture was taken in August or September 1914, just months before Francis transferred to the Royal Flying Corps.

22 April, 1915: 'Flew for & obtained ticket. Good test. Perfect evening.' Francis's aviator licence was issued the same day.

Francis during training in a Farnham Pusher. These flimsy looking aircraft scared many would-be pilots.

Francis with Emile: 'Francis was at Greyfriars, a fine-looking fellow… With his deep china-blue eyes and his brand-new Royal Flying Corps uniform he was my constant envy,' wrote Aldo Cippico, a family friend.

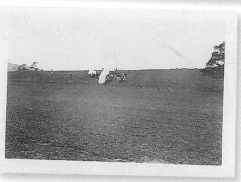

A forced landing close to Greyfriars, a week before Francis was sent to join 16 Squadron in France. 'He flew his Farnham biplane over Greyfriars and then suddenly the machine gave up the ghost at the critical moment and his stick-and-canvas contraption belly-flopped on an embankment,' recalled Aldo Cippico. The aircraft was wrecked.

Date and Hour	Wind Direction and Velocity	Machine Type and No.	Passenger	Time	Heig
TOTAL flying up to going to France 29 hrs. 42 mins.					
FRANCE. Arrived St Omer 24-6-15.					
CHOCQUES. 26·6·15. " C Flight." 16 Squadron. R.F.					
29·6·15. 10·20am	Windy.	MFs 5015	Solo	60	3,00
30·6·15 10·25am	"	MFs 5015	"	15	1,500
MERVILLE 30·6·15.					
30·6·15 5·30 pm.		MFs 5015	"	85	4—6,
3·7·15 12·0 pm	Fine	MFs 5015	1 a/m Bush	90	6-7,
5·7·15 6·30 pm	"	MFs 5015	1 a/m Bush	65	6-40
6·7·16 11·20 am	"	MFs 5015	Lt. Elliot	5	1,00
— " — 11·30 am	"	MFs 5024	Lt. Elliot	145	4-50
— " — 7·0 pm.	"	MFs 5015	Solo.	10	2,00
7·7·15 9·50 am	35-40	MFs 5015	Solo	10	1,00
9·7·15 9·20 am	—	MFs 5004	Self	30	2,00
— " — 10·20 am	—	MFs 5030	Solo	30	2,50
10·7·15 4·20 pm	windy	MFs 5027	1 c/m Bush	135	5-7
		TOTAL in France ....hrs		11-20	mins:

A page from Francis's flying logbook with the four hand-drawn symbols giving some extra visua
detail to describe how eventful his flight had been.

	(MF (shorthorns) 80 h.p. Renaults.)
Course	Remarks
❡ ` ❡ ·	● "archies" ◉ hit ✕ fight. ❢ bombs.

mail-boat. & light-tender.)

ERS – AIRE – MERVILLE – BETHUNE	Bumpy, cloudy. Practice.
CQUES – MERVILLE.	"C" Flight changed station. Raining
TAIRES – BETHUNE. – ARMENTIERES.	Cloudy. Along the trenches.
TUBERT – ARMENTIERES.	After a Hun, but didn't see him.
ENTIERES. – BETHUNE	● Patrol. First experience of "Archie"
co-operation with R.A., but pump spindle broke, & bearings seized
COUTURE. – FESTUBERT.	● Artillery registration, MEERUT DIV. (8 targets)
Aerodrome	Test new engine. Missing.
"	Test engine. Still missing. V.B.
RVILLE – ST OMER.	With 2 Lt. Turner, to fetch new machine.
OMER – MERVILLE.	New machine. & Cloudy.
STUBERT – LACOUTURE	● Artillery registration. Meerut Div:

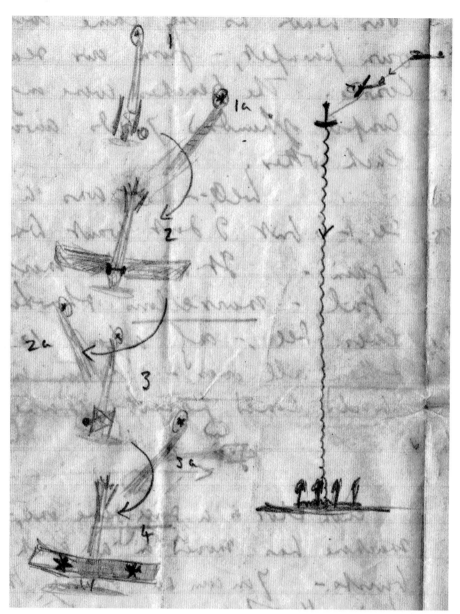

9 September 1915: Francis's drawing of the strafing and crash of a German aircraft he witnessed from a trench.

Francis Mond's wound tags that were attached to his uniform.

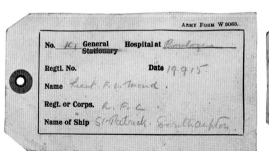

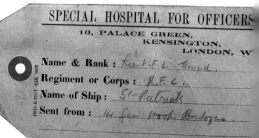

The Mond family gave tea parties and offered their homes for convalescent officers and men wounded at the front. These parties were well attended with hundreds of visitors at each event.

OFFICERS OF THE NTH SERVICE SQUADRON, ROYAL FLYING CORPS

The above squadron has just completed its training at ——, and has now gone to Somewhere in Somewhere. The names, reading from left to rig
Standing—Lieut. F. L. Mond, Lieut. R. J. Stubington, Lieut. M. G. Kiddy (adjutant), Captain F. H. McQuistan, 2nd Lieut. T. H. Ma
2nd Lieut. H. B. Mann, D.C.M., 2nd Lieut. J. W. Atkinson (equipment officer), 2nd Lieut. J. P. Cox; second row—Lieut. N. R.
Captain I. V. Pyott, D.S.O. (a Zeppelin strafer), Major V. A. Albrecht, M.C. (commanding), Captain C. E. H. C. Macpherson, 2n
T. P. N. Stack; in front—2nd Lieut. W. A. Rochelle, "Honeygirl" (mascot), 2nd Lieut. T. Hayes

Francis Mond, with fellow flying officers, possibly 83 Squadron, during training in early 1918. Almost all these officers had previous service overseas, including 2nd Lieutenant John Cox, far right, who had served as a private in France from October 1914 and wears two wound stripes on his left sleeve.

Francis, back in France for the last time.

May 1918: *Caesar* after the third raid on Bapaume that day. 'Crashed on Landing – (not bad)' wrote Mond in his logbook.

The only known picture of Lieutenant Edgar Martyn, taken with his wife before he left Canada for England and the Western Front.

May 1918: a photograph taken by 57 Squadron from 14,000 feet while flying over Bapaume. Francis records three large explosions at an ammunition dump (bottom left). 'From what my observer tells me, our machine was responsible for one of them!' Francis wrote in a letter home.

Close-up of the explosions.

Harold Hill, MC and Bar, the Australian office who crept out to the crashed aeroplane to recover the bodies of Francis Mond and his observer, Edgar Martyn.

The Somme valley, where the river widens into marshes, photographed in 1916. It was here at Smith's Farm two years later, that Francis Mond and Edgar Martyn's bodies were first unloaded.

France
8-6-18

Dear Mr Mond,

Words fail to express just how much I appreciate your letter. Will you accept a strangers sincere, & deepest sympathy in the loss of your beloved Son. I knew him not, but I look upon his death in the most sacred light, knowing so well, that they are the bravest of our men who make these daily flights thousands of feet over the line, with the hope of meeting, & defeating the enemy. The circumstances concerning your Son's death, & the removal of his body behind our lines, I will not touch on here, I know you have been informed by R.A.F, & also my C.O. Col Freeman. I thank you for most kind offer to visit you when on my next leave to England, & I assure you, it will give me great pleasure to meet, & know you.

Yours very sincerely

Harold Hill

31st Batt
A.I.F.

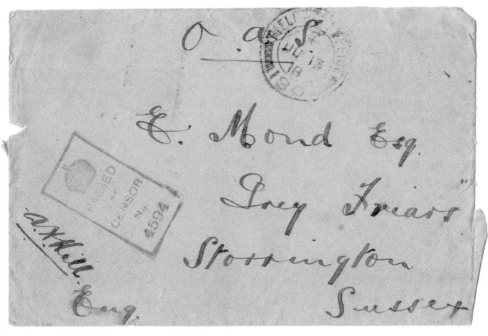

Offering his condolences: the letter written by Harold Hill from the trenches, June 1918.

E. Mond Esq.
Grey Friars
Storrington
Sussex

A H Hill
Eng.

PASSED BY CENSOR
No. 4594

The wreckage of *Caesar* was still lying in the field at Bouzencourt well into the 1920s.

The airframe of *Caesar* with the buildings of Bouzencourt 150 yards away.

The plot of land purchased by the Mond family, as defined in the original legal documents.

The memorial unveiled around 1922, a year before Angela discovered Francis's grave. The broken column signifies the abrupt cutting off of life. The field on which the aircraft crashed was purchased by the Mond family.

Doullens Communal Cemetery Extension No. 2, as photographed by Emile Mond.

The original Graves Registration Report dated 4 October 1920 and amended by hand to show the recently discovered graves of Mond and Martyn.

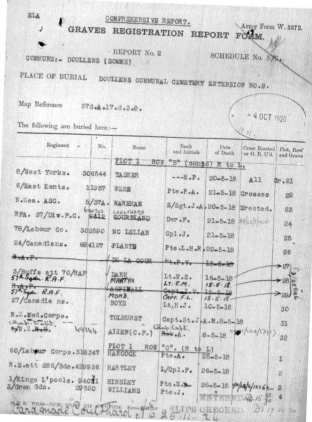

5 May 1924: Emile and ngela Mond stand behind rancis's grave on the fifth nniversary of their son's eath. Francis's parents visited e cemetery at least once very year until the Second orld War.

Emile (right) with Angela, her arm resting on his shoulder. This is one of the last images of Francis's parents. Emile died in December 1938 and Angela in November 1941.

The mural in the entrance hall of the Foreign Office in Whitehall. It commemorates the establishment of the League of Nations and was painted by Angela's brother, Sigismund Goetze, for no fee. Britannia greets America with France and Italy by their side. The Australian in the slouch hat (fourth from right) is believed to be based on Harold 'Bert' Hill.

Most of the men of 68 LC had been in France since February 1917 when the unit was drafted overseas. In the intervening eighteen months, they had seen terrible sights, but the work of battlefield clearance was hardly a job anyone undertook with indifference, although most became desensitised to it over time. But these men were inexperienced and progress was slow; in fact, their work proved unsatisfactory to the IWGC, given the urgency to clear the ground. Across the old battlefields too few men were employed in the grisly task, a point raised at the end of January 1919 to the Army Council by the Commission. The IWGC expressed 'considerable anxiety as to the slowness with which the work of putting graves and cemeteries in order in France [and Belgium] was being carried out'. The issue, the Commission noted, was not with the DGR&E but went all the way to the top, with the Commander-in-Chief's failure to ensure a satisfactory supply of labour. The Army Council wrote to Field Marshal Haig on 28 January but failed to receive a reply that sufficiently addressed the issue of numbers.

Matters escalated to the Secretary of State for War, Winston Churchill, with the threat that unless adequate numbers were employed on battlefield clearance, the Commission would put the whole issue before the War Cabinet. While work was under way in the Fifth Army area around Ypres, noted John Talbot, the Principal Assistant Secretary for the IWGC, 'little or nothing has been done in the Third [Somme] and First Army Areas [Arras, Lys]' to the south.

In mid-April 1919, a conference was held at which the issue was addressed. Apologies were made: there had been serious illness amongst senior officers, especially the ongoing effects of the devastating influenza pandemic that had debilitated a large number of men including officers of the IWGC. Bad weather had also hindered progress. The War Office even suggested bringing in extra labour from home – 15,000 men could be sent out from Britain – but regardless of these reassurances, the IWGC remained unhappy with the prevailing situation. On 17 April, Talbot wrote a confidential note to the War Cabinet:

> The Commission feel strongly that there is no work at the present time which has a more instant claim on the attention of the Government than that of putting into proper order the last resting places of those who have died for their country, and they consider that no time should now be lost in giving such instructions as will ensure the immediate carrying out of the work and put an end to the very regrettable delays which have marked the treatment of this question in the past. … If a scandal is to be avoided, it is clear that the personnel needed for work on the cemeteries must be provided at once. … The Commission are not competent, and would indeed exceed their authority were they to attempt to formulate an opinion as to whether the failure of the military authorities to deal adequately with this vital work during the period referred to [December to April] was due to negligence or insuperable difficulties; they have, however, been most unfavourably impressed by the strong statements made by Dominion representatives on the Commission as to the inability of General Headquarters, France, to make prompt advantage of the offers of considerable numbers of men, for this work, made by the Commanders of Dominion Forces in France.

It would make a terrible impression on the Dominions if a lack of care were perceived, but in reply Churchill complained that he was hamstrung by the speed of demobilisation; a dearth of transport in France only exacerbated the problem, with so many vehicles in a state of mechanical collapse after the Allies' headlong push to victory at the back end of 1918. To make matters worse, a large number of elderly and low category men were being used for duties such as 'care of horses, guards over stores, work in connection with engineer and ordnance services for clearing up and disposal of stores. ... It will be realised, therefore, that, in the present circumstances, the provision of the men in question is a matter of exceptional difficulty.'

More men over the age of thirty-seven, presumably those considered 'elderly', were released for work and the promise of men from England was part-fulfilled, although not the 15,000 once offered but rather less than a third of that number, most trickling across to the Western Front by early summer. Some reorganisation was necessary. In May, the DGR&E took over responsibility for all burials and on 1 July it issued for general use 'complete and able instructions' drawn up 'For the guidance of exhumation companies in the future'. It was written by Captain Charles Frederick Crawford, 68 LC's commanding officer, and was based almost entirely on his unit's experiences and lessons learnt from recent 'mistakes and omissions'.

The unloved science of searching for bodies was known as 'spotting', with best practice passed on for others to follow. Captain Coghlan, an officer employed by the DGR&E, recorded that grass was greener and the grass blades broader where bodies lay undiscovered; others noticed telltale patches of taller nettles. In May and June, as the countryside was in full bloom, with red poppies flourishing everywhere, men noticed patches of yellow charlock indicating more recently dug graves, where seeds, long buried, had been brought to the surface through the churning of soil.

When a body was found, the ground was dug 'to a depth of around 6 feet', Coghlan noted, an officer overseeing exhumations watching as the body was retrieved. A search was made for the soldier's identity discs but if these could not be found then 'the wrists are examined [presumably for an identity bracelet or inscribed watch] and all items of clothing noted. Boots were washed and examined' for a regimental number often found stamped into the leather. If no identification was yet possible then a search was made for other pieces of equipment. 'The helmet is washed, dried and examined for Identification.' Finally the body was placed in canvas, the name (if known) with regimental details written on a ticket by the presiding officer. A precise map reference was taken, showing where the body was found while any personal effects were recorded, bagged up and sent to the Base.

Battlefield formalities concluded, the body was removed by wagon or stretcher to the cemetery and a pre-dug grave, with 2 feet 6 inches separating each new grave from its neighbours. Here the soldier was interred in the presence of the cemetery officer, who took the ticket and wrote out a burial return in his Field Service notebook. The grave was immediately filled in. In theory – though by no means always in practice – a cross was erected at once by men of the Graves Registration Unit (GRU), with the ticket temporarily attached to the cross, pending the stamping of an aluminium tape by an officer. Once the tape was struck, the ticket was taken off and destroyed.

At the end of each day, burial returns were sent by order of the Army Burial Officer to the DGR&E headquarters at St Pol. These forms included the cemetery officer's notes as to the plot, row and grave number in which the remains had been laid. Typed up by clerks, these forms would eventually find their way to Baker Street, London, to become part of the official record of the cemetery.

The process sounded straightforward, precise and, if the correct steps were followed, accurate, though Crawford would later claim that in his experience, the GRUs were 'very seldom' present during the collection and interment of remains. Armed with Crawford's detailed notes, 68 LC remained in the Ypres Salient alongside other labour companies engaged in exhumation work. In April 1920, 68 LC was disbanded, but others stayed, including 126 Labour Company (126 LC), a company regarded as having reached 'a very high standard of efficiency'. It was sensible, then, that when questions began to be asked about 68 LC's early work, this company was asked to examine their efforts. In any peer group review, noted an officer of the DGR&E, there was a not 'unnatural eagerness to find fault' in another company's work, 'a tendency that is observable even where the contents of a grave were not inconsistent with the particulars of the Burial Form'.

Labour companies that came later to exhumation had the advantage of adopting tried and tested techniques, but also, with the passage of time, such work became easier. Further decomposition ensured that those disinterred on the battlefield were largely skeletal, making the job of investigation less traumatic. Further clues as to the identity of the dead man were revealed: an identity disc that sank deep into the putrefying body after death might be revealed now that the flesh had gone.

But 126 LC's review was not simply a question of prudent quality control. Problems had been uncovered at one large burial plot, Hooge Crater Cemetery. This was the first but not the only cemetery where 68 LC had carried the dead. Once a small wartime repository of a hundred graves, post-war Hooge Crater Cemetery had quickly swollen to 5,000 dead and was still growing. A case of grave duplication had been discovered: according to information on two temporary wooden crosses, the same man, a Private Williams, appeared to be buried in both graves. On exhumation, one of the graves was discovered to contain not Williams but a man identified as a Private Hamilton. Other graves were opened and further discrepancies reported between 'the identity established at the time of burial and the particulars inscribed on the aluminum tags attached to the crosses', the Commission discovered, adding kindly that 68 LC had been working under the most 'deplorable conditions' and hence 'indifferent work may have been the result'.

There was mounting evidence that serious identification issues existed within early burial plots and so the men of 126 LC were asked to re-examine a total of 135 graves. From their explorations it was possible to establish the identity of three of eighty 'unknowns' and disprove the identity of five of fifty-five 'known'.

Given these findings, the DGR&E set up a Committee of Enquiry convened at St Pol in January 1921, calling on key participants in the exhumation process to give evidence. These re-examined graves were amongst the first 68 LC had used and initially the DGR&E considered that the percentage of mistakes was low enough not to warrant further investigation: naturally, 68 LC would have been expected to make fewer errors as the men gained experience. This, however, was not the full story.

In the early days of exhumation, a body found under a cross was accepted as the man named on the accompanying inscription without further investigation. This alone had 'led to a lot of duplication', reported Colonel William Sutton, Assistant Director DGR&E, to the enquiry. In other words, if the man buried under a cross was erroneously accepted as the man named above, then it was entirely possible that another body, identified from possessions, would be given the same name on his grave and therefore be buried twice.

The enquiry examined discrepancies between inscriptions on crosses and the remains beneath. In its report they discovered that burial returns were rarely signed by attending officers and only two of hundreds of forms examined were actually dated. There were further revelations. Lieutenant Frederick Cleeves, 126 LC, supervising exhumations, reported that in Hooge Cemetery, Plot I, a body was found 'buried diagonally across' three graves and under three crosses. Owing to incomplete burial returns it was impossible to discover which officer had been in charge on the day of the burial. Further graves were found to be too shallow and on other occasions, bodies lay with feet rather than the head under the cross.

In examining burials made during the week ending 8 February 1919, there were distinct signs of negligence. The body of one unknown British soldier ought to have been identified by insignia on his uniform as belonging to the Lincolnshire Regiment; in another two graves, the bodies had simply been transposed. In a further case of inaccuracy, 'an unknown British soldier should have been identified as an Australian but "unknown British soldier" was probably considered adequate in the case of a soldier of the Dominion Forces.' In another grave, a German had been buried as a British soldier, 'an indisputable case of carelessness'. The report concluded:

> If a date had to be fixed after which identifications can be accepted as reliable, that date would be fixed as the middle of June 1919. Therefore, it would appear that no further exhumation should be considered except at cemeteries brought into use before that date. Records in the office at St Pol prior to June 1919 are by no means complete or reliable.

As for Hooge Crater Cemetery:

> the Committee are of the opinion that the majority of the mistakes occurred in Plots 1, 2, and 3, and are adverse to making any re-opening of graves in any plots other than these, and questions whether the number of identifications that might be accrued by opening more graves in the first three Plots would outweigh the sentimental objection of relatives.

Over 60 per cent of the graves in this cemetery remain to soldiers 'known unto God'.

Concerns over accurate identification rumbled on and were not restricted to the Ypres Salient. The Australians expressed regret over obvious failings, citing their own cases of duplication, including 3475 Private William Collie, 26th AIF, who was apparently buried in both Caterpillar Valley Cemetery and Warlencourt British Cemetery, 5 miles apart on the Somme battlefield. 'Former burial accepted as correct', says a note. No exhumation of the grave in Warlencourt British Cemetery was made, the 'other' man being left 'known unto God'. In another incident, 6794 Private Urban Brown, 24th Battalion, AIF, was recorded as buried in two graves. When the first grave was examined, an overlooked identity disc determined that the remains were that of 2217 Private William Walsh, 24th Battalion. The only problem was that Walsh was buried in another grave in the same cemetery. An Australian request made in December 1921 to examine the second grave was not granted, much to the surprise of an official at Australia House in London, who wrote to the IWGC to complain and to ask for a change in policy.

To complicate matters, there were suggestions that in 68 LC's eagerness to clear the battlefields they had removed a number of isolated crosses but without sufficient examination of the ground to see if a body was there. It was likely that these crosses had been blown down by enemy fire and re-erected at the time but not precisely on the same spot. Perhaps in ignorance of due process and the confusion it could cause, the crosses were collected and subsequently erected in Hooge Cemetery but without a body beneath. During 126 LC's excavations, seventeen graves were re-examined and found to contain no body at all, though sandbags and equipment were present in four.

There were further issues concerning the DGR&E's own temporary wooden crosses, erected generally at the behest of relatives, over graves when the identity of the soldier beneath was 'practically sure' but not certain, and wooden memorial crosses to the missing paid for by grieving families and erected out of sympathy by DGR&E staff close to the location of known death. 'They are not quite in the nature of memorials to the missing as we have got to within a few yards perhaps of the place where the body lies, although we cannot point to the actual spot,' wrote Lord James Stopford, Secretary, Enquiries Branch at the IWGC on 26 June 1920. Rather than abandoned on the battlefields, these crosses were frequently taken to military cemeteries or churchyards.

Such crosses might carry the words 'Near this spot fell ...', or '... buried near this spot', or '... is believed to be buried in this cemetery'. Others bore inscriptions 'In Memory of', and were worded similarly to crosses planted above real graves, and it was not always possible to tell the difference. 'In some cemeteries, I am informed by the DGR&E there are even whole plots containing no actual graves but only rows of memorial crosses. These plots are often in the centre of a cemetery,' wrote Stopford. The Commission was uncertain what to do with them, especially as collective memorials to the missing were being planned: they were certainly against any idea of maintaining 'dummy graves' or that a man might be commemorated twice. If memorial crosses were given headstones, then that appeared to undermine the principle of equality, but if the crosses were removed then the Commission might invoke the ire of parents.

The opportunities for confusion were evident to all. In one incident, relatives searching for their missing son, whom they failed to find, arranged with the maire of the Commune of Neuve Chapelle to buy a small plot of land close to where their son had fallen. Whether in response to a request from the family or not, the maire created a grave mound next to the cross, which was subsequently opened by a passing exhumation party, assuming a body would be there. The maire was asked not to repeat the gesture as this was likely to 'cause a good deal of trouble in the registration and exhumation work to the Commission'.

Cemetery Records of Registration had revealed systemic problems across the Western Front: 'thousands of cases' of grave duplication had been discovered, adding to the burden of work. 'The establishment beyond all doubt of the correct identity is a lengthy process, requiring the close attention of highly trained personnel,' noted an IWGC report, revealing, for example, that in the six months to the end of February 1921, 1,200 graves had been examined for the purposes of revisiting a soldier's identification, though it is unlikely these were all examples of duplication. In a third of cases it was possible to make either a firm identification – the soldier's name – or a partial identification, such as his regiment or rank. Whether it was the extra financial burden of this detailed work or a rapid reduction in available personnel – or both – that halted all but a handful of further exhumations is not clear. Certainly the Commission felt the need, in its own words, to exercise a new 'rigorous control' over the practice, so that from March to the end of August 1921, only a further seventy-two graves were opened for the purposes of identification.

*   *   *

In 1920, the British Army overhauled the method by which it allocated service numbers. From August, all servicemen were issued with seven-digit numbers that were unique to the individual and would stay with him throughout his career, even when he transferred to another regiment. This change did away with an antiquated system found seriously deficient when identifying battlefield dead. Where identity tags were missing, a body was carefully searched for any other clues: a watch with an inscription, a razor with a name scratched on the side, or perhaps a piece of government-issue equipment with a regimental number impressed on it. Clearly, a unique service number would have helped identification greatly, though it could not be relied upon alone.

During the war, army property was salvaged and recycled, except for items covered in blood, and therefore it was entirely possible that a number found, for example, on a piece of leather equipment, might not belong to the last owner. Equally, a man might simply jettison a worn-out or threadbare item in exchange for a better one found on the battlefield or removed from the dead. To complicate matters, wartime numbers were never unique to a soldier. Numbers were handed out sequentially within an infantry battalion. There were many scores of battalions in the British Army, each with a nominal strength of 1,000 men or more. A number, 267 for example, would have been given to as many men as battalions that chose to number in this identical way. Indeed, in this randomly picked example, the Army's Medal Roll, that is, those who served overseas on active service, reveals over 150 men with these three digits. To identify a (dead) man with 'a short number', wrote a War Office official after the war, it would be 'necessary to compile a list of all men who held that number – not merely of those that became casualties – and eliminate those who cannot apply'. An item might have 'changed hands', he said, then gave an example: '[This] is a case which occurred recently. A number was found on a spoon, the owner was traced and said that he gave the article to a friend who was killed the same day.'

Only in 1917 did the army reorganise service numbers for one tranche of the forces, the Territorial Force, and new six-digit numbers were introduced, significantly reducing the number of men with the same number within the Territorial Army, though numbers were still not unique to the individual. Further proof would be needed to determine identity.

An army number along with the recorded location of exhumation could be crucial in putting a name to a body. A map reference eliminated certain regiments from the process simply because they had not fought there. More to the point, if a particular battalion *had* fought over the precise ground where a discovery was made, then if a number or part number could be linked to a cap badge or shoulder title, the chances of identification were significantly improved. Clearly, accurate information on troop movements was key to success. The problem was that the DGR&E did not hold that information themselves, either in France or in London, resulting in frustration and then annoyance with the one man who certainly did. This man was Sir James Edmonds, charged with writing the official history, *Military Operations in the Great War*, a huge multi-volumed work that demanded personal dedication and focus, an undertaking aided by a small department of military experts.

From as early as 1919, Sir James was sent numerous requests from the DGR&E (Effects Branch) in Baker Street, asking for background information on the movements of specific regiments on given dates. The more he responded, the more requests he received, until (though it appeared to take quite a while) his patience wore thin, as he made clear in a letter dated 19 January 1921. His Historical Section existed, he explained:

for the purpose of writing a history of the war, and though I am glad to assist when possible, the work thrown on it by your Department during the past two years has been considerable and seems always increasing.

During the past week I received 78 enquiries from you; they took two experts in classification of the records three complete working days to investigate and answer. 'Where was 10th Battalion Argyll and Sutherland Highlanders operating on 10th October 1915?' This took half an hour to answer. 'Where was 6th Battalion Durham Light Infantry operating 21st to 29th March 1918?' In this case the query would take an hour to answer. It covers miles of ground with constant reference in Diaries to the 'Brown Line', 'Green Line', etc which necessitates reference to Divisional and sometimes Corps diaries and maps. Many times the writer of [the War] Diary did not know where he was and left it at that.

Edmonds appealed to Sir Maurice Hankey, the Secretary of the Committee of Imperial Defence, asking for his advice. The answer was unequivocal. Edmonds was to push on with his History, and refuse to answer any further requests unless the DGR&E provided clerical assistance.

The DGR&E turned to the army's numerous Record Offices in their search for clarification on regimental numbers found. Each regiment was connected to a Home (Infantry) Record Office: the Lincolnshire Regiment's Record Office was in Lichfield, the Cameron Highlanders' in Perth, for example. In each Office, civilian staff dealt with all the administrative records of serving soldiers, everything from issues over pay and separation allowances, to contacting families when soldiers were missing or presumed killed, eventually using their records to send out medals to soldiers or next of kin. After the war, the pressure to discharge men from the army was unrelenting, though large numbers remained in khaki to serve on garrison duty around the world, often engaged in small, localised conflicts. The administration of these men's records was the bread-and-butter work of hard-pressed staff. Yet at the same time that the Record Offices were being assailed for answers from the DGR&E, they were also receiving enquiries from the IWGC, firstly in the Commission's work of collating and compiling the British Army's list of the dead for proposed Memorials to the Missing, and secondly, finalising a list of all the names and addresses of next of kin so that families might be contacted to verify, and add to, the information to be engraved on headstones and printed in cemetery registers.

The pressure was intense. The Commission knew that as time passed the proportion of cases in which the next of kin had died or moved away could only increase. Inevitably, the IWGC wanted Record Offices to furnish lists quickly. 'It is desirable to communicate with all of them [the next of kin] at an early date, even if they may have to wait years for the erection of a headstone or the publication of a register,' wrote the IWGC's Director of Records, and erstwhile officer in the DGR&E, Major Henry Chettle.

The Record Offices baulked at the work being loaded on them. In a curt War Office letter to the IWGC (on behalf of all Record Offices), an official underlined that the primary role of the Offices was 'to keep a record of the services of effective soldiers'. Once they became 'non-effective', the Record Office had 'practically no more interest' in them. As the custodian of next-of-kin names and addresses, they had been asked to forward information on fallen soldiers: the place of burial was equally 'of no concern to Record Officers. Neither is the notification of that place to relatives one of their ordinary duties.'

Compared to pre-war levels, the number of Record Office clerks remained inflated, and paid for by War Office funds. The immediate post-war economic boom was well and truly over and depression was looming. Owing to calls for financial prudency from the Treasury across all government departments, efforts were being made to reduce Record Office numbers. The problem was that any cuts in the labour force were never reflected in a corresponding reduction in work, owing in part to the questions posed to them by the IWGC.

'I can assure you that the labour entailed in searching for the documents of soldiers, especially if the regimental particulars or the spelling of the name are not accurately quoted, is very great,' wrote the War Office official in June 1922. There were other identified issues too, of definition and terminology: the IWGC referred to a man as missing when there was evidence of his death but his whereabouts were unknown. The War Office referred to a man as missing when nothing was known of his fate. The Official finished:

> Speaking quite frankly, as one is able to do in an unofficial letter. What I would like, looking at the question solely from the point of view of Record Offices, would be finally to discontinue all correspondence between the Commission and Record Offices. We simply have not the clerks to deal with the proper functions of Record Offices, let alone work which is altogether outside our province.

There is no evidence that an entirely happy compromise was reached, although alternative sources of information, such as soldiers' records held by the Ministry of Pensions, were suggested to the IWGC to alleviate the work being thrust upon the Record Offices. The efforts made to identify the dead were laudable, but to war-weary staff in Record Offices, being asked repeated questions about men who had died five, six, perhaps seven years ago was at best tiresome and at worst galling. There was an inevitable friction between those whose work remained with the dead and with the past and those whose occupation concerned the living and the future.

* * *

Despite occasional and understandable mistakes – even laxness – during exhumations and reburial, the desire to give both dignity and identity to the dead was sincere, though men were hardened by what they saw. That care did not end with those who were demonstrably British but was extended, in equal measure, to all those from other various faiths and communities who had fought for Britain.

While the war was still raging on the Western Front, the IWGC created the Indian Graves Commission (IGC) to examine how the bodies of Indian soldiers might be dealt with. A committee was established and included the British Under-Secretary of State for India, and Indian representatives including a gifted lawyer, Sahibzada Aftab Ahmad Khan, who spoke for the Mohammedan (Muslim) faith and Sir Prabhashankar Pattani, a renowned politician and close friend of Mahatma Gandhi, representing the Hindu faith.

These men discussed at length how bodies of Indian soldiers ought to be handled: Khan was keen that Muslim bodies should not be exhumed unless absolutely necessary and then a representative of the faith should be present. There was no issue with Muslim bodies being buried among Christians. Pattani was keen that where Hindu bodies were identified, they should, if possible, be exhumed and cremated 'and that the ashes should be scattered into the sea, into a river or failing that to the wind'. Owing to French law forbidding cremation other than in established crematoria, this proved impossible, and Pattani did not oppose reinterment. Both men looked forward to memorials, perhaps a mosque and a temple, in which all the names of the dead from each faith would be listed. Sir Herbert Baker, one of the Commission's three principal architects, having worked for many years in India, was well acquainted with and sympathetic to the architectural requirements of the Muslim and Hindu faiths. He would design the beautiful and intricate Indian Memorial to the Missing at Neuve Chapelle, commemorating 4,700 Indian soldiers and labourers with no known grave.

India had sent over 140,000 men to the Great War, of whom over 8,500 had been killed and upwards of 50,000 wounded, several thousand more succumbing to illness. The first troops had arrived in the autumn of 1914 and many of their dead were recorded as missing owing to the imperfect burial and registration arrangements at the time. In searching for them, it was possible to target areas where the Indian Lahore and Meerut divisions were heavily engaged, in particular, the fighting around Neuve Chapelle. In a statement entitled Major Blacker's Report, dated September 1921, Blacker suggested how the Indian dead could be found using maps and extracts from the War Diaries.

'Added to this should be a list showing just where each particular battalion was in action on any given date during major battles,' he wrote. Exhumation parties would be given a table showing how many men had been killed in an identified section of the line. 'A comparison of this with the numbers exhumed and identified would show how much remains to be done, and to what areas most attention should be directed.' Photographs of shoulder titles, buttons and badges would help searchers. He continued:

It should be made clear that sepoys in France seldom wore pagris [turbans], that Gurkhas usually wore hats and kukris [curved knives], that the only infantry who wore the old 1903-pattern bandolier equipment was that of the Lahore and Meerut divisions, whilst many items of clothing ... afford a ready means of identification. The abbreviations used by regiments for marking identity discs, accoutrements and clothing should be made clear. The fact that new (short) rifles were issued by the R.A.O.C. [Royal Army Ordnance Corps] on arrival at Marseilles, to replace those brought from India, and that the men wore khaki drill up till January or February 1915, might assist to distinguish sepoys' bones. The signet ring that they usually wear should not be overlooked, whilst a list of Musalman and non-Musalman [Muslim] names would help to get bodies buried in the correct cemeteries.

There were physical differences too that might be measured, Blacker suggested. Skull measurements 'might give a clue to the race of the man'. Even leg bones could give search parties an idea as to who the soldier was, as an 'overwhelming proportion of the Punjab Army is renowned for the size of his thigh.

'Since Government has been saved the expenditure on the upkeep of, and the provision of headstones for, several thousand unknown killed, it appears reasonable to expect that it would offer a corresponding sum to establish Divisional memorials to perpetuate the names of the men.'

Over 3,500 Indian soldiers had known graves and due attention was given to establish 'the names of any flowers, shrubs or tree which would be considered especially appropriate for planting in Indian plots, Indian cemeteries or on Indian graves', wrote an officer of the Commission to another, serving in the India Office.

In considering which plants would grow well and in what soils, irises were picked out by Kew Garden horticulturalists as growing especially well 'in blown sand as it [does] in a stiff loam'. The Commission recommended: 'This happens to be one of the plants appropriate for the graves of Indian soldiers, and wherever possible we are planting on or around their graves Iris, Marigolds, and Cypress, all plants which they [the Indian soldiers] regard as sacred and appropriate for cemeteries.'

In years to come, understanding was shown too when it came to grave inscriptions, with concern for religious sensitivities at the forefront of decision-making. In April 1923, in a letter from the IWGC to Sir Frederick Kenyon of the British Museum, some very particular technical advice was sought.

Dear Kenyon

Among the Indians buried in various cemeteries in France are some whose religion is given as 'Animist'. So far as my experience goes Indian Animists appear to worship the spirits of the jungle, water, mountains, etc. What kind of religious emblem should be put on their headstones? I presume it would be best to put up a headstone without any religious emblem, such as is done in the cases of people in this country who object to a cross. The India Office could not help me when I asked for advice.

There is also the question of Buddhist headstones. Here the India Office could not help me either. I suggest inscribing the characters 'OM' such as was put on the Hindu headstones in Meerut Cemetery. I understand this forms part of the usual Buddhist invocation. Can you obtain any advice on this point?

There were repeated checks that everything had been done correctly: had an Indian soldier of Muslim faith been buried in a plot for Indian Hindus and not in the neighbouring Muslim plot? Where a Muslim and a Hindu soldier shared a grave, could two different inscriptions, varying according to the faith of the deceased man, be included on one headstone? 'Possibly there would be enough room to erect separate headstones,' wrote an official in hope. There were other small but important adjustments made to gravestone inscriptions. 'Sohan Singh, 38th Dogras – has a Sikh headstone – was he a Dogra? If so he should have a Hindu stone.' On another grave, that of Ashiq Hussain, buried in Bruay Communal Cemetery Extension, there was a problem: 'Ashiq – the Q is badly cut and looks like an O. Recut.'

In 1924, when further inscription errors were noted, a 'systematic and detailed' examination was undertaken of all names, with reference to lists obtained from the Indian government of known casualties, so as to ensure consistent spellings of frequently recurring Indian names. Even thirteen years after the war, there were additional adjustments: 'Abbeville Communal Cemetery V1 G. (Headstone to Sowar Mool Singh.) The face of this stone on the side facing East is disappearing by erosion, and the inscription before long will be obliterated. The name if recut should read Mul

Singh.' And: 'Bethune Town Cemetery Plot II Kar<u>e</u>m is still on the headstone, correct to read Kar<u>a</u>m.'

There were many minor 'imperfections' when those preparing and cutting the names had no knowledge of the Indian language – imperfections, wrote one Commission employee, that would be obvious only 'to an expert', minor imperfections that did not justify the considerable expense of adjustment there and then. Yet, 'at the same time they are particularly unfortunate in that they detract from the otherwise uniformly high standard of accuracy attained in the Commission's work,' he wrote, and that was important to those who cared, particularly this man, a former army officer who had once served in the Punjab.

* * *

All visitors to the battlefields were awed by what they witnessed: the vast tracts of wasteland, the shattered trees and the detritus of war strewn on the ground, all were visible at every turn. In Britain, images of destruction were seen at the cinema and in newspaper photographs, but it was impossible to grasp the full vista without being there. When these civilians went to France, the appreciation of what a generation of young men had been exposed to must have been profoundly humbling. Standing amid the ruins of the Somme battlefield, when the ground could appear deceptively featureless, visitors may well have struggled to orientate themselves as they were driven over unmetalled roads and tracks from one cemetery to another. Here and there, where villages once stood, clusters of makeshift, temporary dwellings rose from the ground, built by returning civilians using anything that was to hand: 'salvage-made huts', witnessed former Scots Guardsman Stephen Graham; wood stripped from enemy dugouts, corrugated iron from British trenches. 'It has needed courage to come back to your old ten acres,' he wrote in sympathy. In Belgium, near Ypres, most of the Flemish farmers were tenants rather than owners.

Their landlords allow them now three years rent free. From the hut made of salvage starts the re-generacy of the land. In an irregular patch round its gates lies the first reclaimed ground, a mere kail yard, a bean plot. ... Tobacco also has been growing, for the leaves hang wilting from green to yellow on the outside of the unpainted wooden walls.

Not everyone was glad that they had returned. 'I wouldn't never have come back had I known it was like this,' a dejected Belgian woman acknowledged.

Mutual sympathy and respect between grieving parents and bereft civilians was never more in evidence. Everyone had lost, but it was not as if the British had suffered disproportionately; on the contrary, the French had lost one-seventh of the adult male population. More than 300,000 men had been sent back to the firing line after being wounded four times, some of them rural workers who returned to their land, 3 million acres of which had been destroyed, thousands of wells damaged or polluted, often wilfully, in 1918 by the retreating Germans. The vagaries of war had visited death and destruction on swathes of France and Belgium, the trench lines from the Belgian coast to the Swiss Alps settling where they had by chance. During the war the Allied armies had paid their way, in theory at least, compensating civilians when property was used for billets, money paid out to farmers for theft of livestock or deliberate damage, but not for the effective occupation and destruction of their land. Armies and, by extension, governments were a source of revenue for war-affected civilians, though compensation was often resisted or cut by suspicious army officers sent to examine claims. After the war, a complex process of financial compensation would be negotiated between the French state and civilians on a discrete individual by individual basis, but there was no great national plan of reconstruction, no government-driven initiative to bring labour in to help; rather, people were left to fend for themselves, rebuilding livelihoods, forming local co-operatives for mutual benefit and support.

As a consequence, civilians were not especially grateful to the Allied politicians that had wrought carnage upon them. Why should they be? 'The peasants complain that the [French] Government gives them nothing,' wrote Stephen Graham as he toured the battlefields. The French authorities had 'commandeered their [the farmers'] horses at the beginning of the war and in exchange gave them a merely nominal sum. In the stricken areas how few are the horses now!' When a Monsieur Reynaert requested rent from the British for his land occupied by the huts of 126 LC during its work of exhumation, he made sure he claimed for each and every day of occupation from the hour of the Armistice until the huts' disassembly and departure in May 1921. He had been paid two years' rent, but felt entitled to more. In a terse message sent from Paris by the aptly named Colonel Blunt, the Deputy President of the Claims Commission, to the War Office in London, he affirmed that it was 'customary to allow rent only from the date on which half of the total area of the Commune was re-cultivated'. This had been explained to Monsieur Reynaert; nevertheless, he was 'demanding' further payment. The Claims Commission was not minded to pay any more. There was clearly little love lost on either side.

The visceral struggle to rebuild lives in war-torn France and Belgium guaranteed that, somewhere down the line, low-level friction would occur between representatives of those who wished to commemorate the dead, to build cemeteries and memorials, and those whose land had been liberated. Civilians would want to rebuild their lives, preferably without undue interference or hindrance; after all, they had put up with so much during the war, as Lieutenant Colonel Graham Seton Hutchison wrote, using the vernacular of the time:

Everything about peasant life dawn until dusk and long after was an aggravation. The English mules gnawed the bark from trees and destroyed them, poultry went missing, root-crops were unearthed and corn was trampled down. Peasants were knocked up at all hours and there was no one to whom they could appeal for the mitigation of intolerance. ... Picture to yourself, then, a population which from day to day and from week to week did not know what fresh humiliation would fall upon them, to what new inconvenience they would be subjected, who often did not know whether bombs by night would blow them from their beds or a stream of shells would churn up their pastures and lay their cattle low; who were obliged to meet every day men who knew little of their tongue and nothing of their customs. ...

War, of necessity, imposes restrictions upon liberty. No matter how friendly may be an invading army as allies, the restriction and impositions of military exigencies must provoke annoyance and irritation among the civilian population who remain. Grievances are accentuated through linguistic difficulties which produce all kinds of misunderstandings. In France, the Maire [mayor] of a Commune would find himself stripped of authority by aliens, whether British or Germans, who had no time to wait upon ceremony.

The maire held on to one significant power. During the war, the planned use of land for military cemeteries was agreed, through a *délibération* with the commune, including the landowner (where applicable) or, when the land was communal, the maire. These would become official cemeteries, with each of the army's many divisions ascribed map-referenced sites for their use 'at all times' under 'normal circumstances'. Abnormal circumstances were defined as periods of 'heavy fighting' when burial plots, often abandoned trenches, were hastily utilised. In such cases, British Army Instructions ruled that additional plots should be 'sites suitable for permanent acquisition by the French Government'. Nothing was to be within 100 metres of 'groups of houses or ruins and NOT near a well', although some early cemeteries fell foul of these rules.

The amount of land required for official cemeteries was hard to estimate, and occasionally more ground was fenced off than was finally needed, with tin cans placed on top of 10-foot poles to mark the burial ground limits. Sadly, more often than not, additional land was required, with cemeteries growing rapidly beyond agreed boundaries – an issue to be addressed once the cemetery was officially closed. Occasionally, a cemetery grew across commune boundaries. By the end of 1916, Bertrancourt Military Cemetery was adjudged to have overlapped the next Commune by 16 square metres, though it was hoped that no new *délibération* would be required for such a small piece of ground. Very often, new, though not necessarily adjacent, tracts of land would have to be found. At Doullens, the original French military cemetery, known as Doullens Cemetery Extension No. 1, was taken over by the British and gradually filled to capacity in 1918, requiring a second cemetery close by: Doullens Cemetery Extension No. 2.

Although the French law of 29 December 1915 anticipated that most cemeteries would remain where they were in perpetuity, using land agreed for burial plots was not legal ownership. Forceville Cemetery on the Somme was begun soon after the British arrival there in August 1915, the land being acquired by French decree in May 1917 only after the German Army's tactical 25-mile withdrawal from the Somme battlefield. At the time it appeared that no additional land would be needed, but the following year, a new German offensive retook much of the ground, the consequence of which was the reopening of Forceville Cemetery. More land was required for a further 103 graves and the original decree was annulled. After the war, a new application was made for the enlarged cemetery, with additional ground for the architect's intended building work, but approval was harder to obtain from the landowner. He was reportedly 'dissatisfied' with the procedure. It is not hard to imagine that sacrificing further farmland ran counter to his own aspiration to re-establish his rural working life. In the end, the Anglo-French Mixed Committee, set up to facilitate co-operation and discussion concerning all issues affecting war graves, was encouraged to take the matter into its hands so as to smooth over and speed up the process. This would not be the only case referred to them after the war.

The state gift of land was not without caveats; French and Belgian authorities allocated 3 square metres for each grave, for example, plus a certain amount of extra land for 'architectural treatment'. This limitation was recognised and adhered to by the Commission in all negotiations, Major Arthur Ingpen, barrister and the Commission's Land and Legal Adviser, offering his weighty opinion. Considerations of land economy must be at the forefront of the Commission's decision-making process, he advised, 'otherwise, [to] ignore the French and Belgian instructions is apt to create difficulties in the speedy acquisition of sites'. He went further: 'The Commission on the relatives' behalf, have accepted the limitations imposed on the average area of land to be acquired, and if they wish to exceed that area, they should have a special reason, and make a special request.' By their compliance with initial French and Belgian wishes, the Commission would be in a better position to resist any other additional requests made upon them.

By mid-1920, there was pressure from rural communities to resist the presence of numerous small British cemeteries punctuating the countryside, with polite but determined demands from a number of communes for the 'suppression' (the concentration) of some British cemeteries. This was opposed by the Commission, and in particular, Fabian Ware. He was keen to re-emphasise the IWGC policy, as agreed with the French and Belgians, that a cemetery containing a minimum of forty graves was entitled to permanency. Nevertheless, he would be willing, for reasons of hygiene, for the removal of any cemetery established too near a village, or too close to a water supply, but each case would need to be carefully scrutinised. 'Demands on other grounds should be resisted,' and he added later, 'The sensitivities of families in Britain must be pre-eminent.'

For reasons of sanitation, a number of cemeteries were amalgamated. Houplines Old Military Cemetery, with 235 burials, was condemned as the ground on which it stood drained directly into the village well. Nearby, Ferme Philippeaux British Cemetery, with seventy-six sets of remains – primarily casualties of October 1914 and June1915 – was removed as the graves were within the yard of a farm, and close to pigsties and cattle pens. 'It is in exceedingly undesirable surroundings,' wrote an IWGC officer, with some understatement.

These concentrations were inevitable, but Ware also knew that that some municipal councils had 'deliberated unfavourably for want of knowledge of the great importance attached by the Commission to leaving ... graves undisturbed'. Some seventeen communes, including Hébuterne on the Somme and Laventie, near Armentières, close to the French/Belgian border, had pressed for fewer cemeteries. Ware was keen not to oppose the communes directly, but preferred to change minds by 'persuasion'. Nevertheless, the IWGC anticipated a likely trade-off between the need for further grants of land and local demands for the concentration of particular cemeteries. French law could insist that larger, existing cemeteries be respected, but it could not insist that extra communal land be handed over by the maire against the determined resistance of local people. Equally, if the IWGC did not press for more land, it was anticipated that the maire could not insist on further cemetery concentration.

The issue rumbled on for years. In 1926, in a meeting of the Anglo-French Mixed Committee, Ware re-emphasised IWGC policy, while the French members 'explained the difficulty of making the farmers understand this [British] point of view, seeing that these small cemeteries with their access paths divided their fields'. Most municipalities, they said, did not wish to authorise more than one cemetery for each commune.

Under the work of the DGR&E, there had been some attempt to effect an economy of land, moving a few graves within an awkwardly shaped cemetery, or filling in other spaces so as to reduce the amount of land needed overall. This offered financial savings to the French State and, indeed, would make future cemetery designs less expensive to implement for the British. As a general rule, the IWGC was uncomfortable with this style of land economy for fear any change in such practice might be taken as a precedent, and risked paving the way for other more broad-sweeping requests. The Commission's idea of the 'inviolability of a grave' remained key, but as it took over the work of the DGR&E in September 1921, it was obvious some compromise was needed.

The King's Liverpool Cemetery, near Cuinchy, was not only irregularly shaped, but with just 169 burials, it occupied a disproportionate amount of land, extending behind a number of ruined houses. Rebuilding these homes would ensure that the cemetery would be completely shut off from the road, making access and maintenance difficult. Dury Hospital Military Cemetery on the Somme had been established in the grounds of an evacuated 'lunatic' asylum. Now that the patients had returned, including war-damaged veterans, French authorities advised that 'It would be dangerous for families going to pray over the graves of their children or husbands to be in contact with the lunatics. In order to get to the cemetery it is necessary to go through the Asylum itself.' A French military cemetery had already been evacuated for this reason and Ware agreed to put the case for mass exhumation of British graves before the IWGC. This medium-sized cemetery of 446 graves was eventually removed to Villers-Bretonneux Cemetery: the King's Liverpool cemetery was also moved.

It was already a Herculean task to re-establish homes and farmland without being additionally hampered by scores of small cemeteries (with their annoying umbilical cord-like pathways linking cemeteries to roads or cart tracks). There were huge sensitivities at stake, but the villagers were right. What was the point of Allied soldiers liberating France and Belgium from the Kaiser's jack-booted forces if that land were then broken up and made economically less viable, and all to the eternal memory of the dead? It made no sense. As Lieutenant Colonel Graham Seton Hutchison added, in his obvious sympathy for the rural community, the Flemish 'peasants' were hard-working, independent and reserved. 'They regarded the invasion, whether by British or German soldiers, as a monstrous interference with their liberties, as indeed it was; nor was this impression mitigated as the War dragged on. The trumpeted victories of British Armies gave them no relief whatever ...'

On rare occasions, friction spilt over into overt hostility. In March 1922, at Thelus Cemetery, officers of the IWGC found that the approach had been 'practically obliterated', the farmer dragging barbed wire across the track to the cemetery where it met the road, the track itself reduced to a foot's width, making 'progress very difficult'. The cemetery, which had been opened only a year before, 'is now for practical purposes inaccessible as when the crops come up the small existing track will be unrecognisable'. Similar issues were to be found elsewhere. At Berles Position Military Cemetery, the cart track that crossed 42 metres from the road to the cemetery was discovered under plough and impassable. In this case, the IWGC's Legal Branch was consulted and it was revealed that a legal loophole meant that the IWGC could not 'prevent the adjoining owner ploughing across the path nor [could] he [the owner] prevent the Commission remaking the path by walking along it', in the same way that 'rights of way' were traditionally created in England, Major Ingpen pointed out. The Commission was legally entitled to make up a path 1.21 metres wide and of any material considered suitable. A wire fence or hedge could be erected to protect the path, Ingpen noted. Nevertheless, he advised against any provocative action, 'because the farmers being irritated by the permanent path interfering with cultivation, would almost certainly pull such fences down'. In the end, the matter was referred to the sensitive touch of the Anglo-French Mixed

Committee and an unfenced path established through compromise and agreement.

Open pathways to cemeteries were immaterial if visitors were unable to find the cemeteries in the first place. In November 1923, a problem arose in Ploegsteert Wood near Ypres, where the owner was threatening to close the paths leading through the wood 'on account of the number of people roaming about and ... interfering with his shooting of his game'. Three distinct and separate British cemeteries lay within the wood and a lack of direction boards was causing the problem. Ploegsteert Wood was hardly alone in encompassing a cemetery, so would owners in Belgium or France accept permanent rights of way established on their property, fully signposted for the benefit of the casual visitor or dedicated pilgrim? Difficulties 'will undoubtedly arise' in agreeing with landowners a right to establish posts on private land, predicted the Commission's Deputy Controller, Herbert Goodland, and therefore, 'as far as possible, the use of private property [should] be avoided, and we adhere principally to the method of erecting our boards with their foundation standard on road corners on the land which comes under the State Control.' This was possible on first and second class roads but third class roads and tracks had no road margins, and 'we must necessarily encroach on private property, but I think this should only be done as a last resort.'

From the letters it regularly received, the IWGC was aware of the difficulties tourists were encountering. Many struggled to find cemeteries, especially those that were well away from a main road, perhaps hidden from view by trees or a fold in the ground. Direction boards were made in order of priority, with the most important cemeteries, generally the largest and therefore most frequently visited, getting their boards first, while smaller out-of-the-way cemeteries were of lower priority. Even where direction boards existed, there was a struggle to keep them clear of grass and weeds. Alfred Whittle laboured to find the grave of his brother, Private Neil Whittle, buried in Roeux British Cemetery, owing to its secluded location. The cemetery lay a mile from the main road and was screened by a wood. Along the track, before the wood, was Crump Cemetery, 'from here the track appears to be only into the woods,' wrote Whittle, 'and one is apt to turn back, as I did, to look elsewhere for Roeux British Cemetery.' He suggested that a sign at Crump Cemetery directing people onwards would have been useful.

Whittle had eventually found the cemetery, meeting two ladies from Edinburgh visiting the grave of a Royal Scot. 'They complained bitterly that they had been searching for many hours, and had visited many cemeteries before finding Roeux British Cemetery. I have no doubt that this matter will have your attention in due course, and beg to assure you that one or two more direction posts would be of great assistance to visitors.'

Even six years after the war, issues with direction boards, or rather the lack of them, remained common. In May 1925, Fabian Ware, on one of his regular tours of inspection, visited the battlefields seeking to adopt the attitude, as he described it, of both interested tourist and pilgrim, to see at first hand the difficulties they experienced.

Ware found that in many places, direction boards did not exist or were present only immediately outside the cemetery. At the village of Adinkerke he searched for two cemeteries. The first he found within a churchyard extension, but he was 'denied access' – it appears that he was asked to enter the cemetery by a more circuitous route. The other cemetery he failed to find altogether, 'though I searched with the car for a quarter of an hour and enquired, as far as my stock of Flemish enabled me to do so'. At another cemetery near Le Cateau he glimpsed headstones through a hedge, though there was nothing to indicate their presence, while, more generally, he had considerable difficulty in hiring a car in St Quentin to take him to a cemetery where a friend's son lay.

Within the large town, Ware, once more adopting the attitude of a tourist, enquired where the English cemeteries were and was given 'full and detailed' information, which he followed, arriving, 'as I expected', at the French National Cemetery at Vermont. It was clear to Ware that temporary direction boards must be erected before the summer, when most pilgrimages were made, and that all hotels should be given detailed information as to the British cemeteries in the neighbourhood.

Not all Allied dead were buried in military cemeteries. Small numbers, often in single figures, were buried in communal cemeteries during the war, most before the establishment of dedicated military cemeteries. These men would normally remain where they were, not least because local people already cared for them, adopting them as their own. The relative isolation of these graves caused concern amongst some families in Britain, fretful over the permanency of these graves and their long-term status. Would these graves be concentrated together within the cemetery or left scattered? It appeared unlikely that they would be in sufficient numbers to lie under the IWGC's Cross of Sacrifice erected in most other military cemeteries. Cheshire Regiment Captain Ernest Jones had been killed in August 1914 and buried with eleven others in Wiheries Communal Cemetery in Belgium. His family offered to pay for the cross if, as they suspected, too few men were buried there to make that a viable financial option for the IWGC. The family's desire was that Jones stayed where he was but that he and his comrades remained permanently under the shadow of the cross.

British graves in communal cemeteries and churchyards were granted perpetual concessions by French and Belgian governments, although the IWGC was bound by legal agreement to acquire local consent for any architectural or horticultural treatment. As these were existing civil cemeteries, it was essential that the commune's maire gave his approval to all works so that there could be no grounds for controversy or dispute. While local civilians cared for a number of isolated graves, the majority were looked after by French or Belgian gardeners paid for by the civil state. Isolated graves were in effect 'out of sight' and so might also become 'out of mind' and neglected. It was a delicate situation, as the IWGC appreciated. In one communal cemetery where four British soldiers were buried, the grass was observed to be uncut. 'The general effect was one of not exactly neglect but certainly not that of any great care,' wrote an unnamed controller and financial adviser to the Commission. If civil gardeners left British graves poorly attended to, then they would have to be handed over to the IWGC for maintenance. Ever mindful of avoiding insult, the Commission deemed it advisable that concerns should be raised about their upkeep with the Anglo-French Mixed Committee, rather than simply removing the graves from French care without 'sufficient notice'.

A very small number of graves were moved. In 1936, the IWGC received a complaint from the mother of Lieutenant Harry Pell of the Royal Flying Corps. She was concerned that her son's grave was looking unkempt in the communal cemetery of Izel-lès-Équerchin, near the French town of Arras. Pell's grave lay adjacent to that of another flying officer, Lieutenant Eric Pascoe. The IWGC investigated the case and wrote to both families acknowledging it had 'been unable to make satisfactory arrangements for the permanence or the proper care of [the] graves'. Exhumation in the Commission's view 'would undoubtedly prove ultimately the better course' of action and the parents were reassured this would be undertaken with all due reverence. Pell's body was removed to Orchard Dump Military Cemetery, but Pascoe's mother replied that she 'should much prefer' that her son was left where he was. Pascoe remained in the civilian cemetery.

Asserting control and therefore care over isolated graves was not without its additional problems and inconveniences. By their very isolation, IWGC gardeners might suddenly find their burden of work significantly increased. Mr Cutts, working out of Abbeville, had been given partial responsibility for fifty-five cemeteries 'scattered over a wide area', including graves in communal cemeteries taken under the care of the IWGC. 'Mr Cutts is well aware of the importance of isolated graves,' the Commission acknowledged, but as he had only a bicycle, it was inevitable that it would take more time 'to get round to them all': in other words, the grass might still grow tall around graves in isolated communal cemeteries.

Chapter Six

'No one seems agreed as to who had responsibility for the burial, and no records can be found of any graves under those names.'

Angela Mond, letter to the Air Ministry 1919

As Lieutenant Harold Hill lay wounded in hospital in the autumn of 1918, the IWGC made additional enquiries amongst fellow officers in the 31st Battalion AIF, as well as officers in the 8th Infantry Brigade, 5th Australian Infantry Division, under which larger umbrella the battalion served. Given the passage of time, jogging detailed memories of battlefield deaths would normally be problematic. Nevertheless, the circumstances of these pilots' deaths would probably be recalled – a dramatic dogfight directly overhead held a morbid fascination for onlookers, and a plane crash so close to the front-line trenches was not a daily occurrence. A daring rescue by one of the battalion's officers was an event likely to live on in the memory of those who witnessed it, though in Hill's case, it was something he had done before.

Angela and Emile's concerns over the fate of their son and his observer had been first raised in September 1918, and the IWGC enquiries widened in October. By the time a coherent overview had been collected from surviving officers and men, the war had ended and it would not be long before the 31st Battalion, indeed the whole 5th Australian Division, would be broken up, with troops embarked for home and dispersal. There was a pressing need to identify any additional witnesses.

By December, Angela had personally sifted through the available evidence, presenting to the IWGC her own thoughts with names, likely facts and probable scenarios.

The bodies had arrived at the village of Vaire-sous-Corbie, from where the 31st Battalion's assistant adjutant, Lieutenant Cairns, forwarded them by road, under the care of two as yet unidentified stretcher-bearers. These men had carried the bodies across the Somme River and adjacent canal to the 8th Infantry Brigade Headquarters at Vaux-sur-Somme, less than a mile away. Both Battalion and Brigade Headquarters understood that the Royal Flying Corps was in the habit of collecting and burying their own dead and so, at the 8th Infantry Brigade HQ, Major Frank Wisdom telephoned to ask if an RAF tender (lorry) could be sent to collect the bodies. After the lapse of time, he could not be certain whether he rang the 57th Squadron at Le Quesnoy, to where the personal belongings of Mond and Martyn were forwarded, or the nearest RAF squadron at Corbie.

Major Wisdom stated that to the best of his belief, no tender was sent and that therefore orders were given to Battalion Headquarters to bury the men, although officers at Battalion Headquarters denied this, claiming it was Brigade that took the matter in hand. In one sense it did not really matter who buried them; what was important was that the burial details, including a cemetery name or map reference, should have been written down and forwarded to the 5th Division's recently appointed burial officer, Lieutenant Thomas Stapleton. He would as a matter of procedure make his burial record. No such notification of two burials was seemingly received and consequently, no record made by Stapleton.

It was possible that no burial notification was ever written, or perhaps it had been lost or mislaid. After all, Mond and Martyn were entirely unconnected to the 5th Australian Division and just happened to be in the skies above them at the moment of death. It later emerged that shortly after the fatal crash, the commanding officer of 57 Squadron, Major Cuthbert Hiatt, had personally visited the Australian-held trenches at Bouzencourt and had even crept out to look at the wrecked aircraft, according to Angela Mond. He had failed to discover the whereabouts of his two officers but it was likely he reinforced the Australian impression that the RAF did indeed look after their own.

From the outset there was confusion about what had happened to the two dead airmen, but as the RAF was evidently looking, why should anyone else? Was Major Hiatt's presence in Bouzencourt the result of a phone call from Major Wisdom, or of eyewitness accounts of the crash from other pilots of 57 Squadron? This important detail was never clarified.

Mond and Martyn were not the only squadron fatalities that day, and another was to follow five days later. Even Angela acknowledged the realities of war, writing that a search had been made but 'It is doubtful if he [Hiatt] made any exhaustive enquiry.' Major Hiatt had a squadron to command; new officers would have to be brought onto the squadron strength, further vital missions of bombing and observation undertaken. Not that the squadron had given up on its two men. Far from it. After the Armistice, Hiatt's successor, Major Bailey, went 'all over the ground more than once with other officers of the Squadron, and [could] find no traces of any grave'.

The officers of 57 Squadron were not the only ones looking for Mond and Martyn. Lieutenant Harold Hill was back there too. His recovery from seemingly life-threatening injuries had been remarkable, but more remarkable still was his presence in France within weeks of the cessation of hostilities. By mid-December 1918, he had been medically released from his convalescent hospital, Cobham Hall, and placed on sick leave, a week of which he spent at Greyfriars as an honoured guest of the Mond family. It must have been comforting for Emile and Angela to have had Hill in their midst and it seems likely that the curious nature of Francis's disappearance was the main topic of conversation over afternoon tea or evening dinner. The Monds' plight would have been obvious to Hill, heart-rending enough to galvanise him into action. Instead of resting and recuperating in England, he returned to the Somme, days before Christmas, where, according to Angela, he 'spent a week in the Corbie area making enquiries'. He searched a large number of cemeteries.

> He has seen people who remember the occurrence, but no one seems agreed as to who had responsibility for the burial, and no records can be found of any graves under those names. As the ground has neither been shelled nor fought over since May last, it seems incredible that all traces of the burial of two officers duly identified, should thus be lost ...

It was an astonishing gesture by Lieutenant Hill to travel to France in the depths of winter. It is unclear whether he was given any access to transport, but any search would have included much traipsing about in icy conditions, talking to men of the Graves Registration Units, asking whether they had any knowledge of two, almost certainly un-named, graves of RAF pilots killed in mid-May. It stood to reason that if these men were buried, then they must be in, or close to, the village of Corbie, near where the bodies were last seen. While there were numerous British cemeteries in the area, it was also possible that they had been buried in a civilian cemetery or an isolated plot, graves that would be found and consolidated into a British cemetery in due course.

In January 1919, a major working for the DGR&E wrote to Angela to inform her that he had seen Lieutenant Hill, who was proposing to go back to France 'if he can', but 'I am not sure if he will be able to.' It is uncertain whether he was referring to any medical reasons that might hinder Hill. In the event that he could not go back, another officer had been acquainted with the case by the DGR&E. Lieutenant Herbert Everett, a Canadian officer, was due to return to his battalion in France and had been given letters of introduction to the DGR&E, asking them to lend him every assistance in searching for Mond and Martyn. Angela's statement had also been forwarded to Graves Registration Officers working in the Bouzencourt area. 'Directly any information is received I will write to you again,' wrote the DGR&E major to Angela.

Hill, meanwhile, began to contact the privates and NCOs of the 31st Battalion stationed at Littlemoor Camp in Weymouth, awaiting imminent repatriation to Australia. One telegram was sent to Private Charles Garrett, who worked under the adjutant, Captain Frederick Drayton. In reply, Garrett informed Hill that the two bodies had arrived at 31st Battalion Headquarters, where Drayton had told him that 'he [had] made arrangements for a lorry from the Royal Flying Corps to take them across the Somme River away to Vaux'. This recollection of a lorry was slightly at odds with the memory of the battalion's Assistant Adjutant Cairns's memory of two stretcher-bearers, but that did not matter.

More importantly, Garrett revealed that there was an Advanced Dressing Station (ADS) on the Vaux–Corbie road belonging to the 11th Field Ambulance. This road ran to Corbie, curling behind the Somme marshes and roughly parallel to the front line. Corbie was an important medical centre and transit point for men and supplies making their way forward along the road, usually at night, as it was subject to sporadic enemy fire. Any man who had died was taken to this ADS and car loading post, known as Smith's Farm, according to Garrett, and from there for burial at Bonnay (just outside Corbie), although he was personally unaware of what had happened to the two officers once they left Vaux.

As the investigation widened, so did the number of confusions and contradictions. Sometimes these were merely technical: it was easy to discover that it was the 6th and 8th and not the 11th Australian Field Ambulance that worked the area between Vaire-sous-Corbie and an ADS on the Vaux–Corbie road.

Further questions were drafted for the 31st Battalion men waiting at Weymouth, but the respondents were often poorly educated, and semi-literate answers provoked more questions than they resolved. Private Garrett's reply gave new information but even *his* letter was confusing. He referred to a 'Relay Post' in Vaux where the bodies were taken and then to an Advanced Dressing Station on the Corbie–Vaux road, adding, 'I do not know what became of them when they left B.H.Q.' Yet he had just mentioned that the bodies *were* carried to the ADS. 'The R.F.C.,' he writes, 'could not have taken them away.' Away from where? Battalion, or Brigade Headquarters? Or was he referring to the Relay Post in Vaux?

One thing was certain: the bodies were moved from Vaire to Vaux, and from Vaux, there was every reason to believe they were taken by road to Smith's Farm on the edge of the Somme River, where the water widened, creating small inlets and islands. This was confirmed when two stretcher-bearers serving with the 8th Australian Field Ambulance were identified by the unit's commanding officer, Lieutenant Colonel Arthur Clayton, as having carried the bodies. Clayton personally interviewed them: Drivers W.S. Smith and Terence Callinan agreed that *they* had carried the bodies from the boat at Vaire to the Relay Post (also referred to as the Regimental Aid Post) at Vaux before they were taken by another relay of yet unknown bearers to Smith's Farm, then under the control of the 6th Australian Field Ambulance. Both men confirmed that they had seen the bodies between one and two days later (16 or 17 May), though shortly afterwards, an RAF tender had taken them away. Crucially, there is no reason to believe that either man would have known the identity of the men they were carrying, only that they belonged to the RAF.

The evidence as to what had happened to Mond and Martyn was building and beginning to make sense, but there was also a new and tantalising alternative line of enquiry that Angela had to take seriously.

On 27 January, Lieutenant Colonel Clayton was paid an unexpected visit by an officer from the 29th Battalion AIF (8th Infantry Brigade) who had heard of the general enquiries being made into the whereabouts of Mond and Martyn. This unnamed officer reported that any men of this neighbouring brigade who died at the Relay Posts or Regimental Aid Posts around Vaux were buried in a plot adjoining the civilian cemetery in Corbie. If a tender was not sent – or not sent quickly enough – then the pilots might have been taken to Smith's Farm and then buried in or near this civilian cemetery.

This unnamed officer revealed that the padre attached to the 29th Battalion conducted all funeral services for the 8th Infantry Brigade. Crucially, the padre had told him that he had buried two airmen in the cemetery in Corbie on or around the relevant date in May 1918. Crosses were erected, 'and a piece of cardboard with identification details in (indelible) pencil nailed to each cross. This was done in all cases,' said the officer. The padre confirmed at the time that he would write to the RAF squadron with which the two dead airmen served, and give them particulars.

'This he may have neglected to do but from my experience he probably did so,' wrote Clayton. 'My informant is under the impression that one of the officers came from Sussex.'

Greyfriars was in Storrington and Storrington was in Sussex, and this small detail must have distracted Angela's attention. The only problem was that the padre had already left for Australia. In the circumstances it would be far easier for the men working for the Graves Registration Units to carefully examine the near 1,000 crosses in the cemetery extension in Corbie. 'If an opportunity comes, I will do so myself,' were Clayton's parting words to Angela. Was it possible that Lieutenants Mond and Martyn were buried there after all?

Map 2

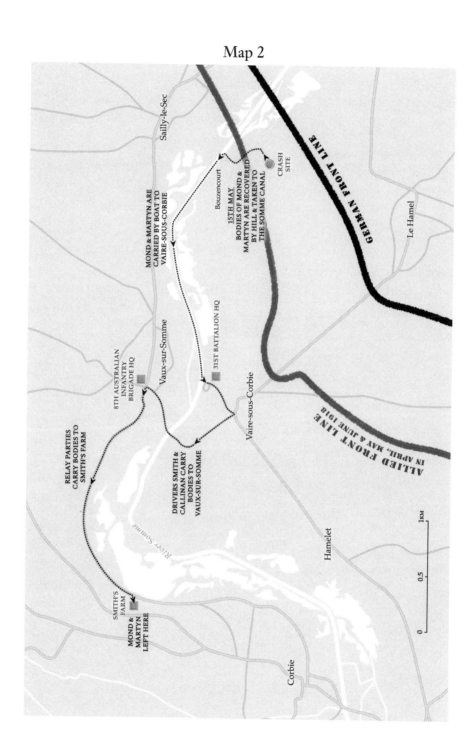

SAILLY-le-Sec

GERMAN FRONT LINE

Le Hamel

MOND & MARTYN ARE
CARRIED BY BOAT TO
VAIRE-SOUS-CORBIE

Bouzencourt

15TH MAY
BODIES OF MOND &
MARTYN ARE RECOVERED
BY HILL & TAKEN TO
THE SOMME CANAL

CRASH
SITE

8TH AUSTRALIAN
INFANTRY
BRIGADE HQ

Vaux-sur-Somme

31ST BATTALION HQ

Vaire-sous-Corbie

RELAY PARTIES
CARRY BODIES TO
SMITH'S FARM

DRIVERS SMITH &
CALLINAN CARRY
BODIES TO
VAUX-SUR-SOMME

River Somme

Hamelet

ALLIED FRONT LINE
IN APRIL, MAY & JUNE 1918

SMITH'S
FARM

MOND &
MARTYN
LEFT HERE

Corbie

0   0.5   1 KM

Chapter Seven

'The policy of searching for lost graves and bodies has been definitely and deliberately abandoned, as some day it had to be.'

Beach Thomas, *Daily Mail*, 14 October 1921

How long could the British Army be expected to search for the dead? Scouring the battlefields for graves was never going to be an open-ended obligation. It was not just the cost of maintaining exhumation parties working in the field, but that of keeping available all the necessary ancillary services of supplies, hospitals, transport, and over such a wide search area. In the end, the financial commitment had proved to be 'an unjustifiable expense to the taxpayer to maintain any longer', a War Office note concluded. In London, the political pressure to hand over the 'care' of British and Empire war dead to the IWGC was mounting. By 1921, dates mentioned for the transition were as early as July and no later than the end of September.

In all, British troops working for the army's DGR&E had been 'spotting' for nearly three years. The battlefields had been combed and re-combed and through hideous experience the men had become expert at reading the land in order to pinpoint the dead. The results had been commendable, indeed almost too good, for they undermined one of the two key arguments for ceasing further work. Financial cost was one; the other was the numerical decline in 'finds', and it was the second argument that was proving problematic, as IWGC figures made clear.

From 13 November 1919 to 17 January 1920, the average number employed on exhumation work (actual working strength, also known as 'pick and shovel' strength) had been 5,766. 'In those ten weeks 40,362 bodies were found or ¾ of a body per man per week,' IWGC calculated.

A year later, the numbers searching had fallen dramatically. In France, the DGR&E had been cut to one Exhumation Company divided into three platoons, each platoon consisting of six officers and 135 other ranks and around sixty additional Belgian contractors. The total working strength was around 200 men for each platoon and therefore around 600 men in all.

The decline in the number of workers reflected the slow but steady withdrawal of the British Army from France and Belgium. With fewer people looking for bodies came an inevitable decline in the numbers found, though figures could fluctuate, depending on variables such as the time of year. What was clear was that the numbers of bodies found per-person-looking had remained broadly steady. Major Henry Chettle, the IWGC's Assistant Secretary and Director of Records, collated the latest figures in mid-July 1921:

Week ending 19/2/21. 374 British and 203 German soldiers found
Week ending 11/6/21. 397 British and 291 German soldiers found
Week ending 18/6/21. 337 British and 228 German soldiers found
Week ending 25/6/21. 381 British and 284 German soldiers found

Though the number of bodies found per person per day had actually fallen in 1920, Chettle claimed that those figures had recently hit a plateau; in fact, there was a small rise in the actual numbers of bodies being found from February to June 1921. Full identification of the bodies found was running at around 20 per cent.

It was perhaps best for all concerned that these figures were for internal and not public consumption when it was announced that all DGR&E battlefield exhumation work would cease by the end of September. In the light of his figures, Chettle wrote a letter to Major Ingpen, the IWGC's Legal Adviser, on 14 July, clarifying the situation: 'It is clear that there is as yet no falling off in the quantity of the results of this work and only DGR&E, France, could tell us whether such definite falling off is likely to occur by the 30th September as to justify the discontinuance of these operations.'

It is unlikely the DGR&E could answer either way with certainty. If there were no decline, if the job were in effect incomplete, what then? Chettle asked Ingpen whether other works performed by the DGR&E should end immediately (15 July) so as to give more time to focus on searching for bodies. Should the DGR&E cease to carry out special exhumations, for example? Special exhumations included the occasional disinterment of bodies for identification as well as to 'settle duplications in grave reports'. The DGR&E could also halt its work on the concentration of cemeteries and graves, requested by the French for the economy of land. These jobs might be carried out by the Commission in the fullness of time, Chettle suggested, though he wished to put on record that the Commission must be compensated by the War Office for such extra work.

The army was keen to stress that it was not abandoning the dead. With a press announcement imminent and perhaps with one eye on allaying expected public anxiety, Colonel James Dick-Cunyngham, Colonel Commandant, British Troops in France and Flanders, set out to the War Office in London what had been achieved. 'The whole of the battlefield areas in France and Flanders have been thoroughly searched and re-searched for isolated graves and bodies. This search has been systematically carried out by taking map squares, and in many cases where areas have produced a large percentage of bodies map squares have been re-searched on two or three occasions.' The farmers returning to their land, and the civilians re-establishing their homes, were certain to discover more dead as they ploughed and tended the land, or as they re-established ditches and hedgerows. Gangs of civilians employed as 'reconstructors' would find bodies as new drains were cut, shell holes filled in, roads remade. 'It is important that this should be realised, otherwise it may be wrongly inferred that the Army have not completed the work,' he wrote, but the army had done all it could be reasonably expected to do.

Trusting in the diligence of the DGR&E and the exhumation parties, the War Office was confident that the battle areas had been cleared of 'all bodies of the dead whose presence [was] in any way visible'. Somewhat contrary to Dick-Cunyngham's view, and as if to further justify their decision to end additional searches, the War Office made an assumption that new discoveries would be made amongst the debris of unreconstructed buildings rather than in the fields themselves. 'Experience has shown that there is now little possibility of bodies being disclosed by ordinary agricultural operations, as it is believed that any lying sufficiently near the surface of the ground to be so discovered have already been found ...' In reality, either from within ruined houses or under shell-shattered fields, the dead would be recovered for some time to come, for how long no one could be sure – some speculated as many as twenty years.

So in the absence of the DGR&E, who would deal with bodies discovered during civilian reconstruction on the old battlefields? Chettle suggested that the continued work of removal and reburial of bodies 'accidentally discovered' might be left to the French *'fossoyeur'* (grave-digger) but in the devastated areas they were not always available. 'Perhaps the Commission gardeners could under-take the work of remains accidentally discovered,' he conjectured.

The IWGC were not going to run around the country carrying out exhumations. Colonel Herbert Goodland, Deputy Controller, was adamant that that was not the IWGC's role. The IWGC would supervise, he said, but:

> the whole labour, transport and reburials will be done by a contractor i.e. the same contractor who is doing the French exhumation work and who is called the *'Adjudicateur'*.

The cost is so much per body, inclusive, with a coffin, and there is no question of employing our gardeners or any other Commission employees in dealing with exhumation at all. The necessary supervision will be done by the Area Superintendent, using whosoever he has available for such work if the Area Registration Officer is not available, or if he cannot be spared.

Major Ingpen said that he had the matter in hand.

With the withdrawal of the men of the DGR&E, all battlefield searches would cease, with the exception of special, requested searches based on specific information, usually garnered by grieving parents. Otherwise, the British government was effectively handing over the job of locating and reporting the fallen to French and Belgian civilians. The IWGC would not have the manpower or the transport to continue the search. Instead, it would react to reports of bodies as it focused on its primary role of establishing cemeteries and offering help and advice to battlefield pilgrims and tourists. It would continue the DGR&E's work of concentrating cemeteries, with an eye on requests made by the French authorities for land economy, as well as exhuming bodies within cemeteries for regrouping.

Dick-Cunyngham had robustly praised the work of the DGR&E, but he was also keen to point out that the IWGC must be ready for its new role once the army was gone. In expressing his views, he could not but sound some notes of caution.

Civilians, he said, had always come up and spoken to army exhumation parties, pointing out isolated graves, and owing to the on-the-spot presence of soldiers, cases had been dealt with rapidly, 'chiefly', he wrote 'because personnel and transport have been detailed at once'. Dick-Cunyngham expressed his view that the IWGC, through no fault of their own, might not be prepared to deal promptly with the discovery of isolated bodies and this was of particular concern; he warned of potential problems and risks.

I am unaware of the arrangements to be made by [the] IWGC to deal with these cases quickly, but I would like to point out that unless bodies can be removed and buried rapidly, there is great danger of some 'traffic in bodies and effects'.

Within the last few months there have been articles in the English papers, advertising effects and whereabouts of bodies, criticising the work of the DGR&E and IWGC, and I feel sure that there are individuals in France and Flanders who would only be too ready to seize upon any opportunity of making money by this 'traffic in bodies'. This may be an extreme view, but it is one that must be guarded against.

Perhaps the IWGC gardeners may be able to deal with most cases, but here again I think they must have some means of transport ready at hand to remove a body. It would never do, for instance, if a gardener was discovered removing human remains in a sandbag by a British traveller, removing human remains in a sandbag on his bicycle.

It would not do at all, and Colonel Goodland had been adamant that it would not happen.

In September, a press release was issued on the final cessation of the DGR&E's work, giving optimistic reports as to what had been achieved. Without any prior notice, the press release announced: 'The Exhumation Parties hitherto employed under the War Office have now been withdrawn.' It went on to reassure civilians across Britain that there was every confidence that 'all further discoveries will be reported by French or Belgians to IWGC who will deal with [presumably supervise] "reverent" interment in existing military cemeteries'.

There was always going to be public concern and even hostility to the cessation of work by the specialist exhumation platoons, particularly amongst families whose loved ones were still missing. It was easy to appreciate the anxiety of others who feared that what was taking place was a permanent breach with these men.

In September, Charles Cornick, father of Corporal Frederick Cornick who had died on the first day of the Third Battle of Ypres, wrote to the newspapers to express his feelings.

Sir

I lost my eldest son in Flanders in July, 1917, and for four years no tidings of the position of his grave was obtainable. About a month ago, however, the War Office informed me that his will had been found, and further enquiries directed to the Imperial War Graves Commission elicited the information that my son's body had been found during the clearing-up operations around Zonnebeke, and had been re-interred in Tyne Cot Cemetery, Passchendaele.

Your article states that hundreds of thousands of bodies lie unrecovered on the several battle areas and I cannot help thinking that what has been possible in the case of my son is possible also in hundreds of other cases.

I have within the last week, been able to visit my son's grave, and whilst at Ypres I was informed that from 200 to 300 bodies were being recovered weekly in the Ypres Salient, and that a large proportion of these were identified. I was also informed that the whole of the Englishmen who had been employed on this work were to return to England during this month. ....

If this is due to the 'Economy without exception' stunt that is being waged at the present moment, I consider it a crying shame. Many hundreds of bereaved fathers and mothers would willingly give their last pennypiece if by doing so the recovery of the body and reverential burial of a son could be accomplished, and I cannot believe that any Britisher worthy the name would begrudge any sum of money spent in this direction.

Yours, C.F. Cornick

Corporal Cornick's remains had been found close to the German front-line trenches outside the village of Westhoek, 1½ miles west of Zonnebeke. He had been identified by the fortunate survival of his AB64 Soldier's Pay Book and Will. Later his father was able to add an inscription to the base of the grave. It read: 'Ever Loved But Lost Awhile.'

In October, national newspapers, reflecting the concern of the British public, continued to follow up on the War Office's abrupt announcement. The proactive search for the dead had ended, so what, they asked, were the repercussions of that decision?

On 6 October, Colonel Herbert Goodland, the Commission's Deputy Controller, contacted the IWGC in London to let them know that Beach Thomas of the *Daily Mail* was heading to France to see for himself the effect of the changes. Thomas intended to discover the truth as to whether bodies found since the completion of the DGR&E's work were not being collected quickly enough and worse still, that some bodies were being left exposed for days, to be fouled by animals. Beach Thomas had contacted Colonel Goodland at the IWGC headquarters at St Omer to find out where he might go and whom he might see. The Commission decided to offer an infantry officer and priest, Reverend Edward Gell, Assistant Director of Records, as a source of calm, thoughtful advice and information. 'The important places are the Salient and Albert. If Colonel Gell could accompany Mr Thomas it might prevent the latter from getting an exaggerated impression ...' Meanwhile, just to be clear, the IWGC manoeuvred to head off possible criticism by stating a few facts.

The Commission has a sufficient organisation to deal with the disposal and burial of any body that may be discovered by French or Belgian inhabitants and reported; they have not however any organisation or exhumation staff to go round searching for bodies. This duty was carried out by the War Office, and if the War Office is of opinion that the time has come to cease the work, the responsibility is theirs and not the Commission's. We have no knowledge as to the future intentions of the War Office in this respect.

On 14 October, Beach Thomas's article was published. He had finished his tour of inspection, ending at a site of Somme infamy, Delville Wood, 'still almost impenetrable', before visiting the 'vast' cemetery that adjoined it. His stated purpose was 'to test the truth of many vague reports about the neglect of cemeteries, isolated graves and unidentified bodies'.

His view was forthright, measured and, if anything, sympathetic to the IWGC.

> The facts are these. ... The policy of searching for lost graves and bodies has been definitely and deliberately abandoned, as some day it had to be. Hitherto a select body of soldiers has been engaged in the work of probing and peering below the surface of the old battlefields and ruins. Some of these men became curiously expert and by their trained observation found, not once or twice, the body of a lost soldier. The men had even designed special instruments of their own with which they practised the strange work of the humane and beneficent ghoul.

That irreplaceable expertise would be lost while 'many thousands, probably several tens of thousands of dead still lie unidentified'. He continued:

> The French and the Belgians have no searchers. They trust, as we are going to trust, to the groups of workmen engaged in reconstruction in clearing buildings and fields and woods, and they pay to the workman who finds a body the sum of two francs. We give nothing in the pious hope that discoveries will be reported nevertheless ...
> The search for bodies is not of the Commission's work. They must trust to the reconstructors, who, by the nature of the job, are much more likely to make discoveries than even the deliberate and specialised searchers. Since this is so, we shall justify every report, we shall deserve blame

as perpetrators of a sort of negative sacrilege if we do not take every means to make sure that discoveries are duly reported. ... Does the knowledge of every discovery reach the ears of our Commission? Two francs, or one shilling, is not a large sum. Why is it refused?

Beach Thomas had not been critical of the IWGC, but he had picked up on a point that would have to be addressed. If there was an expectation that workers would, either out of good consciousness or more nebulous feelings of debt, report the discovery of a body, then expectations were over-high. Some would, no doubt, if it was not too inconvenient, but reporting was bound to be irregular without some financial incentive.

On such a sensitive issue it was important that everyone was on-message. Beach Thomas's article had been judged by the IWGC as not 'unfavourable', though it was noted that while he was being escorted he had 'asked very few questions and was forming his own conclusions as to what he saw, which, from the nature of the articles that have been appearing from his pen of late, do not appear to have been unfavourable', wrote Colonel Goodland, the IWGC's Deputy Controller. Still, newspaper men were always to be regarded with just the right amount of suspicion.

'I'm afraid that these newspaper men, when they come out here, have an extraordinary knack of gleaning little bits of information here and there and retaining it in their minds, afterwards writing about it,' Goodland cautioned.

The British government was nervous. Those who had given their all, were they expected to rot, undiscovered and forgotten? The potential for public outrage was high, high enough for the new Secretary of State for War, Sir Laming Worthington-Evans, to ask for specifics with which to rebut any awkward questions he might face in the House or from journalists. How many times had the key battlegrounds been searched? How were the search parties organised and what was their methodology? Examples would be useful, he stated, such as pumping out shell holes to find bodies 'and other interesting facts which may occur to you. Please report in writing as soon as possible.'

A week later, and possibly at the behest of the Secretary of State, the Army Council sought to allay public fears and to answer questions.

> Since the Armistice the whole battlefield area in France and Flanders has been systematically searched at least six times. Some areas in which fighting had been particularly heavy were searched as many as twenty times. In the spring of 1920 the work was easy and rapid owing to the number of surface indications, but since then in approximately 90% of the bodies found there was no surface indication.

And now that exhumation parties had been withdrawn:

> The owners and inhabitants are now resuming possession of their houses, fields and gardens, and reports of the discovery of bodies by such owners and occupiers must be awaited before exhumation and re-interment in an approved cemetery can be undertaken.
>
> In cases where relatives or friends can produce from their own knowledge evidence that the body of an officer or soldier may be found in a particular locality, special search will be made under the instructions of the IWGC if the Commission is satisfied that a good prima facie case has been made out.

It may have felt distasteful, even disturbing, to talk about money for bodies but equally was it not lamentable that British bodies were apparently *not* worth paying for? The IWGC pressed the British government to fund bounties. The French and Belgian governments paid two francs for every French, Belgian or German body found. 'We', the IWGC complained, 'pay them nothing.' In Flanders, the Belgian government contracted gangs, each around 250 men under a foreman, to reclaim devastated areas. Each gang was split in two. One was responsible for roughly levelling the ground while the other dug it over. Each gang was expected to cover about 2½ hectares a day and was paid by piecework, in other words, results. This presented a problem: gangs were under orders to report bodies but, in practice, many did not as they would lose time and therefore pay. The DGR&E used to attach two soldiers to each gang but the Commission had no spare personnel to do the same thing.

Major Arthur Ingpen estimated that each gang would find about eight British dead a day. It was 'anticipated' that around twenty-five sets of remains would be reported by each gang every week if there were no extra pay, and seventy if there were. As between 10 per cent and 20 per cent of bodies discovered were identified, that would mean that each week, dozens of British soldiers risked being abandoned, unknown, when they should have been buried under a named grave. The IWGC was very keen that men should be paid and it also asked for the employment of twelve former DGR&E exhumers to be attached to the gangs for purposes of identification. Furthermore, it requested that special staff be employed to deal with reports of discoveries until at least July 1922. One exhumation officer and six assistants should be employed and drawn from the DGR&E to help in identification and disposal of remains.

Newspaper pressure helped ensure that funds were finally made available to pay a bounty of two francs, but was that sum even enough? In the spring, a minor dispute had broken out within the IWGC when a Scottish Unionist MP, Walter Elliot, contacted the Commission with reference to a disturbing letter he had received from one of his constituents, Reverend James Gillies, whose son had been killed at Serre on the Somme in November 1916. The body of Second Lieutenant Halliday Gillies had not been recovered and identified.

Gillies had been in touch with Thomas Chapman, a former officer in the Army Service Corps who was making 'his living on the battlefields' near Serre and was witness to the restoration

of the land and the discovery and exhumation of bodies. As well
as running a small restaurant with his French wife, catering for
both labourers and tourists, Chapman worked as a tour guide,
and appears to have been given some IWGC authority to pay out
money (two francs) to reconstruction workers who reported the
discovery of a body. It was in this capacity, working as an informal
go-between, that Chapman had offered a bounty of 500 francs
on behalf of the Reverend Gillies to any workman who could
identify his son's body. But there was another issue that Chapman
wished to bring to Gillies' attention.

> Now what I want to ask you is this, cannot some pressure
> be brought to bear on the Government to look after this
> exhumation better? ... There are so many things which happen
> with the bodies, one really feels disgusted ... A man finds a
> body, he comes and reports and I pay him [two francs] (after I
> have ascertained the truth) but frequently he finds some thing
> of value and puts it in his pocket.

Chapman revealed that even 'today' he had confronted a labourer
whom he suspected of stealing a cigarette case from the body of a
British soldier. 'Well, I threatened and frightened him with the
Gendarmes and at mid-day [he] produced it and inside is a photo
of the poor fellow with his name and address.'

A bounty of 500 francs would be a significant encouragement for
a labourer to report the discovery of Lieutenant Gillies, property
and all, but a small fee of two francs was so low that the temptation
to take items of value could only prove irresistible to some people
struggling to make a living in such an inhospitable place.

> I would like to point out that within a few kilometres from
> this town [Albert] there are hundreds, possibly thousands,
> of British bodies that have never been recovered, and which,
> by the process of clearing ground, are now being exposed

not only to daylight but to the searching and desecration [by those] who are doing the work of clearing the ground.

A man is not likely to leave his work and walk perhaps two kilometres to report a body for two francs, thereby losing perhaps six or seven francs time lost. In my work out here I take tourists to all places, and when they say, 'There is a body lying there,' I have to say, 'yes, it is not English.'

In every case I find a body I report it to the IWGC here in Albert and I must say that action is taken immediately. The fault does not lie with the IWGC here, they are only allowed to pick up 'found' bodies ...

Elliott's intervention saw Chapman's concerns spiral up the military chain of command. Field Marshal Sir Henry Wilson, who had only just resigned his position as Chief of the Imperial General Staff, received then forwarded Chapman's letter to the Adjutant General, who sent it to Sir Fabian Ware, adding that he might wish to be 'cognisant of' the letter's details, 'though, of course, they are probably very much exaggerated'.

The reaction of the IWGC was to aggressively challenge Chapman. In a pointed response, the IWGC in France were asked to review the case.

Mr Chapman who carries on a somewhat precarious business in close proximity to Serre Road Cemetery No. 3 has been interviewed by a representative of the Commission from St Omer. He admitted:

1. That the pictures drawn by Dr [Rev] Gillies [based on what he heard from Chapman] bears no resemblance to the facts.
2. That there are no grounds for believing that 'thousands of Unknown British are being cast up, etc.'
3. That some 60 bodies have been reported in the region of Serre since the Commission took up the work of reinterment.

4. That every report of remains found had been promptly dealt with by a Commission representative.
5. That he was with the Field Assistant when the cigarette case was reported to have been taken and that it was eventually returned as a result of the prompt action of the <u>Field Assistant</u>.
6. That in his opinion the machinery of the Commission is quite adequate to deal with the reports of isolated British remains that are now being made.
7. That no identifications are being lost through any neglect on the part of the representatives of the Commission.

Mr Chapman promised to write to Dr Gillies in this sense.

Chapman may have exaggerated his case, though to what possible personal advantage is unclear. The IWGC was evidently rattled by the accusations that there was not enough supervision of the reconstruction gangs. As Ernest Gell, the Assistant Director of Records, writing on behalf of the Deputy Controller, pointed out:

It is possible that quite unavoidably some identifications have been lost. The limited staff at the disposal of the Commission make it quite impossible to watch without intermission the work of each individual of the hundreds of reconstruction workers employed in different areas from time to time. No effort is spared, however, in keeping in touch with the different gangs and impressing upon them the necessity of reporting the presence of any remains that may be uncovered.

Yes, but that did not mean that they would oblige without greater financial encouragement, and in a sense, that was Chapman's point.

* * *

Towards the end of September 1921, the departing DGR&E gave the IWGC a certificate of their work to date, re-emphasising that if they had cleared an area of visible graves, it did not follow that the area was totally clear. To an extent, everyone was covering their backs on this issue. What even constituted a 'visible grave' was not clear: walking the fields, a tourist or battlefield pilgrim would see little or no evidence of unretrieved bodies whereas an experienced search party crossing the same land quite possibly would.

That summer of 1921 had seen so many bodies reported by civilians and gardeners that the outgoing DGR&E had created 'two small flying squads' to race round and pick up the dead. Even then, they could not keep up with the work. 'Numbers of these reports have had to be left untouched, on account of the closing down of the DGR&E and the subsequent disposal of the Exhumation Parties,' an army memo noted. On 15 September, a list of the most recent and so far 'untouched' notifications was passed on to the IWGC, including map references and notes:

A portion of cross with G.R.U inscription slips reading '2nd Lieut. J Jotcham, 1/8th Worcestershire Regt. K.I.A. 9th August 1917'. Only the upper portion and cross beam remains. The body may have been taken away but the portion of cross is left and this usually [denotes] the presence of a body.

Remains of British soldier behind ruined house used as shelter and Pillbox. Grave is situated on left side of road when proceeding in a N.E. direction. These remains were exposed to view but have been covered with Macintosh sheet.

Body of an English soldier wrapped in canvas and situated approx 100 yards beyond St Julian Cemetery towards Poelcapelle, on the right hand side of the road. I have covered this body with cart and erected a temporary cross which I marked 'Not to be touched'. As civilians are at work cutting away the road, this body should be removed immediately.

Part remains of British officer or soldier. As Belgian civilians are clearing the ground and making roads in the immediate vicinity of this spot, the body should be removed as soon as possible.

The list was long and likely to get longer once the takeover was completed. Each season, in nature's changing landscape, new telltale details emerged of graves that the previous season had hidden and the warmer weather naturally encouraged greater outside work and further finds.

Less than three months into the IWGC's expanded role, the Assistant Director of Records took a trip round the battlefields to see how the collection and burial of the 'reported' dead was being undertaken. He kept a journal throughout the week, being accompanied by two others, named only as Wells and Dowse Brenan. First stop was the village of Villers-Faucon, and recently discovered bodies found on the Arras battlefield.

13 December

It was growing dark when we arrived at Villers Faucon M.C. [Military Cemetery]. Here we found three men (British) civilian labourers employed by Wells, burying seven bodies which had been brought in during the day. Only one body remained to be buried; these remains were contained in a sandbag. All these bodies had been found at Fins in a grave in which one only had been reported by a civilian. One was identified as belonging to the Northumberland Fusiliers and one to the Leicester Regiment. There was a cross erected over his grave to 'Gills or Gillies' but it was impossible to single out this soldier from the others ...

16 December

To Bourlon Wood to see the condition of it, as report goes that large numbers of bodies are still missing there.

We worked our way through a part of the wood, but soon the tangled undergrowth became so thick that progress was impossible. Brambles grow in such profusion, that I give it as my opinion that no systematic search is possible. I do not believe the wood has ever been searched properly, let alone re-searched. From time to time bodies have been reported in the country round, and some within the limits of the wood, but there is no likelihood of remains being found there in any numbers until the undergrowth has been cleared away.

The gardener (Lloyd) lives at Bourlon in a ruined cottage, which backs on to the little Bourlon British Cemetery. He told us that he spends many of his Sunday afternoons walking through the less dense parts of the wood. ... This gardener, like so many of the Commission's gardeners, is a man of obviously good character. Local civilians spoke to me about him in terms of the highest praise. His life, however, must be a lonely one, and very silent, for his French is monosyllabic.

20 December

To Tower Hamlets (Gheluvelt). Body reported by one of a gang. This was not identified even partially, though very careful search was made, the boots scraped and the coloured silk handkerchief examined. This was probably a 1914 soldier as the date of his boots was 1914. It is, therefore, remarkable that the silk handkerchief should have been so well preserved, but I am amazed that there is nothing other than metals which resist decay better than silk. In this case every bit of cloth was completely decayed, but after washing the silk handkerchief would be as bright and good as the day it was buried ...

21 December

In Kemmel French Cemetery there was a large pile of light-coloured wooden coffins which are to be used for the removal of French bodies to Notre Dame de Lorette shortly.

There are a certain number of German graves at the back of the cemetery. Towards the road there is first a collection of 150 or so British graves (only 15 of which are knowns), and then about 300 French graves which are all to be moved. When the French have gone this will be an awkward little bit of a cemetery within a few yards of Klein Vierstraat British Cemetery. From the point of view of construction and maintenance these 15 known and 150 unknown would be better placed in Klein Vierstraat if the acquisition is straightforward. The gardener here, who was for 14 years in the 1st Somerset Light Infantry before coming on to the Commission, is doing his work well, but looks exceedingly gloomy, poor fellow. He lives (alone at the moment) in a dismantled [military] vehicle and seems to spend his whole time in this wilderness with the exception that he goes on Saturday to Kemmel to buy his groceries.

To Tyne Cot, picked up a blanched skull just outside the Battalion H.Q. dugout in the embankment of the Broodseinde Cutting. This will be reburied tonight in La Brique, but will not be registered. An entombed R.F.A. observing officer was found close by this spot today, in an old O.P. [Observation Post] that had been knocked in by a shell. The telephone and receiver were beside him.

Despite the desolate nature of the land, there were reasons why a man might wish to remain in France. Survivors' guilt was certainly one reason he might devote years, even a working life, to fallen friends and comrades. Seeing the battlefields transformed from shell-pitted wildernesses to vibrant, verdant fields again, would be cathartic. Watching the cemeteries grow from drab, filthy burial grounds to pristine grassed graveyards, was perhaps a balm for troubled, guilt-ridden souls. Meeting visitors in France, helping widows find graves of a beloved husband, provided some redemption for having lived when others had died. Of course, there could be more prosaic reasons: maybe a desire not to return to the pedestrian life of old, a dull career already retarded through war service. There could be an awareness of faltering job prospects in England, of high unemployment amongst former servicemen: a potential job for life working for the Commission would be tempting. Equally a man might have a love of the outdoor life, perhaps he remained a keen horticulturalist, a would-be tour guide, or he had simply met and married a local girl.

Whatever the backstory, living on the Western Front could never be easy. In the early days, back in 1919, former Scots Guardsman Stephen Graham had become intrigued by the men who had worked as exhumers, 'the weather-beaten Tommy, in old flannel shirt and sagging breeches'. Talking to these men, Graham had been told that the job was not too bad, though they could have been paid more. 'We gets used to it,' he said, Graham noticing that these men had 'become as matter of fact as can be'. Yet these exhumers lived amongst the ghosts. When Graham asked one man whether he had seen any, he just smiled affably. He had seen none. He had felt the presence of none. 'Imagination did not pull his heart-strings. If it did, he would go mad,' Graham wrote.

It was inevitable that some men would struggle with their demons and what we would call post-traumatic stress disorder. From the days of the first exhumations, DGR&E men had reported themselves sick. The actual, rather than paper strength of exhumation parties was indicative not just of the ghastly job they endured but also of likely mental health problems. In the week ending 17 January 1920, the nominal strength of those men tasked with combing the battlefields was 8,559 but the number of men actually employed that week in the field was 6,342. The difference of 2,217 could be accounted for by a mixture of leave (700) and a daily sick attendance rate of around 500. This still left just over 1,000 men who were noted as already being 'sick in hospital' or were logged simply as 'absentees', while an undisclosed number were undergoing 'Field Punishment' for unspecified misdemeanours. The number on the daily sick parade had stubbornly held at 500 for weeks.

Freed from wartime dangers but still surrounded by their consequences, is it any wonder that some men took to the bottle, and not just those responsible for the exhumations, but those also responsible for their collection? A number of incidents were logged:

In September 1920, near the village of Niergnies, south-east of Cambrai, the discovery of five bodies within the Commune was reported by the mayor to British officers and NCOs on at least six occasions, according to an IWGC internal report. Despite the serial notifications, nothing was reportedly done.

The Mayor [said] that unless we took some action it would be assumed that we did not trouble about the graves of our soldiers and these particular graves might be lost. He said that on each occasion the Garde had pointed out the position of the graves, and he had himself, some months ago, taken an officer round, only to find that he went off to the local 'estaminet' to get half drunk, so that he was not surprised that nothing had resulted from the information he gave.

In July 1921, the IWGC Area Superintendant near Albert, a man named Captain Meikle was reported 'incapacitated' as a consequence of a motorcycle accident sustained while drunk. This accident came after a 'series of erratic incidents', including, when in 'a fit of depression, driving off to Amiens in the middle of the night and returning to Albert the following morning'.

The same man was reported as appearing at camp regularly 'intoxicated'. On one occasion he and two other men, named as Ford and Christian, were in the staff mess drinking heavily at midnight. At least one of these two men was supposed to be on duty. 'During the drinking Ford produced a revolver and threatened to shoot Christian.'

This state of affairs was allowed to drag on, with further accusations that Meikle was not doing his job. Finally, the Commission's Deputy Controller, Colonel Goodland, confronted Meikle who, though he denied wrongdoing, resigned in March 1922.

Meikle wasn't the only officer to go. Captain Francis Bluett-Duff had served in France from May 1916 with the Royal Flying Corps and had joined the IWGC with excellent references. He was removed from France 'forthwith' in April 1922, his contract terminated. The reason cited: erratic behaviour owing to excessive drinking and 'worry', both 'financial and domestic'. His work for the IWGC had been 'practically nil', according to Colonel Goodland, and he could no longer rely on him.

> I have had him removed from the Hotel de Commerce to our hospital at the Camp, where he will have proper treatment and nursing. The Doctor had reported to me that since last Thursday, when he took to his bed, he has had no solid food, simply stimulants – coffee and brandy. On Saturday he was a complete wreck ... The Doctor states today that now he is cut off alcohol he is suffering from insomnia.

Like Meikle, Bluett–Duff also rejected the allegations and furthermore claimed the dismissal would 'entail the complete ruin of a long and honourable career of which you yourself [Goodland] have the record'. His contract remained terminated.

Even those who had given sterling work to the IWGC could struggle with the emotional stress and pressure of work. Colonel Edward Gell, the priest and former infantry officer, and one of the most senior people in the IWGC, had had problems. In August 1914, he had gone to France with the 1st Battalion, Royal Fusiliers, being awarded both the Distinguished Service Order and Military Cross. And yet, weeks before showing the journalist Beach Thomas around the old battlefields, he had been taken ill. In August 1921, in a letter to Chettle, Colonel Goodland wrote:

'I have sent Gell away on leave as if he did not get a couple of weeks' rest he would crack up, and he has been showing signs of a breakdown for some weeks past. Thorn has brought me your confidential note of him in reference to exhumation.' Gell returned to meet Beach Thomas and to carry on his hitherto outstanding work.

* * *

The Western Front remained a world apart. And in this strange world, human magpies appeared – unscrupulous individuals keen to make money from any opportunity.

Dick-Cunyngham's view that an illicit 'traffic in bodies and effects' might occur once the army had left was not entirely without substance. He had seen articles in the English papers, 'advertising effects and [the] whereabouts of bodies'. The work of the DGR&E and the IWGC had been criticised. It was easy to imagine that a market in personal items might prove lucrative for rogues. Many a signet ring or fob watch had gone missing during the war, as soldiers' belongings were collected and returned to parents. But a traffic in bodies, was that not too far-fetched?

At the end of the war a decision about the final resting place of military bodies would have to be taken, though in reality, the evidence demonstrates that the decision had already been made. Once certain conclusions were reached as to the preservation, expansion and architectural treatment of British cemeteries overseas, it was clear the dead were going nowhere. Nevertheless, a public statement to this effect would need to be made.

There had been no legal prohibition on the removal of bodies from the battlefield in the first months of the war. Around forty bodies – all officers – had been collected and taken back to Britain for burial in family mausoleums, cemeteries or crypts. Even the suggestion of there being one rule for rich families and one for everyone else could not be allowed to continue and the army's

Adjutant General prohibited the removal of any further bodies from the Western Front: this restriction, reconfirmed by Haig in December 1917, would last as long as the conflict did. By the very nature of a circumscribed ban, expectations may have been raised amongst families that it would be lifted once the Armistice was signed. There may have been a belief that families would be permitted to do whatever they saw fit with *their* dead. There was no precedent by which to judge.

An important question had been posed: to whom did the dead belong? Did families own them? Or did the bodies of servicemen and women remain in passive, eternal servitude to the army and, by extension, the government? They were, after all, in military service and under military law when they died. Did death release a body from continued service only to be automatically re-enlisted into the ritual of state-organised and state-controlled remembrance?

After consultation between the IWGC and the government, it was decided that the best policy was to act swiftly, and permanently ban all exhumations undertaken with a view to bringing the body home. Before any announcement would be made in the press, the legal ground was prepared, with the French obliging on cue: under a decree by the Paris government, the exhumation and transportation of the bodies of officers and men buried in France was forbidden, a decree that was quickly incorporated into Article 2 of the Anglo-French Agreement of 26 November 1918. The following year, the Belgians followed suit, arguing that exhumations would be an interruption to reconstruction, dangerous to public health and impracticable.

The French decree was a useful legal tool to block all applications to exhume bodies for transfer to Britain and elsewhere, such as Canada or Australia. It would also help deflect criticism by allowing the British authorities to stand, conveniently, behind the French decision. There already existed around 100 applications for exhumation and this list was only going to lengthen, and so on 29 November, an announcement was made in *The Times* under a headline: 'Comradeship in Death, Soldiers' Bodies not to be Brought Home'.

Wilfrid Thompson was one of those who had applied to exhume the body of his son, Second Lieutenant Albert Thompson, killed in August 1917. He now received a polite brush-off from the Inspector of Works at the IWGC: 'I deeply regret to inform you that permission cannot be obtained from the French Authorities for this exhumation to take place.'

It appeared to some that an easy collusion had occurred. When another father, William Dawson, later applied for the return of his son's body, Colonel Bob Dawson, commanding 6th The Queen's Own (Royal West Kent Regiment), he too was given the same reply. 'I told him about the decree of the French Government prohibiting the removal of bodies from France,' confided an internal IWGC memo. Dawson smelt a rat and wrote again, only to be rebuffed. 'He [Dawson] wishes to know whether this decree was "absolutely spontaneous" on the part of the French Government or not. As you will see he writes in a somewhat bitter strain.'

For those who had waited patiently for the conclusion of hostilities, the breaking news was earth-shattering:

Sirs

I was shocked beyond words and grieved more than I can say, as I read the decision of the Imperial War Graves Commission (in the daily papers for Friday the 29th alto.) ...

First of all, let me say here that I protest most emphatically against that decision, as I consider the parents at least might have been consulted before you sat in council to discuss what shall be done with the remains of our sons. I speak plainly, (as I have a right to) being one of many mothers who have been called upon to sacrifice an only child, in the defence of our country. Is there no limit to the suffering imposed upon us, is it not enough to have our boys dragged from us and butchered, (and not allowed to say 'nay') without being deprived of their poor remains? ... The country took him, and the country should bring him back.

The author of this letter, Ruth Jervis, had lost her son, Gunner Harry Jervis, aged twenty-two, in 1917.

'I am <u>not</u> satisfied with your answer to my request re. the removal of my son's body to this country,' Ruth told the IWGC, furious that bereaved families had been sidelined while such decisions were made behind closed doors.

> Militarism has destroyed his body and it seems to me if some people in this country had the power they would deal with his soul also, but thank heaven that at least is beyond you. If we mothers of England marched on Downing Street in thousands, like the munition workers and suffragettes, then we might receive some justice.
>
> Therefore in conclusion I tell you once more, (and I think we've come to a pretty state of things when a mother has to beg for the remains of her own boy), I want my boy home and I shall be satisfied with nothing less, and who has the right to deny me more under heaven?
>
> I beg to remain
> Yours faithfully
> Ruth Jervis

An IWGC letter in reply was just as firm:

> I am to express the regret of the Commission that you are unable to feel in sympathy with their decisions. They are confident that these decisions are the most satisfactory in the painful circumstances with which they have to deal and although they have the deepest sympathy with your desire, they are strongly of opinion that it would be unwise to allow of any exceptions to their policy.

Throughout the war, many of the dead *had* been buried in Britain: wounded men deemed fit enough to travel home on hospital ships but who eventually succumbed to their wounds. Conversely, when a soldier was believed to be mortally wounded and not fit enough to travel, then families, under certain circumstances, were permitted to visit.

One man who had travelled to France had been William Dawson. His son, Colonel Bob Dawson, was mortally wounded in late October and his parents were granted a travel warrant to see him just before the Armistice. During their poignant hospital meeting, Colonel Dawson had asked that in the event of his death his remains be brought home. After his son's death on 3 December, William Dawson's request for repatriation was turned down. Angered, Dawson then asked the IWGC by what law his position 'as the Legal Representative of my deceased son' had been superseded. The answer from government lawyers was simple: the body of his son was not his 'legal property'. In May 1919, Dawson wrote again, but only the outline of the IWGC reply survives, the Legal Adviser suggesting 'that Mr Dawson be informed that the Commission has nothing to add to their letter of the 14th Instant, and that it is open to him to take such legal action in the matter as he thinks fit'.

An opportunity to challenge the authorities' ascendancy over the dead came after the Versailles Peace Treaty of 29 June 1919. When the text of the treaty was released, Dawson read it carefully, particularly Section II of Article 225.

The Allied and Associated Governments and the German Government will cause to be respected and maintained the graves of the soldiers and sailors buried in their respective territories.

They agree to recognise any Commission appointed by an Allied or Associated Government for the purpose of identifying, registering, caring for or erecting suitable memorials over the said graves and to facilitate the discharge of its duties.

Furthermore they agree to afford, so far as the provisions of their laws and the requirements of public health allow, every facility for giving effect to requests that the bodies of their soldiers and sailors may be transferred to their own country.

The third paragraph appeared to offer hope and he was not the only father to notice. Lieutenant Albert Thompson's father, Wilfrid, had spotted it too. Both Thompson and Dawson wrote to the IWGC, pointing out the clause. The reply to Dawson does not survive, but it probably followed along the lines of that sent by the IWGC to Thompson:

I am directed to inform you that Article 225 Section 2 of the Peace Treaty with Germany is concerned only with the transfer of bodies from Germany to any one of the countries of the Allies and vice versa. The Article in question has no reference to the transfer of bodies from one Allied country to another.

I am further to quote for your information an answer made by Captain [Frederick] Guest in the House of Commons on the question of bringing home bodies of soldiers and sailors who have died in France and Belgium during the war.

'If permission to exhume bodies for subsequent reinterment in all parts of the Empire is given to some, it must be given to all, and I am sure it will be realised that such a proposal is quite impracticable.'

Impracticable was right, on every level. Even if the huge cost of repatriating hundreds of thousands of bodies was judged acceptable, what exactly would be sent home; a full skeleton or an assortment of bones in a sandbag? In the case of a family dispute, who would own the bones? The parents or the dead man's wife? How fair would such a policy of repatriation be to those with no body to mourn, those who were blown literally to pieces? And what message did repatriation send to the countries that had offered up their land in perpetuity for fallen heroes? That their land was not as worthy as Britain's?

To Dawson, and to others, the IWGC's interpretation of Article 225 appeared selective and unfairly used to bolster their stated position. This caused understandable bitterness. 'I am afraid,' wrote Dawson ominously, 'there is going to be great and grave trouble over this question unless your Commission, instead of thwarting, endeavour to assist me to carry out my son's expressed wish. And there must be hundreds of similar cases.' The prediction of 'grave trouble' was not meant as a pun.

There was clearly concern that some people might be driven to desperate measures, and that Dick-Cunyngham's anxiety over a 'traffic in bodies' might turn out to be prophetic. On 24 July 1919, Major Arthur Ingpen, the IWGC's Land and Legal Adviser, wrote from Brussels to London talking of his own pre-emptive measures.

I have taken such steps as I hope will result in a circular being issued to Bourgmestres calling their attention to the law forbidding the exhumation and transport of Military bodies, and requesting them to post notices in the areas under their respective control calling the attention of the Civil population to the fact that the disturbance of Military graves is forbidden by law and is contrary to the interests of the relatives of the deceased and to their own interest for hygienic reasons. It is hoped that there will also be included in the notice a statement to the effect that isolated bodies of soldiers will be eventually removed by the properly constituted Military Authorities to Military Cemeteries.

In October 1919, as the first anniversary of the Armistice was approaching, the United States of America, under pressure from civilians back home, announced that it would repatriate bodies requested by family members. This made something of a mockery of the French decree and may have influenced the wording of the

Belgian decree, issued the following month, which made no mention of sentiment but rather of the public health issues of exhumation.

The sight of American mass repatriation of bodies undermined the British belief in a brotherhood of the dead: that the fallen should remain together in cemeteries as a perennial memorial to their fight against tyranny. Stephen Graham, former soldier in the Scots Guards, saw the coffins and was not impressed by the message this sent.

> At Calais now the boxes are stacked on the quays with the embalmed American dead. At great cost of time and labour the dead soldiers are being removed from the places where they fell and packed in crates for transport to America. In this way America's sacrifice is lessened. For while in America this is considered to be America's own concern, it is certain that it is deplored in Europe. The taking away of the American dead has given the impression of a slur on the honour of lying in France. America removes her dead because of a sweet sentiment towards her own. She takes them from a more honourable resting-place to a less honourable one. It is said to be due in part to the commercial enterprise of the American undertakers, but it is more due to the sentiment of mothers and wives and provincial pastors in America. That the transference of the dead across the Atlantic is out of keeping with European sentiment she ignores, or fails to understand.

The American decision might have been out of keeping with European sentiment, but it did more than that, as an IWGC memo predicted. Questions were expected to be asked in the House 'about the possibility of the transfer of bodies', wrote one official, 'and I am sure we shall have the same problems to face which the French Government have been wrestling with since the Americans forced their hand ...'

The memo predicted that the French would be coerced into allowing bodies to be moved.

> It is impossible to give a figure which has any real value at this stage and I can only refer to figures already given in reports, that out of a total of 1,000,000 dead in France, about 400,000 will be asked for and that the cost of exhumation, encoffining and transport of each body would approximate to 500 francs. Total cost 200 millions of francs!

This would have been the equivalent of around 4 million sterling. And that was the cost of moving a body from one part of France to another, never mind across the English Channel! And then, of course, there were the British bodies lying in Gallipoli, Africa, Salonika and Mesopotamia.

Beyond the confines of government and the offices of the IWGC, there was active civil opposition to the repatriation of the dead, and public debate on the issue was played out in the press. Many people felt that the dead should remain where they were, with their comrades. Partial repatriation would denude cemeteries and consequently appear to lessen the sacrifice of those remaining. Letters were sent to newspapers, and an open and frank discussion began in public.

'Would it be wise to bring these bodies here?' wrote Clara Graves, mother of a dead son, in October 1919.

> Think what it would mean to take up bodies who have died in full flesh and have lain for a long time. It would cause our hearts to bleed afresh, and perhaps bring sickness and death in its train. Our boys themselves would not wish it, but would rather we let their bodies lie where they are.
>
> I have lost a son [Cedric Graves] out in Egypt. I wish his grave were in France where it would be possible sometime to go and not so far away in the desert. If I thought it was

him that was there I could not be comforted, but it is only his shell and it makes no difference where it lies. Our Father keeps the reunion before my eyes.

Another son of mine has returned safe, and he tells me how reverently our boys have been laid to rest. French ladies, he says, take flowers and place them on the boys' graves which will be well looked after. Mothers! Take comfort; your sons WILL NOT soon be forgotten, but they will be remembered while the world lasts. Let us remember them as they left us, their bright, sunny, laughing faces, for they themselves would wish it so.

C. Graves

Brighouse 29th October 1919

Reading the published letters, one 'Ex-Soldier' from Leeds contributed his view on 6 November 1919:

I have read with interest the series of letters published in your columns of late with regard to the subject of 'Our Dead in France' and I have come to the conclusion that most of your correspondents are not in the least conversant with the difficulties of the situation.

I speak from personal knowledge when I say that thousands of our gallant dead were buried in close proximity to the firing line both on the Somme and around Ypres. Everyone who knows what shell-fire is and anyone who has experienced the uncomfortable whizz of rifle and machine gun bullets knows full well how difficult it is to bury the dead. In fairness to the living soldiers it was impossible to hold imposing funeral services. There was absolutely no question of callousness. How can any decent minded civilian think of such a thing?

In the cases of our dead at Ypres and in the Somme at any rate, there can be very little question of the bodies being exhumed and brought back to this country. As regards the big cemeteries well behind the lines, they were and are being kept in a good state of presentation.

Others wrote in support of exhumation:

I lost my all, and am keenly interested in the letters advocating that the bodies of our dear ones should be brought over to the country they died to save. This would be of great comfort to thousands of poor mothers and wives.

I think that the government snubs us when we ask questions on the matter but they did not snub us when we gave our all, and when the lads left home and all they loved to defend their beloved country. That was quite different.

They should now try to comfort the bereaved, and the country should put all its strength towards achieving the object of recovering the bodies to be laid in British graves.

One of the Sufferers

Ackworth 26th October 1919

William Dawson's assertion that there were 'hundreds' of families wishing to repatriate their dead was confirmed when the British War Graves Association (BWGA) was established, a band of bereaved parents dedicated solely to that end. It was formed on the eve of the first anniversary of the Armistice and was led and held together by the insuperable personality of Sara Ann Smith, the Association's Honorary General Secretary and Treasurer. Her son, Frederick Smith, had died of wounds in September 1918 and was buried in Grevillers Cemetery on the Somme.

Sara Ann Smith was fifty-nine years old, from Stourton in Leeds. A twice-married mother of five children, she was not unused to bereavement: her first husband died in the 1890s and she lost a daughter, Frances, aged eighteen in 1907. She had become tenacious through adversity, and out of Sara's drive and energy, the Association grew, as the *Yorkshire Evening Post* reported on 12 February 1920, referring to the BWGA as 'Claiming the Fallen':

> The Yorkshire Association of Claiming the Fallen held their monthly meeting at Tabor House, Stourton, Leeds, when new members were enrolled, and Mrs Bertha Coats of Paisley, was elected an honorary patron.
>
> This association has been formed with the object of obtaining the return to the homeland of the bodies of those who have fallen in the war. It is felt that the sorrow of the bereaved might be greatly alleviated by a frequent visit to the graves of their loved ones. This association hoped to obtain for British families the same privilege as granted to the Americans.
>
> A branch has been opened at Wakefield.

The Association always knew it would have a battle on its hands. The American decision had been helpful, and made things awkward for the British government, but appealing to the British government alone for a change in policy was not going to work; a multi-faceted approach was needed. Perhaps in the foreknowledge that a Belgian decree concerning the dead was imminent, Sara Smith immediately appealed to the Belgian King Albert for his support.

> Your Majesty
>
> I have been asked by many who like myself, have suffered loss in the war, to appeal most earnestly to allow us to have the bodies of our dear ones who have fallen in France and Flanders brought to this country, at our own expense if necessary.
>
> It has always been the view of every English family that their beloved dead belonged to them alone and we feel it would be a great consolation to have their bodies put in the family vault here so we could visit and tend the graves ourselves.

We pray and beseech your gracious Majesty that the right which has ever been the privilege of the bereaved may not be denied us.

Your humble and obedient servant

Sara A. Smith [Honorary General Secretary and Treasurer]

The Association had a number of branches, mostly in the north and north midlands, and while it is not clear precisely how many members there were, the *Yorkshire Evening News* reported in June 1920 that there were 2,000 members of the Leeds and District Branch alone, albeit this was the highest profile and most vociferous of all the branches. There were some high-profile supporters. The president was Leeds Central MP and racehorse owner Sir Arthur Willey, whose son was killed on the first day of the Battle of the Somme. Lady Maud Selborne was patron. She was the eldest daughter of the three-times Prime Minister Robert Cecil, Marquess of Salisbury, and wife of the 2nd Earl of Selborne and former First Lord of the Admiralty, who had also served in Asquith's government during the Great War. Her son, Captain Robert Palmer, had been killed in the Middle East in 1916.

At the Association's first mass meeting on Armistice Day 1920, the resolution to press for the rights afforded the fallen American troops was passed unanimously. A petition and details of the resolution would be forwarded to Queen Mary in the hope that she would exert some pressure over her son, the Prince of Wales, the President of the IWGC. Re-emphasising the deep hurt that was felt by a privilege 'granted to other countries [but] denied us', Queen Mary was urged to give the resolution her 'kind consideration', but the Queen's 'consideration' was to ask her Private Secretary to pass on the letter and resolution to the IWGC. The IWGC would not alter the stated policy.

No matter how many letters Sara Smith sent, how many resolutions were passed, the BWGA was never going to alter a decision that had long met with general acceptance. In a note dated

January 1922, the Secretary of State for War, Laming Worthington-Evans, wrote that he was 'not interested in this Association or in the writer [Mrs Smith]', while a note attached to the Secretary's views asked his Principal Assistant Secretary: 'Do you think you could draft a letter which will stop Mrs Smith writing any more?'

The BWGA was effectively sidelined and ignored. On 2 July 1923, its president, Sir Arthur Willey, died after collapsing the previous day – the seventh anniversary of his son's death. 'I find the work of the Association almost too much,' wrote Sara Smith to Lady Selborne in June 1924, 'but nobody will take my place and I feel I must carry on.' Smith then confided to Lady Selborne: 'It seems we cannot have our first object [returning the bodies of the fallen] and all we can do is try and give help and comfort and band ourselves together.'

The United States eventually repatriated around half of its 116,000 dead. The BWGA managed just one, officially: Tom Backhouse. He was British born, from Leeds, and had emigrated with his brother to the United States, becoming a naturalised American in 1913, though he died fighting with the West Yorkshire Regiment. His family still lived in Leeds and his body was exhumed and brought back and buried in Holbeck Cemetery. Sara Smith was a friend of the family and it was the Leeds Branch of the BWGA that secured his return. At the funeral, his coffin was draped with the United States flag, with both the British Legion and American Legion present at the graveside. A wreath was laid by BWGA and one on behalf of the British Legion by 6-year-old Cyril Hant wearing the medals of his father, killed in 1918 when his son was two months old.

This repatriation would be their only success.

21st June 1924

Dear Lady Selborne

I believe I sent reports re American soldier. I now enclose one of our recent visits to Flanders. I managed the journey much better than I expected but I was ill on the Monday and had to keep to my room.

I have got unsettled though and want to go again. I wish I had a domicile there, and would have, had I the means, not that I love France at all, but I fancy I might help our members and probably find some means of getting our boys home eventually. ... We stayed at Bapaume in a nice little French hotel and about ½ an hour's walk from the cemetery (Grevilliers) where my boy lies ...

Sara Smith

Moved by Sara's words, Lady Selborne wrote to the new Secretary of State for War, Stephen Walsh, a Labour MP who had himself lost a son in April 1918.

June 26 1924

Dear Sir [Rt Hon. Stephen Walsh MP]

I have appealed to every Secretary of State for War since 1918 to let these poor women bring home the bodies of their dead sons.

It seems to me the most heartless and unnecessary official woodenness that prevents them. This poor old lady has been helping a friend whose son was killed while fighting in the American Army, to bring home the remains of her boy. The American Government has been sympathetic and helpful, and as kind as possible. If she had applied soon enough they would have paid all expenses, but of course private people are not in possession of information always, and they did not know that America was so much more humane than Great Britain.

I am

Yours very truly

Maud Selborne

The BWGA knew that their primary aim would be forever thwarted, and it gradually morphed into an organisation of mutual support and friendship, frequently leading trips to the battlefields for bereaved relatives, and taking on the self-appointed mantle of guardian of the cemeteries. The BWGA frequently wrote to the IWGC to point out problems or issues with stonework, or cemetery paths and access, sometimes to the obvious frustration of the IWGC. Sara Smith continued to visit her son's grave every year but one until she could no longer travel. She died in June 1936, aged seventy-six. The BWGA continued at least until the late 1940s.

The BWGA had failed in its primary objective but not without five years of agitation and flashes of considerable guile. There were several attempts to test the authorities both in Britain and overseas, probing to see whether local knowledge on the ground was aware of the exhumation laws.

The IWGC had always maintained that Article 225 of the Versailles Peace Treaty permitted the exhumation of bodies only where the individual was buried in the cemetery of an 'enemy' nation. This would mean that a British soldier, for example, buried in Germany, could be returned to Great Britain, although no evidence survives that this ever took place. But what happened if a British soldier was buried in an enemy cemetery in France or Belgium? Could he also be transferred home? In 1919, the IWGC had refused a request by Reverend Frederick Guy to transfer his son's body to England. This was to be expected. But his son, Captain Christopher Guy, happened to be buried in a German cemetery at Wynendaele in Belgium, and so, in February 1920, Reverend Guy made a separate and local request to have his son exhumed. This was accepted and a 'necessary permit' issued by a Colonel Chapman. Only at the last moment did Major Arthur Ingpen discover that the intention was to transfer the body to Britain. Ingpen, on the authority of the Brigadier General, DGR&E, hastily wrote to St Pol in Belgium 'that authority had only been given for the body to be moved from Wynendaele to Poperinghe'. Article 225 had made 'no reference to the transfer of bodies from one Allied country to another'. Captain Guy's body was buried in an Allied country already, Belgium, so that was where he would remain.

In November 1922, the Association directly approached the Belgian Defence Ministry and requested the exhumation of Private Arnold Dyson of the Lincolnshire Regiment, buried, with twenty-nine others, in the Communal Cemetery at Roisin. This was not a military cemetery, although all the men had IWGC headstones. The request was made on behalf of the boy's mother, Ada, and concluded with the words 'Perhaps you would also give me some idea of the cost of removal and transport'. Permission appeared to be taken for granted, and that was probably the idea. The Belgian Defence Ministry was not fooled and immediately informed the IWGC of the request, triggering a sternly worded message from the IWGC to the Association: 'The Communal Authorities at Roisin have been specially warned in case an effort should be made to exhume and remove the body.'

The story of illegal battlefield exhumations was not revealed to anyone until the *Sunday Express* uncovered the story in May 1931. The IWGC had every ground to keep the story quiet. They knew that there had been a series of illicit exhumations between 1919 and 1922 before attempts were made to smuggle the bodies 'home' either to Great Britain or Canada.

It is not known whether the BWGA ever threatened such measures, but they were not trusted by the IWGC, owing in part to their known attempts to test and even subvert Belgian law. Even so, the blanket decision to allow no one to be exhumed drove a few individuals to dig up their loved ones, successfully in a small number of cases, while in others the attempt was thwarted.

One successful case involved the body of Major Norman Mcleod Adam of the Royal Field Artillery, son of Major General Mcleod Adam. He was killed in August 1918 and buried in an isolated grave near Fontaine-lès-Croisilles near Arras. The Major General had been in dispute with the authorities concerning his son's pension, a protracted case that became embittered. It was perhaps with this battle in mind that the Major General decided that he, not the authorities, would have his son's remains. Major Norman Mcleod Adam was buried in an isolated grave, which significantly helped with the exhumation. In June 1922, the Major General co-opted the help of the local mayor and the body was taken clandestinely to Scotland and Glasgow Necropolis. Under police questioning, the mayor later claimed ignorance of the law forbidding exhumation.

In the aftermath of this exhumation, the IWGC wrote to the Ministry of Health, the Home Office and the Scottish Board of Health. A decision was taken that no further action would follow but all would strive to ensure nothing like that happened again.

An illicit exhumation usually relied on local help, whether that help was knowing or ignorant. Corporal James Burgess was smuggled back to Britain and buried in Englefield Green cemetery close to his mother. Burgess had married a French lady, Germaine Marie Victorine, in June 1918, but tragically, the following February, he died of the flu epidemic that swept Europe. He was buried in a civil cemetery in Paris but just three months later, his wife obtained an exhumation authority from the Paris Prefecture of Police and his body was taken to Britain.

Most attempts ended in failure. Herbert Baron travelled from Hull in an attempt to dig up his brother Frank. Herbert had visited the British Consul in Antwerp claiming he had permission to exhume the body buried in Westoutre Military Cemetery, and asking for details as to how to proceed. He hired a hearse and with local civilian help had actually exhumed and placed his brother in a coffin when two passing gendarmes approached him; he was arrested, prosecuted and fined, and Frank Herbert was immediately reburied.

Sara Smith had lost her son in September 1918; Herbert Baron's brother Frank had died in the same month. Major General

Mcleod Adam had lost his son in the same year, and most of the leading lights of the BWGA had also lost their loved ones in the final year of the war. This was no coincidence. The agony of bereavement was acute, too recent to be ignored, clouding their judgment. Perhaps, too, losing a loved one so close to the end of the war increased feelings of desperation and bitterness. It is easy to see why some people in this position might become fixated with recovering their dead.

Chapter Eight

'There are no likely UNKNOWNS in any of these cemeteries; neither do Exhumation reports for the same area reveal anything at all likely and I am unable to make any progress …'

Unidentified IWGC officer, November 1919

Genuine hopes had been raised that Francis Mond's body might be buried in the British cemetery extension in Corbie. A padre had recalled burying two unknown airmen there in May 1918 and one of the dead, he believed, had come from Sussex. This cemetery was widely used by Australian Field Ambulances in 1918, and the majority buried there that year were men of the Australian Imperial Force. Angela waited for confirmation.

But the news was not good. There was only one grave of a member of the Royal Flying Corps and that belonged to an observer, Lieutenant Charles Wells, 62nd Squadron, a man from Norfolk, not Sussex, killed the day after Francis Mond. This news must have been bitterly disappointing. The search for Angela's son was stalling. By February 1919, it had been established that Mond and Martyn had reached Smith's Farm and that the bodies had probably been taken away in a lorry for burial, as likely as not on 18 May, but clearly that lorry did not belong to 57 Squadron.

In March 1919, 'after much difficulty', Angela said, she was given contact details for a man named Sergeant Alfred Hempel. He served with 6th Australian Field Ambulance and was the man in charge at Smith's Farm (his two superior officers being temporarily away) when the bodies of Mond and Martyn arrived and were left in his care. Hempel confirmed that he had told the two men who had taken the bodies from Vaire to the Relay Post in Vaux, Drivers Smith and Callinan, that an RAF lorry 'was expected' when both men visited Smith's farm a day or two later. Smith and Callinan had clearly shown at least a passing interest in the bodies, which suggests that they may not have been completely covered up.

During his interview, Hempel added some interesting detail. He had received the bodies at Smith's Farm but he was adamant that identification labels, if ever attached, were now missing and that both bodies were very badly injured, making facial identification 'impossible'. Although he did not know who the dead men were, he was told to expect a tender from 57 Squadron.

Later that day, as he walked along the Corbie–Vaux road, Hempel met a car containing two RAF officers. He spoke to the men, assuming, for no other reason than that they were RAF personnel, that they came from 57 Squadron. He politely 'reminded them' to send a tender to collect the bodies and they agreed to do so. Hempel never mentioned 57 Squadron and so the two officers were under the impression that they were simply arranging to pick up two dead and unknown British pilots. The trail could easily have gone cold at this point for Hempel never enquired as to the identities of the two men in the car. Fortunately, he did recall one small and very useful fact. One of the officers had a wooden leg and from this small, idiosyncratic detail, Angela was able to identify Captain Cedric Gordon, Brigade Major of 5th Brigade, RAF.

Gordon remembered the brief meeting and confirmed he sent a lorry the next day, 18 May, though in his own deposition to Angela, he 'could not remember to whom he gave it [the order], nor what followed'. A day later, Hempel handed over the bodies to a sergeant, as 'Flying Officers Unknown', once again assuming that the sergeant came from 57 Squadron and that he would know the identity of the dead men. Hempel took a receipt, as was the rule, a receipt he subsequently lost 'in action'.

Clearly, the lorry was not from 57 Squadron, but to whom had Gordon given his order? With time to mull things over, Gordon's vague recollections became clearer, as a letter from the Air Ministry in London to the IWGC confirmed: 'It has been definitely stated by the Brigade Major ... that orders were given to the 22nd Wing' to collect the bodies. The problem was that every wing had an equal number of squadrons under its command and 57 Squadron did not belong to 22nd Wing. Asking the wing adjutant if he recalled the despatch of a tender thirteen months earlier was unlikely to yield much and by June 1919, all Angela's enquiries were returned without result. Soon afterwards, the wing itself was disbanded, many of the wing and squadron officers leaving the service.

In the case file held by the Commonwealth War Graves Commission, there is a four-month hiatus in the paperwork, as if Angela herself was considering her options. In fact, she made two visits to the Western Front, walking round dozens of cemeteries, peering at pressed metal strips attached to rows of wooden graves: in all, she helped 'methodically and systematically' search between forty and fifty cemeteries, enquiries fanning out ever further from Corbie.

The paperwork began again in November 1919. 'Further investigations have been made ...' a note stated. French civilians returning to their land were questioned and the maire of Vaux had conducted numerous enquiries. Not that anyone was living in the vicinity at the time of the crash as the civilian population had been evacuated, but had they seen anything since the war as the community re-established their farms and smallholdings? The answer was, predictably, 'no'.

In desperation rather than real hope, cemeteries much further away were examined: Freancy, Vignacourt and Villers Faucon ... nothing. 'I have made an extensive and exhaustive search of all cemeteries round a wide area of Smith's Farm with negative results,' wrote one officer charged with maintaining enquiries. 'There are no likely UNKNOWNS in any of these cemeteries;

neither do Exhumation reports for the same area reveal anything at all likely and I am unable to make any progress ...'

The Graves Registration Units were requested to keep a lookout for men still buried in isolated graves, but then that was their job. The fact remained that the search seemed as far from being resolved as ever. Mond and Martyn had vanished, and back in England, Angela was left with little alternative but to place speculative appeals in *The Times* newspaper in the hope of jogging someone's memory:

ROYAL AIR FORCE – To all officers, Chaplains and non-commissioned officers of the R.A.F. INFORMATION urgently desired as to the NUMBER of the SQUADRON who sent a flight sergeant and lorry to fetch the bodies of two flying officers from a dressing-station known as Smith's Farm on the road between Corbie and Vaux-sur-Somme on the 18th May, 1918 ... The Officers were probably buried behind the lines as 'Flying Officers Unknown'.

The Times newspaper ran this appeal on 1 November 1920. There was not a single reply.

* * *

By early 1921, Angela was at an impasse. She had been searching for two and a half years and could get no further than Smith's Farm and a last definite sighting of her son and his observer, Martyn. New details trickled in, but they appeared to offer only slender possibilities – filling in the gaps – but nothing that offered a new avenue of exploration with any prospect of success. Memories were fading, key witnesses moving on, disappearing into civilian obscurity.

Angela was the only person willing to drive this search forward because she was the only person who wanted to, her desperation ever more evident to those who looked on, her requests for help and information ever more unlikely to bring meaningful results. We shall never know what Emile felt about Angela's search, whether her youngest children felt neglected: May was fourteen when her brother was killed, Stephen only ten. Nor is it clear how much time in each week, in each month, Angela devoted to her search, or whether she could enjoy other pursuits or interests. She attended family functions and she went to Sir Alfred Mond's Cheshire home for Christmas, but could she ever escape Francis's shadow? Emile appears only rarely to have been involved in the search, and does not seem to have made any attempt to stop her, probably assuming such a move would be pointless. As a scientist, his natural inclination to see things rationally, dispassionately, logically, would have told him that the chances of finding Francis were almost nil, but this search had always usurped logic and it was certainly never dispassionate.

Anyone who was inclined to help Angela must have considered her next appeal with raised eyebrows. It was the definition of speculative.

Unwilling to leave any stone unturned, Angela requested that a list be drawn up of every officer in 22nd Wing, the squadron they served with and their last known address. These men were now spread far and wide: Lieutenant Colonel Jack Cunningham, 65 Squadron, was now living in the Transvaal in South Africa; Squadron Leader Keith Park, 48 Squadron, was at the RAF School of Technical Training in Manston, Kent; and Squadron Leader Stanley Goble, 205 Squadron, was now working with the Air Board in Australia. Angela intended to write to these men and every other squadron leader in the wing. She was also given names and addresses of officers who had served in neighbouring wings and the address of Major Cuthbert Hiatt of 57 Squadron, for good measure. Angela was becoming well acquainted with the complex structure of the RAF and its Order of Battle.

22, Hyde Park Square, W2
11th June, 1921

Dear Sir [Lieutenant Colonel Antony Byng, 5th Balloon Wing]

According to information received through the Air Ministry you were commanding the 5th Balloon Wing of the R.A.F. in France, in May 1918. This Squadron was, I believe, in the 5th Brigade and the sections operating on this date were:- Coy. 13 – Section 3 & 29, Coy. 16 – Section 12 & 43, and Coy. 14 – Section 14 & 19.

I am searching for the grave of my son, Captain Francis Mond … Can you recall any circumstances at that date [May 1918] which could lead to the discovery of who received the order to fetch the bodies from Smith's Farm, and, where they were buried, or suggest any channel (other than official) by which I may receive information? Enquiries by advertisements have apparently been exhaustively made in the United Kingdom and Australia with disappointing results.

It has taken me over two years to get as far as this, and I have also been twice in France, and examined some thirty to forty cemeteries.

Angela's latest list of enquiries brought in a trickle of responses between June and September 1921 from 22nd Wing's squadron leaders. Further lists of names were drawn up and a précis of correspondence and replies supplied to the IWGC. Under headings 'Sections of Brigade', 'Name of Officer', 'Date of Reply' and 'Remarks', Angela collected her 'Correspondence Re: Missing Grave'.

Major Park, 48 Squadron, replied on 14 June: 'Will show letter to Capt. R[aymond] Whitaker who was Staff Capt. of 5th Brigade. If he can throw any light on the matter will write again.'

Major Gordon, SO2 15th (Corps) Wing OC, was interviewed directly by Emile Mond: 'Thinks it unlikely that the Balloon Wing would have been asked to send lorry.'

Lieutenant Colonel [Ivo] Edwards, 15th (Corps) Wing: 'Suggests writing O.C 10th Wing. Sailing for England from India in a few days and would make personal enquiries at the Air Ministry.'

Second Lieutenant Stone, OC 4th Reserve Lorry Park: 'Suggests getting hold of the logbook kept (every car journey being entered). States his lorry park was at the service of 5th Brigade. Write to his Orderly Room Corporal, re Corporal T.L. Corking.'

And so, Corporal Thomas Corking was contacted: 'Certain no car or lorry was detailed from the park to do this duty, but Captain Gordon may have given an order to one of the lorries when out on another duty. Will make enquiries of Captain Reed and will send other addresses later.'

The Air Ministry was asked about the lorry park logbooks of 5th Brigade RFC, but these potentially enlightening volumes were missing and a search did not locate them. Meanwhile, Captain Reed replied on 6 September: 'Regrets unable to help.' A follow-up letter was received from Corporal Corking, 'giving addresses of Sergeant W.H. Mackenzie, Sergeant E. Wood'. Wood replied, suggesting a letter 'to a friend of his, George Pickhard, in 57th Squadron', and so on and so forth. The contact list grew longer by the day, and the nagging fear, never allayed, was that someone might have overlooked a crucial detail, someone might forget to reply, or a critical link in this human chain of contacts be missed. And then there was always the possibility that the key person involved in the transfer of the bodies from Smith's Farm had not survived the war.

The options for opening new channels of investigation were getting ever more tangential, ever more 'hit and hope'. Angela could afford to continue her search ad infinitum; she had the money, she was influential and she had time to give, but that created its own predicament. How long was it sensible to look, who would make the decision to finally stop and why? Angela was not the only parent seemingly damned to a search without end, in an endless, restless and ultimately fruitless hunt. It was a curse peculiar to the middle and upper classes, not to the poor. They could not count on networks or contacts: those without influence could appeal to the IWGC, they could write to the regiment or the Records Office, but official doors closed more quickly, gently but firmly, so as to discourage further correspondence. This may have appeared harsh but, in reality, it was probably the best option for all concerned. For the vast majority of those whose loved ones were missing, whose death was presumed, or those known to be dead but whose bodies were lost, there was little chance of resolution, and life had to move on. Rich or poor, all were trapped; it was only the mechanisms by which they coped with grief that was different. Poorer people might leave back doors permanently unlocked in the hope that one day their loved one would walk in, wealthier people pursued their fruitless searches, some well into the 1930s, but very few of any class found solace through success, and almost certainly not through their own efforts. With hundreds of thousands missing, the dead were being found every day; some were identified. It was just down to luck as to who heard good news.

Angela's search for her son was always different because the events surrounding his disappearance were so unusual, but by the end of November, the lists were exhausted, all contacts of contacts written to. Nothing substantial had come of the enquiries. On 28 November, Angela wrote to The Secretary, IWGC, requesting a nominal roll of sergeants serving with 57 Squadron in May 1918 and known residential addresses. Letters were posted; nothing new was added to the story. Angela could write to every sergeant in every squadron in 22 Wing, an IWGC memo suggested. Angela replied that 'she had all the names but that it would be a very big business and the prospect appalled her', which suggests she took on much of the personal responsibility herself even though she could well afford secretarial help. Nevertheless, she would be prepared to work through the names.

'If the Sergeants cannot help I am afraid there is not much hope of finding M & M's graves,' an IWGC official ruefully noted.

There are no likely graves – that is, we have none reported which are worth opening for investigation. The difficulty is – we do not know where they might be buried. The bodies, if taken away in the tender, might be 20 or 30 miles from Smith's Farm …

If all the Sergeants, serving in the area in question on the date, are still alive, and if the bodies <u>were</u> taken away in a tender in charge of a Sergeant then one of them <u>must</u> know <u>something</u> about the matter.

'If', 'if': the opportunities for finding Francis Mond and Edgar Martyn's bodies appeared exhausted.

Just before Christmas 1921, Angela went to the IWGC's offices in Baker Street. There was a meeting in which an official, no doubt in an effort to appear helpful, suggested that as the bodies of Mond and Martyn were handed over without identification, perhaps the search for 'unknown officers Royal Air Force' was too narrow an approach. Perhaps, he said, 'some light might be thrown on the matter by considering the reports of the burial of "unknown officers"'. Angela's heart must have sunk at the thought. The suggestion was made that she could start with Heath Cemetery, a few miles south-east of Bouzencourt. This cemetery started after the war through the concentration of Allied graves found in various small cemeteries, including those belonging to the enemy, as well as churchyards and isolated graves found in the area. There were quite a number of unknown officers in there, apparently.

So the focus of Angela's search needed to change: she should be looking for the graves of *any* unknown officers, from *any* infantry regiment or corps buried within a 10-mile radius of Bouzencourt to start with, in a cemetery in the heart of the 1918 Somme battlefield. Well, good luck with that.

* * *

During Angela's visits to France, there was one place where she could always visit and know that she was in the right location. That was the village of Bouzencourt, and just outside the village, the precise spot where her son died. The wreckage of *Caesar*, Francis's DH4, still lay in the field where it crashed and Angela took keepsakes from the mangled airframe, some connecting wire and a fragment of the wooden propeller. The idea of erecting a private memorial to her son and his observer was not an original one: other families had bought plots of land in France, sometimes to leave sacred and inviolate the ground on which a relative was known to have died, his body missing, more often to establish a memorial that could be visited for years to come.

Shortly after the Armistice, the Mond family set about purchasing the 1,900 square metre field where Francis's plane remained entangled amongst weeds and grass. French families had returned to their land, re-establishing homes and replanting crops. The fear was that the crash site would be put back under the plough. In order to speed up the purchase process and to circumvent any problems that might arise for a foreign family acquiring French land, Auguste Galland, a Parisian music teacher and a close friend of the Mond family, offered to buy the ground from the owner, Louis Leroy. The sale was agreed and concluded in October 1919, the same plot being sold on to the Mond family after a suitably respectable period of ownership, in May 1922.

Angela and Emile Mond designed a monument for their son and for Edgar Martin. It was simple in concept: a broken column, symbolic of the abrupt cutting off of life in its prime. The column, rising from a plinth, was inscribed to the memory of the two airmen and the date of their deaths. The monument was surrounded by an iron chain railing strung between low, white stone pillars and the enclosure (54 square metres) was planted with flowers, shrubs and trees. The upkeep of the plot was entrusted to a returned civilian, Madame Lecat, living in Sailly-le-Sec, a neighbouring village to Bouzencourt. If Emile and Angela never had a son they could bury, they would at least feel close to him at his memorial.

Chapter Nine

'Our whole trouble arises from the fact that the Belgian people do <u>not</u> realise what Ypres means to us, nor how great our sacrifices have been here.'

Lieutenant Colonel Beckles Wilson, July 1919

Ypres held huge symbolic importance to the British people. For four years, many of the country's finest troops had fought to keep the Germans at bay, refusing to relinquish the city. Any strategic value in holding it became inextricably entwined with the army's active preservation of fighting men's morale: Ypres was Britain's Verdun.

By the time the Armistice was signed, there was not much left of the once beautiful centre, of the mediaeval Cloth Hall, or the neighbouring cathedral. The city walls were badly damaged; the entrances across the centuries-old defensive moat, the Menin Gate, the Lille Gate, through which most men of the British Expeditionary Force had passed at one time or another, were shattered. From the air, the definition of a city was clear, and it was clear too that this was a historic city on the brink of historic oblivion, with every house damaged or destroyed. The author and former soldier Stephen Graham visited Ypres in 1919.

Back thunders the empty lorry – on to the Menin road – and faces Ypres. You see the grey contour of the tower afar, but doubt whether you are approaching a city, so flat has all become. Yet certainly it is Ypres. You enter by a series of new-painted wooden taverns and hotels. You walk up a wide main street and there is Ypres.

A great dust storm is raging here whilst the sun shines out of a perfect sky. Here are no rushes, no wild flowers, no moisture, but only infinite debris and the shatterings of old masonry. There is a suggestion of the desert. A notice says 'This is Holy Ground', and a barbed wire fence runs round the whole centre of old Ypres.

Holy Ground was right, perhaps too holy for its own good. In the same way that French farmland had to be returned to its rightful owners on the Somme, what was the point in holding Ypres in order to pursue the defence of violated Belgium, if the streets, or what was left of them, were not given back to the people who had lived there? But such was the sanctity of the ground that withholding Ypres from its rightful owners was exactly what was anticipated by some: Ypres, they felt, ought to be jointly owned by the dead and the pilgrim.

A grand scheme to leave Ypres as a mausoleum was proposed by the one man who was prone to bigger picture ideas, a man who liked a grandiose plan and, dangerously, the sort of man who might just make it happen: Winston Churchill. He had put forward the view to the assembled great and good of the IWGC, sitting amongst whom was the government's Director of Works, Sir Alfred Mond, uncle of Francis. On 7 February, Sir Alfred wrote from the Office of Works to Churchill, then Secretary of State for War.

HM Office of Works
7 February 1919
My dear Churchill

I have been thinking a good deal about the very striking suggestion you made at the last meeting of the IWGC, namely, that we should endeavour to get the Belgian Government to present Ypres to this country as a lasting war memorial.

If this suggestion could be achieved, it seems to me altogether an admirable one. I observe that the Belgian Government has decided not to rebuild Ypres, which removed one of the difficulties. From a report I have received from one of my Principal Architects, who has recently visited Belgium on behalf of the Government, I am afraid that the remaining picturesque ruins of the town, particularly the fragments of the Clothworkers' Hall, will not be adequately dealt with by the Belgian engineers, and may develop into a number of mounds of debris, entirely losing their meaning. I am sure if this site were give to the British Government, it would be possible to retain what remains of these ruins in a permanent form ...

Yours sincerely

Alfred Mond

Churchill was clearly taken with the whole idea and as was his impatient way, he pursued Fabian Ware at the IWGC, writing to him on 24 February. This was Churchill at his delegating best:

What have you been doing about my suggestion for acquiring Ypres as a British mausoleum, and what steps do you recommend me to take to bring this idea into actual operation?

A letter should surely be written to the Belgian Government asking on what terms they would give or sell the ruins of the town to us.

I am surprised not to have had a paper from you showing me how my wishes in this respect could be advanced. I have had a letter from the First Commissioner of Works supporting the scheme, but not a word apparently from you or your branch.

WC

Winston Churchill had been under fire. He was assailed by disgruntled soldiers, upset by what they saw as his unfair scheme of demobilisation 'What's Churchill's Game?' they taunted, and even booed him when he visited the British troops in the Occupied Rhineland. At the same time, the IWGC had raised serious concerns about the slow pace at which bodies were being collected from the battlefield. Paradoxically, Churchill was put under pressure by the IWGC, anxious that there would be no lorries available for the collection of the dead if demobilisation sucked in all available transport. The Secretary of State was threatened that if this issue were not satisfactorily addressed, the Commission would go direct to the Cabinet. It is no surprise that Fabian Ware had scant interest in Churchill's bigger schemes in Ypres while bodies lay exposed on the battlefields. Two days later, Fabian Ware wrote a testy and obliquely barbed reply.

> I am sorry you should have thought that I have been idle in this matter, but that is not the case. ... The Commission has already on hand more than it can do ...
>
> I think, however, they [the Cabinet] might come to see that a grand scheme of this kind [in Ypres], in addition to its own intrinsic merits, might be most useful for attracting public attention and withdrawing a good deal of idle curiosity and criticism from the work that the Commission has already undertaken.

In other words, sterling work by the IWGC, as Ware believed, with scant help from anyone else and 'criticism' that might be more justifiably levelled at Churchill himself.

Fabian Ware pointed out that Sir Alfred Mond had felt the 'grand scheme' should be carried out by the Office of Works and not the IWGC. He also warned that he had heard that the Belgians would be very reluctant to cede the British 'any exclusive rights in Ypres' and that Churchill might take care about how he pursued his idea by talking first to the Sir Frank Villiers, the British ambassador to Belgium.

Finally, Churchill was reminded that he had not replied to a letter Ware had sent weeks before. Perhaps Ware could be 'spared' ten minutes to talk about Ypres.

The truth was that the Belgian government was undecided about the future of Ypres and understandably it was not going to be rushed into a decision. In early March 1919, the IWGC's Land and Legal Adviser, Major Ingpen, reported that there was 'strong pressure being brought to bear by owners of property in Ypres to be allowed to rebuild their houses on the old sites'. The current Belgian scheme was to leave 'the Cathedral and Cloth Hall and the buildings around them in ruins, clearing away one or two buildings between them and the Plaine d'Amour [an open piece of town land used for a riding school before the war] and making a great international Cemetery on the latter'. This scheme would require the exhumation and transfer of bodies from many existing cemeteries in the Salient, an idea that the Commission would never have endorsed. The Belgian plan was designed not to interfere seriously with the 'desire of the inhabitants of Ypres to rebuild', except, of course, that the centre of their beloved city would remain in permanent ruins.

There was genuine concern in Britain that Ypres would be repopulated by stealth and that civilians scenting a business opportunity would invade and set up shop. There were severe restrictions on what could be erected within the city walls, and only temporary wooden structures were permitted. Even then, there were those who saw any reconstruction as tawdry and disrespectful of the dead.

Fifty-year-old Lieutenant Colonel Henry Beckles Wilson, working in the Town Mayor's Office in Ypres, was disgusted by what he saw. In July 1919, he wrote to the one man he thought would have the connections and the interest to take up the matter, Field Marshal Viscount French of Ypres, the former Commander-in-Chief of the original British Expeditionary Force in 1914, a man whose men had

Ypres and the Ypres Salient immediately after the fighting ended. Servicemen had near-exclusive access to the former battlefields before pilgrims and tourists began arriving in ever greater numbers from the summer of 1919.

Around half of all those killed in the Great War have no known grave. These crosses mark the graves of Private John Shaw, Royal Engineers, killed 20 August 1917, and Corporal Samuel Fellows, 8th Alexandra, Princess of Wales's Own (Yorkshire Regiment), killed 8 June 1917. Their original wooden crosses are rapidly deteriorating on the rim of this flooded shell crater. In the end the bodies of both men were never identified, their names being inscribed on the walls of the Tyne Cot Memorial and the Menin Gate respectively.

Men of a Graves Registration Unit working in Klein-Vierstraat Cemetery, south-west of Ypres. This cemetery was begun in January 1917 but was regularly enlarged during the war and then again afterwards through the consolidation of two smaller cemeteries and the battlefield exhumations. Some 895 bodies are buried here, 109 unidentified. Note the men's lack of engagement with the camera: theirs was a grizzly occupation.

igh Wood on the Somme, 1919. Bodies still littered the ground, waiting for collection and burial. Some
rly visitors to the battlefields were shocked at finding skeletal remains still inside discarded boots.

An unusual battlefield cross, as it includes an attached photograph of the dead man, 23-year-old Sergeant David Fenwick, Royal Garrison Artillery. The cross was erected by one of his brothers, either Arthur or John Fenwick. Sergeant Fenwick is buried in Mindel Trench British Cemetery near Arras. Families could make an application for the return of the wooden cross to Britain once a gravestone had replaced it.

Aveluy Communal Cemetery Extension clearly signposted for visitors. Awkward, hard-to-reach cemeteries were not always so clearly identified. Note the sign underneath recording that this cemetery was now 'Closed' for further burials.

A group of pilgrims from Nottinghamshire is conducted around Aveluy Communal Cemetery Extension by what appears to be a former serviceman. Several in the group had lost relatives in the war. The lady on the left is still wearing widow's weeds.

Battlefield tourists play with the conflict's rusting detritus. During the war, a number of soldiers feared the advent of tourism: sightseeing jaunts rather than respectful pilgrimages. However, it is possible that some of those pictured here also fought in the war and saw no contradiction between paying their respects to dead comrades and also having some fun.

Promotional literature from the patriotic-sounding Britannic Tours: this company was just one of many battlefield operators working in and around the Ypres Salient.

The Hotel Splendid in Ypres, in the early 1920s. Most of the early hotels were hastily erected out of wood to cater for the rapid rise in visitors making their way to the Salient, or south to the Somme. Not all were as splendid as this one.

GEN. GRIERSON'S GRAVE.

The grave of Lieutenant General Grierson in Glasgow Necropolis. Grierson was the first of around forty servicemen, all officers, brought home from France before a ban stopped any further repatriations. By an extraordinary coincidence, the last man brought home, in 1922, was Major Norman Adam (right, photographed in his school days). Major Adam was clandestinely exhumed by his father, Major General Frederick Adam, on 20 June 1922, and smuggled to Scotland, where he was taken to the same cemetery and placed in the family vault.

Sara Ann Smith, indefatigable leader of the British War Graves Association, which campaigned for the right of families to bring back home for burial the remains of their loved ones killed in the war.

Kemmel Château Military Cemetery during construction. Note the Portland headstones stacked up and waiting to be erected, replacing the wooden crosses. The cemetery was designed by Sir Edwin Lutyens, one of the three principal architects working for the Imperial War Graves Commission.

Temporary regimental crosses adorn the battered ancient burial mound, the Butte de Warlencourt, a well-known feature on the Somme battlefield. The British front line rested just yards to the west of the Butte when the fighting ground to a halt in November 1916. Many units erected such memorials but never expected to take on their long-term maintenance after the war.

The remains of Ypres' medieval Cloth Hall with new wooden huts erected for returning civilians in the foreground. The Secretary of State for War, Winston Churchill, originally proposed that the Cloth Hall, indeed Ypres itself, should be left in ruins as a permanent monument to those who had died in the Salient.

The Cloth Hall in scaffolding: the Belgian authorities had already begun to save the Cloth Hall and surrounding buildings prior to their eventual restoration, a project that would take fifty years to complete. Subsequently, the British Government opted to focus its attention on the nearby Menin Gate and the proposed memorial to the missing.

Throughout the 1920s and 1930s, a series of memorials dedicated to the fallen was erected across the Western Front. On 10 October 1926, the South African Memorial in Delville Wood was unveiled. The wood was the scene of desperate fighting in the second half of July 1916, in which the South African Brigade suffered grievous losses.

Thiepval Memorial to the Missing, under construction in the late 1920s. A Lutyens masterpiece of architectural design, the memorial was unveiled in August 1932 and commemorates over 72,300 men missing during the fighting of 1916.

Divisional memorials began to spring up across the battlefields, including this one dedicated to the battalions of the 51st Highland Division, which took the village of Beaumont Hamel in November 1916. In the distance it is possible to make out the new buildings of the reborn village.

A veteran pilgrimage back to the battlefields: here a former officer, Lieutenant Colonel James Mulholland (far left) of the 14th Royal Irish Rifles, presents a shield to the mayor (centre) of the village of Mesnil on the Somme. The clock hands on the shield were originally taken from the church tower.

Gardeners working for the Imperial War Graves Commission, 10 May 1922. They are standing outside their billet near the Somme village of Bazentin-le-Petit.

Bazentin-le-Petit Military Cemetery, June 1925. The Cross of Sacrifice has been erected but the wooden crosses are still to be replaced. Nevertheless, the beds are suffused with flowers and the grass lawn has been laid.

An IWGC nursery at Albert, where thousands of plants were propagated, waiting for distribution to military cemeteries.

The IWGC camp in Albert. Men can be seen working with heavy rollers in the background.

Out with the old and in with the new: June 1921 and a cross kept as a monument outside Cheddar Villa Cemetery (later renamed Seaforth Cemetery, Cheddar Villa) at St Julien, near Ypres.

The memorial erected by Emile and Angela Mond on the edge of Bouzencourt village. It is believed that the memorial was positioned on or adjacent to the site of the plane crash. A small piece of *Caesar*'s propeller sits at the foot of the plinth.

Bouzencourt and Doullens, France, 15 May 2018; 100 years on

Doullens Cemetery Extension No. 2, 20 miles from the site of the crash. Francis Mond and Edgar Martyn lie side by side.

fought such a tenacious defence of Ypres that autumn when the Germans had almost broken through.

> Our whole trouble arises from the fact that the Belgian people do <u>not</u> realise what Ypres means to us, nor how great our sacrifices have been here. It is, of course, inevitable that, in view of the incoming of tens of thousands of tourists, many former residents of the town, not of the better class, will wish to return and rebuild their shops and estaminets: what is earnestly hoped by us and in fact by the whole world is that the noble Grand Place and adjoining ruins shall not be vulgarised and desecrated by the erection of cheap and gaudily-painted barraquements ... Even as I write, six new huts are in process of erection – all estaminets. One which is painted sky-blue boldly calls itself 'The British Tavern' which exposes us daily to the rebuke of Belgian and French visitors who imagine we are responsible for this type of eye-sore ... At present these thoughtless entrepreneurs are defeating their own interest by utterly spoiling a glorious site, far more interesting and splendid than the Forum or Pompeii ...

Beckles Wilson went on to lament the lack of information, records and maps available for battlefield 'tourists' and the relatives of the dead, a situation he personally hoped to rectify.

Sir John French 'fully' sympathised with Beckles Wilson's anxieties and his desire to preserve the city, French forwarding the letter to the Foreign Office with a supportive covering note. Whether he engaged in any further correspondence with Beckles Wilson is unclear.

'Ypres is terribly empty,' wrote Stephen Graham, continuing his own, more heartfelt eulogy to the city.

> Hundreds of thousands of eyes [might] look on it but there are few people who come to look at it – just ones and twos who

stand diminutively in front of the great ruins and peer at them like the conventional figures in an old print. This absence of the living intensifies the strange atmosphere. It is said that the city will build itself up again, but it is possible to feel some doubt on that point. Perhaps Ypres will never be built again. At present it has some hundred and fifty places where they sell beer to two where they sell anything else. Its string of wooden hotels with cubicle bedrooms do not pay …

On his travels around the battlefields, former Scots Guards Officer Wilfrid Ewart entered Ypres one evening at dusk.

Electric arc-lamps at intervals lit the thoroughfares: there were few people about; but from a brilliantly illuminated white-fronted restaurant near at hand came the thumping notes of a piano playing ragtime. Being hungry, anxious about a bed, and seeing no other hostelry in sight, I entered by a side-door [and] sat down unwittingly in this 'Temple of Joy', seeing vaguely the tragic outline of the Cloth Hall through the window.

It was clearly a moment for some melancholic reflection.

'This Ypres is a terrible place still. There is no life when night comes on but tavern life,' wrote Graham.

Those who live and work here have lost their sense of proportion. They are out of focus somehow. 'You lookin' for dead soldiers?' says a Flemish woman to you with a glaring stare, wondering if you are one of the exhumers. Death and the ruins completely outweigh the living. One is tilted out of time by the huge weight on the other end of the plank, and it would be easy to imagine someone who had no insoluble ties killing himself here, drawn by the lodestone of death. There is a pull from the other world, a drag on the heart and spirit. One is ashamed to be alive. You try to sleep in a little bed in a cubicle with tiny doll's house window …

You lie listless, sleepless, with Ypres on the heart, and then suddenly a grand tumult of explosion, a sound as of the tumbling of heavy masonry. You go to the little window, behold, the whole sky is crimson once more, and living streamers of flame ascend to the stars. An old [ammunition] dump has gone up at Langemarck. Everyone in Ypres looks out and then returns to sleep – without excitement …

By November 1919, the Belgian government was seriously considering two schemes, both of which envisaged leaving the Cloth Hall and cathedral in ruins, but in one case allowing the rebuilding of houses around the Grand Place, in the other, creating a belt of trees surrounding the Hall and cathedral, including the Grand Place.

Whatever was proposed, there appeared to be little direct consultation with the people of Ypres, other than with the Bürgermeister, who wished the city to be largely rebuilt. The British government, having an idea to buy land from civilian owners, was advised by Ware to refrain from becoming involved financially just yet, as news of British money would no doubt push up prices. Ware was still sceptical that the Belgians would be willing to sell and suggested that the British government stood back, but in doing so it might ask the Belgian government to consult with it before a final decision was made.

No one could reasonably stop civilians returning to their city and attempting to restart their lives and businesses. The following year, in May 1920, *The Evening Standard* sent a journalist to see what was happening.

No private person is allowed to build within the ramparts at the moment. It is obvious that the Government plan for the new Ypres could not possibly be carried out if the families who are returning every day were allowed to have free play. The only notable building done by private people is that of hotels. Last year, ground landlords, who many of them had never lived in Ypres, scented profit in hotels and quickly built large wooden huts of two stories which have sprung up everywhere amid the ruins [including the Plaine d'Amour].

There are 4,000 workmen employed by the Government at work on the new Ypres. As many as possible are housed in wooden huts, some dwell in dugouts made by roofing over exposed cellars, while the remainder live in nearby villages and cycle to the scene of their labours. This is the bulk of the present population. The returned private families are mostly small shopkeepers who are trying desperately hard to get businesses working once more. Of the 500 habitable structures in the desolation, not counting the huts on the outskirts, 450 are said to be hotels or estaminets; and I can well believe it.

There was still no final decision as to the future of Ypres centre, even if rebuilding was going on elsewhere. In July 1920, the Cabinet again asked the Belgians not to carry out any formal plan of reconstruction without the British government expressing its view. Behind the scenes, the British were quietly scaling back their ambitions, looking towards the Menin Gate and a great memorial to the missing, costing £150,000. By early September 1920, a decision had to be made by the Cabinet, as a memo made clear. 'Shall we now definitely tell the Foreign Office that we only want the Menin Gate and the immediate surroundings, and that our embargo on the other buildings is taken off?'

On 22 September, the Belgians were told of the British decision, although the Cabinet still asked for the city centre ruins to be left for the time being, 'to be on the safe side'. The Menin Gate was to be the 'National British Memorial' in Belgium and final confirmation thus given that all other interest within the city walls was to be withdrawn in November. In point of fact, the Belgians had already begun to rebuild, the Cloth Hall being surrounded by scaffolding. Ypres was being raised from the ground, though it would take fifty years to complete the job.

In the years ahead, memorials to the dead would come in all shapes and sizes: leaving Ypres in ruins would have made it just the biggest and most imprudent.

* * *

During the fighting, memorials had been erected to honour the dead and to commemorate the action in which they fell. After the war, the British government was made aware of sixty-six such memorials, mostly built of wood. There was no shared belief amongst those who raised them that these memorials would survive. On the contrary; a number of units were approached by the British government and asked if they wished to make them permanent, but most replied in the negative, concerned that they would be committed to their lasting preservation. Equally, there were other units that had begun to sound out the French government in order to erect permanent memorials of stone, enquiring as they did so about the acquisition of land.

In order to deal with the whole issue of battlefield commemoration, the Army Council set up the Battle Exploit Memorials Committee (BEMC) in November 1918 to co-ordinate 'claims'. There was no appetite for a slew of memorials to every battalion and battery, the Committee openly stating that it hoped proposals would be submitted for the 'erection of memorials to divisions or higher formations only ..., [the] exploits of smaller units can then be recorded on these memorials'.

All interested parties were to forward their 'claims' to the BEMC, who would refer them on to the Historical Branch of the Committee for Imperial Defence (CID).

'Claims,' the BEMC said,

> must be accompanied by an accurate sketch plan of the
> ground, the exact map reference of the site on which the
> proposed memorial is to be erected, a design of the memorial,
> if chosen, together with a note as to the area it will cover and a
> full statement as to the historical facts in respect of which the
> memorial is to be erected. In submitting claims units should
> state the sum of money which they guarantee for the erection
> of their memorial, including the acquisition of any land that
> may be necessary for their purpose.

If the Historical Branch of the CID was happy with the proposals,
then they were forwarded to the IWGC, responsible for channelling
all plans to the French and Belgian governments. In the summer
of 1919, the Belgians offered land at twenty-three sites in the Ypres
Salient, suggesting that monuments were best located at crossroads
in towns or villages. Dominion troops too were naturally keen to
be involved before they went home and as a result, their requests
were processed first.

Most applications were accepted unless two claims were made
for the same location, in which case submissions were encouraged
to amalgamate into one joint venture. To avoid a plethora of
memorials, the BEMC proposed that each unit should have
no more than one site in each theatre of war, the Committee
undertaking to carry out negotiations with the landowners and
foreign governments on behalf of the units concerned. In the
event, a number of sites were offered for free by landowners,
including sites on the Somme, such as at Fricourt and la Boisselle.
After construction, the IWGC would look after the memorials
as 'they were the only permanent body with machinery suitable
for such duties'. In all, the total number of 'claims' received
was 110.

In response to questions asked in the House of Commons in June 1920, it was recorded that twenty-eight divisions, five brigades and thirty-six 'lesser formations' had applied to the Battle Exploit Memorials Committee for permission to erect, at their own expense, one or more permanent memorials in France and Flanders.

It was perhaps surprising that more divisions did not step forward at the time to 'claim' their memorial and not all that did were able in the end to raise the money required. The 11th (Northern) Division, which suffered 32,000 casualties during the war, proposed a memorial at Thiepval – giving a specific map reference of Sheet (map) 57D, R. 20. D. 9. 6., to commemorate its actions at Mouquet Farm, Zollern Redoubt and Stuff Redoubt over the period 26–30 September 1916.

In their submission, it was noticeable that under the category 'Sum of money guaranteed' there is no mention of funds, and no design was submitted. The Historical Section, CID, did not remark on the absence of monies, and supported what was a very 'strong case' for a memorial. 'The only point is that the capture of Thiepval by the 18th Division is so closely mixed up with the 11th Division's operations that it seems a pity there should not be a joint memorial.' However, 'The 11th Division do not wish to join with other claimants for Thiepval and in any case the 18th Division [has] not claimed Thiepval but [has] plumped for a Somme based memorial at Trones Wood a few miles away.'

Nothing much happened for the following two years. In October 1921, Major Ingpen of the IWGC wrote to The Secretary, BEMC, to say he had received 'no information about it [the memorial] either from you or the IWGC', adding that the proposed site was 400 or 500 metres from any road and that even then, the nearest road was little more than a track 'and not good for erection of a memorial'. By the following May, the location had been altered and in June 1922, Ingpen accompanied the division's erstwhile commanding officer, General Henry Davies, to the new proposed site. The site was being levelled but Ingpen saw that 'nothing yet [was being] done to find owners of the land'. By June the following year, the idea of a memorial had been abandoned.

> I am now writing to tell you [Ingpen] that we have decided to give up the idea of an 11th Division Memorial altogether, as the money we have collected is not enough for an adequate memorial. I have already told the Battle Exploits Committee this officially ...
>
> H. Davies [President of the 11th Division War Memorial Committee]

The strength of Divisional Identity varied significantly in the British Army. The 11th Division, which had an undergone a sobering baptism of fire on Gallipoli (where a memorial at Helles was erected to its efforts), did perhaps not feel as keen a link to the Somme when so many of its original officers had already fallen. During the war, a number of battalions within the division had left or even been disbanded, and post-war money was extremely tight. The dead might demand recognition, but painful decisions of economy were also made.

* * *

As part of the post-war project of remembrance and commemoration, the British government proposed to erect twelve free-standing Memorials to the Missing on the Western Front. Two would be in Belgium: the National Memorial, the Menin Gate in Ypres, and a small, 8-metre high memorial at Nieuport on the coast, where 547 names were inscribed commemorating the activities, in the main, of the Royal Naval Division in the autumn of 1914. Both these memorials were constructed without demur from the Belgian authorities.

On a much more ambitious scale, a further ten memorials were envisaged for France at key battle sites, all of imposing size, several close to towns. Unlike the setting of the Menin Gate in Belgium, there was no obvious location for the second National Memorial in France, though it was agreed that the further away from Ypres the second memorial was, the greater the impression would be made (by dint of distance) of the army's commitment to the cause.

British troops were engaged on several battlefields and so a plethora of suggestions were made by its senior command. Field Marshal Haig thought Pozières and Thiepval on the Somme were good locations, as well as Bullecourt at Arras and Villers-Breton-neux, where the Germans were held in the spring of 1918. General Rawlinson suggested Épehy, near Arras, as well as Pozières, and General Horne suggested Messines, Albert and the Butte de Warlencourt amongst others. Sir John French suggested La Ferté-sous-Jouarre on the Marne, where he had been in command in 1914, or, alternatively, a memorial for August 1918 when the tide of war decisively turned in the Allies' favour. Opinions varied but there was a consensus amongst these officers that the site should be high and isolated so as to amplify the impact.

National Memorials would also be required in Salonica and Gallipoli as well as in France and Belgium, and with this in mind, the Cabinet approved a construction budget of £300,000 in late 1920, with France and Belgium receiving the lion's share of the money. When news of the sums earmarked for these projects was given to Sir Alfred Mond, he was concerned. There was a general review of expenditure being undertaken and this large sum had been promised without parliamentary sanction or with his own Department of Works being consulted.

I feel I must ask the Committee to reconsider the sum allotted, more especially in regard to the Ypres Memorial which seems to me far to exceed what would appear reasonable in view of the fact that the Government do not propose, so far as

I know, to erect any War Memorial in this country beyond
the Cenotaph.
  Alfred Mond
  First Commissioner of Works
  December 13th 1920

He had a point. A lot of money was being lavished on projects a
distance away – across water – far from the veterans and the families
of the fallen. His immediate concerns were allayed by the triumph
of the Cenotaph and its almost universal approval amongst British
people. Nevertheless, spending considerable sums on the dead met
with some rancour at home when many of the living were struggling
to survive the peace. Frederick Young, a member of the conservative
and patriotic 'Comrades of the Great War', was uncomfortable
with what he saw as an excessive dividend for the dead. He had
met on a daily basis former 'non-commissioned officers and men,
who, having lost all they possessed, are at their wits' end to find
employment, and in many cases are actually in want of food'. By the
government's own 1920 estimates, around 70–80 per cent of the
male unemployed were ex-servicemen.
  Young added ruefully:

People appear to forget that, whilst all honour is due to the
fallen, yet a vast number of the survivors have run the same
risk, and are equally entitled to their gratitude. Indeed,
what is wanted is not so much a monument to the dead, who
are at rest in the hands of the Almighty, as a memorial to the
living … Surely if a war memorial is required, the first to be
considered should be those who have taken part in the war
and brought it to a successful issue.

Discussions about precisely where the National Memorial in France
would be built dragged on but, finally, in 1923, a decision was made
that it would be on the Somme, at Pozières, on a site chosen by chief

architect Herbert Baker. It would be placed in a central position on the battlefield of 1916, the same land that was swept over by first the Germans and then the British in 1918. And where better than the highest point, the Pozières Ridge, with a monument close to the principal arterial Albert–Bapaume road? It would certainly make a statement and it would be visible for many miles.

But from the start there were peculiar difficulties in obtaining the site, not least the fact that twenty-two or twenty-three different people were identified as owning the land, some mere infants. Negotiations to purchase the ground stalled and legal difficulties appeared insurmountable. In October 1925, the Director of Works suggested that if there was 'no reasonable hope of obtaining this site very soon, that Major Ingpen [in his capacity as the Land and Legal Adviser] should be asked to suggest sites himself where the acquisition of the land would be comparatively a simple matter ...'

It did not take long for Ingpen to reply:

Up to the present I have been quite unable to get any acceptance of my proposals to buy, and my hands are tied by the question of price. Mr Baker had a long conversation with me in my Office, during his recent visit to France, and he said he was perfectly willing to take some of the money from construction, with a view to my being able to offer more money for the land.

In light of this, Ingpen doubled his offer, but to no avail.

Apart from the issues of negotiating with so many interested parties, there may have been wider opposition to such a colossal structure being built so close to what would be primarily single or two-storey homes: the memorial would be the same height – within a foot – of the great Arc de Triomphe in Paris. There were wider political concerns too that great and impressive memorials would not only overshadow local towns and villages, but that they would put French war memorials in the shade. At the regular meeting of the Anglo-French Mixed Committee, concerns were raised amongst French members and discussed with British representatives including Fabian Ware and Major Ingpen. The French position was explained:

> Would [it] be possible to request the British Government to design monuments which would not appear so large by the side of the poor little monuments which we are obliged to erect to our own dead. It is not a question – and here I am venturing on very delicate ground – of drawing a comparison in any way in regard to the human sacrifice of the two allied nations, nor of wishing to have on the battlefields lasting monuments showing the extent of such sacrifices ...

Here was the issue: the French were unhappy about the size of certain monuments but did not wish to openly offend her allies, so immediate concerns were couched in gentler, more palatable fears over long-term historical perspective.

> ... there would be a certain number of French people, not at once, but perhaps in 100 or 150 years who would make an unkind comparison between the monuments erected by France and those erected by Great Britain on French soil. We have therefore been asked to request the British Government to examine this question from that point of view.

This was not a disingenuous concern, just one that was easier to sell at that delicate time.

Both Britain and France were aware of the lasting legacy their monuments established and how future generations would 'read' what they saw. It was partly with this in mind that Britain had forbidden the private removal of remains from the Western Front (and elsewhere), lest cemeteries shorn of officers would give the appearance, perhaps a thousand years hence, that other ranks alone had made the supreme sacrifice, or at least disproportionately so.

And so it was with the French, that British memorials, including those proposed by other Allied nations, such as Canada and Australia, might deliver the wrong historical message to future generations.

Major Ingpen, speaking on behalf of the IWGC, stepped in to suggest better communication between all sides might allay fears. The proposed Canadian Memorial on Vimy Ridge was cited as an example. The French were concerned not just about the imposing height of the memorial (40 metres), but were unclear about what lay behind the sculptor's vision. 'There is evidently a symbolical idea to which the sculptor desired to give expression' but which escaped the immediate comprehension of the gentlemen of the Commission (des Monuments Historiques), the views of which were represented at the Committee. 'There are various figures which appear to be climbing up a kind of pylon. What do these figures symbolise, I do not know, and it would be desirable to have this explained to us.' Lack of clarity was the reason cited why the French had not immediately approved its construction, though permission would eventually be given.

Most monuments were given the green light for construction; the memorial at Soissons, erected to the region's British dead of the 1918 Spring Offensive, was agreed with 'no difficulty': it is 'small and it will be very well situated in the town', was the Committee's French view. However, concern was expressed over the proposed Arras Memorial and its 'imposing, colossal dimensions'. In reply, Ingpen pointed out to the Committee's representatives that 'If you have 40,000 names to inscribe, a wall surface sufficiently large is required to contain them all'; likewise, the Soissons Memorial was small because it would commemorate fewer than 3,900 names.

The eagerness of all representatives to maintain cordial discussions was very evident. General George Macdonogh, speaking for the British representatives, thanked General Edouard Castelnau for having presided over the meeting 'with so much good will'. It was a 'great honour' to 'have as President one who had always shown such great friendship towards us'.

This obvious warmth ensured that compromise was easier to find. The design for the Arras Memorial would be significantly modified, while concerns over a memorial at Amiens were allayed when a decision was made to 'tack on' a high wall to the cemetery outside Pozières to commemorate the missing 25,000 Somme dead of 1918. Indeed, additional cemetery walls became the preferred option, so that the total number of freestanding memorials to the missing in France was slashed to four. Not unreasonably, the French had gently objected to so many monolithic constructions when great tracts of land had been very generously given 'in perpetuity' for Allied cemeteries.

The decision to abandon the Pozières memorial was, with the benefit of hindsight, prudent. A memorial close to a major thorough-fare would hardly have proved a proper place for pilgrim tranquillity and reflection. A new site was chosen: Thiepval, a high promontory overlooking the ground over which so many Allied troops had fought and died in 1916, and it was quickly approved by the French War Ministry. Acquisition proved relatively straightforward and work began on the onerous task of assembling the tens of thousands of names that would be inscribed on the memorial's panels, while Sir Edwin Lutyens busied himself on final architectural drawings.

Almost everyone had an emotional investment in the country's memorials, and no one could predict how they might be received once designs were made public. The astonishing success of the Cenotaph in Whitehall was acknowledged only after the memorial was first built in wood, with no expectation that it would last longer than the first anniversary of the Armistice. The public acclaim for the Cenotaph ensured that it would be replaced a year later in stone, to remain for evermore. The plain, sombre structure was a Lutyens masterstroke, a structure commissioned by no less than the government's First Commissioner of Works, Sir Alfred Mond.

The Cenotaph appears to have received near universal welcome, an extremely rare reaction to any significant architectural structure, let alone one that would be at the epicentre of an annual act of national remembrance. As with the cemeteries on the Western Front, there were those who would seek a physical cross in Whitehall, but their wishes were but a small and diminishing minority compared to those who found that the Cenotaph's austere beauty and quiet, gentle pragmatism tapped directly into their deepest heartfelt emotions. If there were others who had more negative thoughts about Lutyens's work, then they appeared to have kept them largely to themselves. The same could not be said of the design for the Menin Gate. When the architect's drawings were revealed to public scrutiny in 1924, they were not met with unqualified acclaim.

Sir

I have seen an illustration of the Memorial Arch which it is proposed to erect at the Menin Gate at Ypres.

As a member of the great British public I would appeal to you to reconsider your decision regarding this design.

It seems to me that the architect responsible for this work has completely failed to express the brave chapter of English history enacted before our sight during the five struggling years of the war.

The heights of glorious sacrifice. The depth of human agony and endurance, the press of strife and tumult whereby the nation's youth and manhood so proudly and magnificently died – these have no meaning and no substance in the design for the memorial which is supposed to interpret and immortalise the Empire's gratitude, remembrance, and devotion to the Empire's faithful dead.

Look at the design! It is made up from the stock of architectural commonplaces and meaningless trappings, lacking that imaginative, sympathetic handling visible in all great works, bereft of the enthusiasm and patience which should endow it with the impress of life, lacking power and significance, missing utterly, that quality which would prove it has been played over in every part of the sensibility of human intelligence and emotion.

Your architect has not seized this high opportunity to erect for the country a fitting expression of the country's loyalty and love towards those who died for her.

I would appeal to you to realise this! Begin afresh, put the design aside, do not stand upon ceremony or any false feeling of obligation. Your obligation is to the Empire's slain sons, and your duty is to see that what is erected to their memory is wholly worthy of them and their fine sacrifice.

If it is invidious to ask another single architect to attempt the work, call for a design from the whole architectural profession in competition, that the Memorial Arch may be splendidly conceived in the spirit of highest aspirations.

Yours faithfully

Mary Atterton

January 1924

The problem was that Mary Atterton, while decrying the architect's design, did not offer any solutions as to how the Menin Gate might meet her nebulous aspirations to encapsulate within its edifice the 'heights of glorious sacrifice'. That may not have been such a bad thing, because others did offer up ideas as to how precisely a memorial might look, down to minor details, details that were so astonishingly personal and idiosyncratic that there was no chance that they would ever be adopted.

Lena Hunter grieved for her fallen son, Captain Nigel Hunter, holder of the Military Cross and Bar. He was killed on the Somme during the German offensive of March 1918 and when she heard that the IWGC were soliciting ideas from the public for a memorial to the missing, she immediately wrote from her Winchester home. 'I beg to send the following suggestion,' she began.

The monument should be in granite or marble of a soldier lying dead, with a half circle of angels standing around him with bent heads – and the text beneath 'He shall give his angels charge over thee' – Ps XCI. II. I might tell you that I had a vision of my son, the late Captain N.D.R. Hunter, climbing a hill with determined face, with a half circle of five angels behind him; and he met his death, when climbing an embankment to locate the enemy's machine gun, which was enfilading his men ... his body could not be recovered.

Should the suggestion be adopted I would ask that the monument might be erected in the cemetery nearest Bapaume, where my son fell.

Yours truly

Lena Hunter

The design for the Memorials to the Missing would vary greatly, but they all had one thing in common: they would be adorned with stone panels and inscribed upon them long columns of names. It would take time to collate all the names for commemoration, and meanwhile, other more immediate questions had to be resolved.

On each memorial it would be right and fitting that the missing be listed under the title of the regiment in which they had served. But should all men from one regiment appear on one designated memorial? Or should they be commemorated by regiment on a memorial closest to where they fell? Close to where they fell was felt more appropriate. There was another linked complication. Should a man be commemorated with the regiment with which he originally served or, where relevant, the one to which he was subsequently attached? Again, the decision was to follow the second option.

Men were to be listed in order of rank but some battalions within regiments, such as the King's Liverpool Regiment, referred to their most junior ranks as riflemen, as opposed to privates, but lists of names, some prefixed by Rifleman, some prefixed by Private, would appear confusing and unsightly. The decision was taken that in all cases men would be referred to as privates, but in memorial registers, where appropriate, they could be listed as Rifleman.

Most importantly, how would men with the same surname and initials be distinguished from one another? How would individuality be guaranteed when there were scores of common names: Smith, Jones, Davis, Williams ...? As one IWGC officer observed (in June 1926), 'The Joneses in the South Wales Borderers will be more painfully numerous than ever, and none but the officers will have any recognisable individual place.' Every regiment would have similar problems. In drawing up final lists of the missing for the Menin Gate (August 1925) it was noticed that the King's Own Lancashire Regiment had four 'Jones A.'. 'It seems that these, one under the other, would not express the real object of the Memorial to the Missing, as there is no identification to the individualities of the <u>Jones A.</u>,' noted the Commission. Should a first name be used, perhaps, or an abbreviation of it? That would not work. Three of the four 'Jones A.' were named Arthur, men also of the same rank: private. The only way to distinguish one man from another must be to include the regimental number.

In putting together a definitive list of the missing for the Menin Gate, many errors were noted and corrections made. An initial list identifying 57,464 soldiers was received from the Director of Records and this was subsequently cut by 1,693 names owing either to the discovery and identification of remains since the conclusion of hostilities, or because a missing man was to be commemorated on a Memorial to the Missing elsewhere. Further amendments were made: today, 54,614 names are commemorated on the Menin Gate.

Where an up-to-date contact address survived, Memorial Register forms were sent to the next of kin to check details, in large part to correct the misspelling of names, but also to double-check regimental details. This seemed a straightforward formality but the process had an unexpected consequence that threw the Commission into turmoil. A considerable number of next of kin were disputing the date of death. The Suffolk Regiment, specifically the 1st Battalion, had twenty-eight cases where the date of death according to the many-volumed *Soldiers Died in the Great War* was 8.4.15 or 9.4.15. The battalion was serving in the Ypres Salient in April so the names were assigned to the Menin Gate. Yet five next of kin had amended the date of death on the final verification sheets to read 26.8.14, and on a further scrutiny and appeals to the relevant Home (Infantry) Record Office, it was discovered that all twenty-eight men had been recorded in the Battalion Ledger as 'Missing, presumed dead' in 1914. As no further news about their whereabouts was forthcoming, their legal death was 'accepted' by the Infantry Record Office almost eight months later. It was this second date that had been accepted, eclipsing the actual date of death, a date that automatically changed the memorial area for these men from the Menin Gate to La Ferté-sous-Jouarre, much further to the south. In another battalion of the Suffolk Regiment, next of kin challenged a further twelve dates of death, and these men too were removed to Bethune Memorial. If forty cases had been discovered so easily in one regiment, how many more were there to be found amongst other regiments and on other memorials?

The IWGC blamed the overworked Infantry Record Office for not amending the dates in their own records in the first place, and furthermore accused the Office of not showing instances where men had been 'attached' to other regiments, further complicating the process of accurate commemoration. This indeed did lead to additional errors.

One other significant memorial to the missing was proposed in Belgium. The Menin Gate would not be big enough to contain the names of all the missing in the Ypres Salient. Instead, it would hold the names of all British and Dominion servicemen who fell up to and including 15 August 1917 (the last day of the Battle of Pilckem Ridge). The names of all subsequent British and New Zealand 'missing' would be engraved on a semi-circular flint wall at the back of the vast Tyne Cot Cemetery. If the date of death was not properly noted, soldiers could appear on the wrong memorial. It was deemed too late, for example, to change the inscriptions for 800 men of the

London Regiment 'who should properly be commemorated at Tyne Cot' but were discovered on the lists for the Menin Gate.

Small numbers of missing names could be added in supplementary panels. When the sister of Bombardier William Cannell wrote to the office of the Director of Works in 1925 referring to her brother, he was found to have been omitted from *Soldiers Died in the Great War*, and his name was not known to the IWGC. Woolwich Records Office, home of the Artillery, verified his service and his name was approved to be added to the Menin Gate. By mid-May 1926, an additional 420 names had been discovered for inclusion on the memorial, including 123 names of men belonging to one battalion, 2nd The Duke of Wellington's (West Riding Regiment). As the schedules for carving names had already been placed with contractors and the majority of names already cut, it was decided that blank panels would be added for aesthetic purposes – 'tidy and inoffensive' – until the Director of Records had completed his work 'for the whole of the Memorials to the Missing', at which time additional names could be carved 'in situ'.

Certain errors could not be corrected. The 14th (King's) Hussars would for evermore be known on the Menin Gate by the abbreviated title the 14th Hussars. This was not the fault of the IWGC, or the Director of Records, or indeed anyone other than the regiment itself. When the title was checked with the then Honorary Colonel of the Regiment, he had confirmed it as the 14th Hussars. When, in November 1926, the error was spotted, there was a brief flurry of correspondence between former officers of the regiment and Fabian Ware. Perhaps, the word 'King's' could be added in brackets after the title, as there was still room to do that, apparently.

9th Dec 1926
Dear Ware …
 It is a great pity that we cannot get the Regimental title right, as it will go down for all time incorrect! I am sorry that

the WGC did not write to me instead of the Colonel, who is appointed in an honorary capacity and knows little about Regimental history.

I still hope you will be able to have a new stone put in with the correct title of the Regiment.

Yours sincerely

R.V.K. Applin

He added: 'The correct title is "14th (King's) Hussars" ... but 14th Hussars (Kings) would not be the title at all. I am sure there will be no discontent at the error, as we must accept the responsibility of our Colonel's original letter to you.'

Reginald Applin had retired from the army in 1921 and had been elected Conservative MP for Enfield. His regiment, which he had commanded until his retirement, deserved better, he felt.

It was aggravating that the name was wrong but it was also of great concern to the regiment that 'for centuries' to come, the 'inscription might be quoted to prove that the title "King's" was not given until after the Great War'.

The Director of Works at the Menin Gate was hurriedly contacted. Could a new stone be inserted?

It is, of course, possible to put in a new stone to replace that already fixed, but there would be a great danger of damaging the surrounding panels when hacking the stone out, and the danger would be repeated again when placing the new stone in position. I should therefore be reluctant to recommend that the stone be replaced.

E.H. James

The omission of 'King's' had clearly concerned the regiment, although other regimental names were similarly truncated. Another cavalry regiment, the 4th (Royal Irish) Dragoon Guards, lost the descriptive 'Royal Irish' from its panel on the Menin Gate, though whose error it was is not known, nor whether the regiment was overly concerned or not.

The unveiling of the Menin Gate was originally scheduled for the end of May 1927, but the date had to be postponed owing to the contractor overrunning on time. 'The completion of the work is long overdue,' according to a letter to Sir Reginald Blomfield on 13 January 1927, claiming that the Commission had been lenient with this contractor before. 'I cannot impress upon you sufficiently the very grave importance that the Commission attach to the work being completed in the early part of the summer of this year. If this is not done, I anticipate with the gravest apprehension the result of such delay.'

On 19 June 1927, the first of the Memorials to the Missing was unveiled: the great flint wall in Tyne Cot Cemetery. Five weeks later, on 24 July, the Menin Gate was unveiled. Over the following five years, twelve further memorials were completed, dedication ceremonies being held at each one, ending with the numerically greatest of them all, Thiepval, on 1 August 1932.

These freestanding memorials, anticipated so keenly after the war, reflected the desire to honour the dead, with suppressed concern for monetary restraint. It would never have been shrewd for any politician to appear too miserly, to caution financial responsibility when public emotions remained elevated. These great memorials were very visual reflections of the nation's respect for the dead, touched too, perhaps, just perhaps, by collective guilt over their selfless sacrifice made in frequently atrocious conditions. The Menin Gate and Thiepval could not be slimmed down, apologetic memorials, because above all others, they were always designed to be at the epicentre of British remembrance.

Nevertheless, by the mid-1920s, there had been a timely overlap between French objections over the number and size of the freestanding memorials and a British drive for economy. The addition of walls dedicated to the missing was the unintended expression of growing financial conservatism as the new economic realities bit hard. Austerity at home was visited upon the IWGC abroad, with swingeing cuts to its overall budget proposed by the Treasury. In a desperate effort to save money, several ideas were put forward, but none was more extraordinary than the idea in the early autumn of 1924 to partially abandon the cemeteries, some of which were still under transformation.

To see what was possible, Treasury officials had asked the IWGC 'to consider and report on the organisation and establishment necessary for the permanent maintenance of the cemeteries, graves and memorials'. What they meant was: 'Where can we save money?' The IWGC looked to its Finance Committee for answers, a committee on which sat a financial adviser from the Treasury. He was there to give 'the benefit of his experience, in accordance with the arrangements made with the British government on 20th June 1919', noted an IWGC letter sent to Fabian Ware. In meetings, this Treasury adviser's 'experience' led him to suggest that the Commission be asked 'to consider whether, in future, a very much lower standard [of cemetery maintenance] should not be adopted'. It must have appeared to Fabian Ware a fairly radical idea from such a normally conservative body.

The IWGC contacted Kew Gardens' horticultural experts. Kew had been central to the establishment of the cemeteries, and it was only sensible to ask them their views, and from their answers it was clear what they felt about the Treasury's suggestions. In September, Kew's experts had been asked to look at 'a more economic system of maintenance' for the cemeteries, not least a proposal to scythe cemetery grass on an occasional basis.

On 7 October, William Bean, Kew Gardens' curator, replied:

We have the honour to submit the following comparative report based on the present policy of maintenance, the Grass Lawn Treatment, and the present proposal, the Scythe or Field

Treatment. This latter may be designated as a system opposed to the accepted method of fabric construction of the cemeteries, having no regard to the general fine and delicate design that the Principal Architects have devoted their attention to in order to produce a worthy monumental character commemorative of the object in view.

In the first place it should be recalled that at the very commencement of the work of the Commission, careful consideration was given to all systems of horticultural treatment of cemeteries, and the arguments, in fact the arguments embodied in this report, were in favour of the present accepted treatment, as being the most economical.

The report went on to say that nothing had altered their view: 'It is not believed that the proposed radical change would in reality achieve the presumed object of the proposal.'

Nevertheless, it was incumbent upon Kew to set out the options:

Present System
Green lawns regularly attended (British personnel)
Suggested system
Scythe, treatment periodic attendance (local personnel)

Present System
Narrow borders along headstones facilitating mowing and
    planted with flowers
Suggested System
To be done away with

Present System
Hedge boundaries, clipping twice a year
Suggested system
Left uncared for except at scything times

Present system
Occasional beds of flowering shrubs
Suggested System
To be done away with

Present system
Trees (staking until fully established)
Suggested system
Left to take care of themselves

'Left uncared for', 'done away with' and 'left to take care of themselves' said everything that needed to be said about Bean's view on the proposed alterations. 'There is no half way house method between these two systems: the suggested system is entirely against the Laws of Nature in that rank and coarse growing vegetation stifles all growth of more delicate plants.'

William Bean had over forty years' hands-on experience in horticulture, and it showed. He spelt out the consequences:

Appearance more or less neglected except for the short period following the scything. ... Clipping round each individual headstone would become necessary. In the case of close-set headstones this becomes practically impossible. It is impossible to estimate the time but it is left to the imagination; the clipping round the 10,000 headstones in Lijssenthoek Cemetery ... The hedge enclosure of the cemeteries would run riot and be extensively spoilt by the rank grass in the body of the hedges. ... Headstones would suffer deterioration from rank vegetable growth up against the faces; the stones would be kept more or less permanently moist, exposed to moss and lichens growth and frost damage, intensified weathering; the personal inscription would not be legible owing to the impossibility of scything ... The grass would soon become full of rank weed, thistle dock etc … the surface of the cemeteries would become irregular (mole hills etc).

To support Bean's conclusions, the IWGC sanctioned a confidential visit to the cemeteries by Captain John Parker, the Chief Horticultural Officer in France and Belgium. For three days in mid-October, Parker toured the battlefields before reporting back. He savaged any suggestion of radical change. A proposal to scythe cemetery grass just twice a year would ensure coarse grass and a great increase in weeds. The grass would grow 'tufty' and would look rougher than on an ordinary field trodden down by grazing animals. Grass would inevitably grow up against the headstones.

In considering six or even eight scythings a year, he was prepared to concede that the grass would 'probably' be kept reasonably tidy but that the ground would be uneven, and clipping around headstones, walls and kerbs would be necessary. Where headstones were close together, clipping would have to be by hand and therefore very time-consuming. Clipping in the summer would be more urgent than at any other time of the year and if done but twice, would leave a very untidy appearance.

Money could be saved by giving up the scheme of planting flowers and there would be a saving in the expense of supply. 'The saving would be represented by the time at present occupied in pricking, planting, weeding and removing the dead flowers and plants.' As a consequence, British gardeners could be replaced by cheap and unskilled French or Belgian labour, but this was clearly not something he would recommend.

The Treasury's proposals were astonishing and were not made public, though had they been adopted, the public would have seen the consequences soon enough. The guns on the Western Front had not been six years silent, the great memorials to the missing not yet built let alone dedicated, but the dead of the cemeteries, it would have appeared, were already ripe for short-changing.

In mid-November 1924, the IWGC's Finance Committee met again. Fabian Ware was present, as was Viscount Richard Cross representing the Treasury. Cross was brimming with ideas, as the minutes from the meeting make clear. What if the cemeteries were laid with gravel as opposed to grass? The IWGC could path the cemeteries with spoil – he said 'material' – from a copper or lead mine. By smothering the ground with 'material', nothing would grow in a cemetery 'thus treated' and 'it would need nothing more than occasional visits to see that the copings were not falling off the walls'.

Viscount Cross was playing devil's advocate. He told the Committee that the Chancellor of the Exchequer was bound to ask him 'what alternatives there were to existing standards of maintenance'. He made 'layman' suggestions to the Commission, such as cutting the visits to a cemetery from once a week to once a month: with his proposals, one man would do the work of four. 'If reductions were made on that basis over all, the staff could be reduced by three-fourths and it would make a heavy cut in the cost.'

Sir Henry Maddocks, speaking for the IWGC, was horrified and pointed to the great difference between his own and Cross's views, as the minutes recorded. 'Put into plain words, Lord Cross's suggestion was that having expended large sums in making monumental cemeteries the Commission should now abandon them ...'

In response, Viscount Cross 'observed that the cemeteries would stay exactly as they were except that instead of having grass and flowers they would have grass and gravel'. He did not think the flowers would make a great deal of difference because flowers could not be grown if the lawns were not mown regularly.

Sir William Garstin, a former civil engineer and member of the IWGC Finance Committee, said that the Commission and its work 'was of such importance that, if the Treasury adhered to its view, then the Government should decide what to do. He was of the opinion that an endowment should be set up so that the Commission did not have to go to the Exchequer every year to get its money.'

The IWGC had proposed an annual budget of £226,000. Viscount Cross believed the figure was 'excessive' and that a more 'appropriate' amount would 'be a sum not exceeding £140,000 per year'. He thought the Commission could get along with very many fewer officials of the higher grades and these at very much lower rates of pay. He thought the Commission was paying far more in supervision than they would save in actual damage that might take place if the cemeteries and memorials were allowed to look after themselves. He pointed out that the Treasury maintained pre-war graves all over the world for a sum of £1,200 a year.

Admiral Morgan Singer observed that from his personal knowledge of these graves, they were not maintained at all, and Sir William Garstin referred to the neglected condition of the Indian Mutiny graves.

Viscount Cross said that he thought the estimate of £96,250 for 550 gardeners in France and Belgium could be usefully discussed.

When over 40 per cent of the IWGC's budget was spent on paying gardeners for their work, it would inevitably come under close scrutiny. The Finance Committee agreed that £3 per week was the lowest possible wage for desired labour, i.e. 550 gardeners costing an annual wage bill of £85,800. A pledge 'had been given to relatives as a reason for not allowing the bodies to be brought home, that the graves should be cared for by their countrymen', the Committee noted. If that pledge was to be honoured, then wages had to be kept up. Yet even that small cut in wages would save £10,450, a £19 per gardener pay cut per annum, their wages dropping from £175 to £156.

All this talk of cuts and the diminution of standards must have felt tawdry to many who sat on the Finance Committee, and there was huge relief when the decision was reached that standards set for the cemeteries were to be broadly adhered to. In his report, Kew Gardens' curator, William Bean, had forcefully pointed out the mechanics of proposed alterations: how scything the grass was in fact a skilled labour; how scything took three to four times longer than mowing, and longer too in raking up long grass. His report had been key to enlightening everyone to the false economies that would accrue from radical change. But he made another telling point. Cutting British staff at cemeteries would cut the guardianship of them too, and the help these men gave to grieving families to find the grave of their loved one. It was hard for anyone to forget that death and loss had been egalitarian. Everyone had paid into those cemeteries one way or another.

Chapter Ten

'I have tried, as you know, on my side, to do all that is humanly possible to locate these graves ...'

Angela Mond, 10 April 1922

The mystery of Francis Mond's disappearance along with that of his observer, Edgar Martyn, had remained a conundrum for over three and a half years, a family tragedy exacerbated by an avoidable wartime failure of process: missing identification labels, missing lorry park logbooks, missing receipts. Could there be one further error: mistaken identity?

Two bodies had been taken away from Smith's Farm in a lorry belonging to the Royal Flying Corps, of that there was little doubt, but where had the bodies been taken and why could their burial plots not be identified? Many named graves had been destroyed in later fighting, but this case did not fit that scenario because the Germans had been stopped in front of Corbie and would advance no further; indeed, they would soon be pushed back across the Somme region.

In January 1922, a new line of investigation was tentatively opened. From the Air Ministry's Casualty Department, a man with the surname Wallis was curious about the combat deaths of two other airmen on 15 May. Shot down in a Bristol Fighter over the Somme battlefield, the bodies of Captain John Vincent Aspinall and Lieutenant Paul Victor Dornonville de la Cour had been recovered and brought to Corbie. They were identified and then picked up by a tender on 17 May and removed for burial 20 miles away at Doullens. The similarities in the two cases were unsettling. 'It is curious,' wrote Wallis, 'that there should be some uncertainty about the removal and re-burial of two lots of airmen from about the same place at just the same time.'

Wallis had been to see Lord Stopford, Secretary, Enquiries Branch, at the IWGC. 'He [Wallis] does not suggest yet that a mistake has been made ... But of course it is just possible,' wrote Stopford in an internal memorandum. It was possible that a tender had picked up four bodies, not two, and that Mond and Martyn were buried in Doullens cemetery as 'unknowns'. The cemetery needed to be searched. 'I fear from my recollection of the reports of the cemetery there was rather a confusion in registration at that particular time,' he noted. Wallis could not find any evidence of a tender taking four bodies.

What struck Wallis was that there remained residual doubts as to where Aspinall and de la Cour had been killed. Mond and Martyn had fallen into no man's land; Aspinall and de la Cour, from eyewitness accounts, appeared to have been brought down behind German lines, in which case their bodies could not have been retrieved. As soon as Wallis had seen Angela, she immediately realised the ramifications of this news and proposed that the Doullens graves be opened and the bodies assessed for their identity. Wallis sounded a note of caution.

We cannot possibly open graves like this unless we have very strong evidence to show that the registration is wrong and that the persons buried are certainly not those we think. Until therefore we have definitely established the fact that Aspinall and de la Cour were brought down in a Bristol Fighter behind the German lines we cannot take any steps to open the graves in Doullens C.C.E. [Communal Cemetery Extension].

Even before considering whether Aspinall and de la Cour had crashed behind enemy lines, this new development had much to attract Angela. It would help explain why nothing could be discovered after Mond and Martyn left Smith's Farm. The missing logbooks of 5th Brigade, for example, were now rendered irrelevant because Aspinall and de la Cour flew with 11 Squadron in 13th Wing, 3rd Brigade. All Angela's attention had perhaps been devoted to the wrong wing; no wonder she had heard nothing.

No one was about to sanction the opening of two graves without detailed evidence of error. There were just too many graves on the Western Front that might become the focus for speculation and mistrust. The British people had been through enough and it was in no one's interest for millions of grieving civilians to believe, for one moment, that their loved one might not be in the grave named to their son, husband or father. Wallis's initial thoughts and Angela's wishes were put before the IWGC and were firmly rebuffed by an unidentified official in the Registrar's Department: the job of the department was to keep all records of graves and burials:

> As I have previously stated the only action possible is – ask the Sergeants. Why not ask the 11 Sergeants of the 57th Squadron first? They are most likely.
>
> Please see note flagged 'A' re Aspinall and de la Cour. There is nothing in our records that raises a doubt respecting the burial of these officers, in fact we hold a perfect burial authority – a Burial Return signed by the Rev. R.W. Dugdale attd 13th Wing RAF.

Dugdale's burial return did indeed state that three men had been buried, specifically Aspinall and de la Cour, as well as an officer named Lieutenant Wilfred Dann of 70th Squadron, killed on 16 May.

The men were buried in graves 27, 28 and 29, plot 1 in Doullens Cemetery. 'It seems hardly likely that an R.A.F. Chaplain would make a mistake in burial, however, if we are working on these lines, our best plan would be to ask the Rev. Dugdale particulars of the burial ...' wrote Wallis to Angela.

While contact was being made with the Reverend Richard Dugdale, the Air Historical Branch of the Air Ministry was asked to compile a list of all known losses on 15 May, and to examine each one carefully, eliminating those whose burial places were 'definitely accepted' and those whose burial had taken place behind German lines and whose identity was unknown.

In all, twelve British aircraft were lost on 15 May: two Sopwith Camels, four Bristol Fighters, three DH4s, two DH9s and one SE5a. Interestingly, while Mond and Martyn were listed as 'killed' in the RAF's Headquarters' War Diary, Captain Aspinall and Lieutenant de la Cour were listed as 'missing' in the Casualty Book kept in the field. Initially their fate had not been known; only later was 'M' substituted by a 'K', a suggestion that their fate was not definitively known, a hint perhaps that they might have died behind enemy lines.

German sources in Berlin were contacted to cross-check records. They recorded the crash of two Bristol Fighters and the correct identification of the occupants, Napier and Murphy, Glover and Fitton; both planes belonged to 48 Squadron. A third Bristol Fighter was shot down and the occupants also named as Lieutenant Herbert Sellars, who was killed, and Lieutenant Charles Robson, who was captured. Crucially, Sellers and Robson flew with Aspinall and de la Cour in 11 Squadron and so Robson was a likely witness to the deaths of his comrades. A subsequent statement from him would be all the more important as it was discovered that the fourth Bristol Fighter – it had to be assumed flown by Aspinall and de la Cour – was destroyed, falling in flames, and the occupants buried as unknown. The contemporary German report mentioned that this Bristol Fighter had a white cross on the upper wing. Would Robson confirm that detail?

In the Air Historical Branch of the Air Ministry, Wallis was trying to discover which unit had taken the bodies away from

Smith's Farm. The Lorry Park logbooks for 13th Wing, 3rd Brigade were found, and indeed a tender was sent to the 'region of Corbie' by 11 Squadron to pick up two bodies, which were brought back to Doullens Military Cemetery. Was it possible that the bodies of Aspinall and de la Cour were retrieved and sent to Corbie? A summary of 'particulars' concerning all four men was set out.

Lieuts Mond and Martyn	Captain Aspinall and Lieut. De La Cour
Brought down. Near Bouzencourt 4,500 yds from Corbie	Near Corbie
Date and time. 11.55 am 15.5.1918	4.15 pm (approx) 15.5.1918
Bodies sent back 18.5.1918 ? 17.5.1918 for burial by R.A.F. tender	17.5.1918
Squadron 57 – Le Quesnoy 3rd Brigade [13th Wing]	11 Remaisnil 3rd Brigade [13th Wing]

According to the Air Ministry, there was no record of a second plane being brought down near Corbie on 15 May. Furthermore, all arrangements for the removal of the two bodies had taken place over the telephone and there was the chance that details had been misheard. 'A further argument is that "11" and "57" are not dissimilar over the telephone,' according to the Air Ministry official. 'Yes,' came a reply from another official, 'but it is not easy to make a mistake in the two sets of names.'

A further request was sent to Berlin on 10 March 1922 asking for details of the aerial scrap with 11 Squadron. If Aspinall and de la Cour were brought down behind German lines, their bodies unidentified (not least because they were burnt), then, naturally, there would be no record that could identify these officers. Lieutenant Sellers, who was brought down in the same skirmish, was killed and identified, would have a record, and where he and his surviving observer (Robson) crashed would also indicate the approximate position of Aspinall and de la Cour's plane.

The Air Ministry had not contacted Lieutenant Robson, but they had been in touch with Captain John Chick, who led the 11 Squadron patrol that day. In a completely unconnected enquiry dated January 1919, Chick had received a detailed letter from Robson about the fight on 15 May, in which Robson had been taken prisoner and his observer, Sellers, was killed.

Robson had been shot down early on in the engagement.

After getting height over Amiens, I imagine we must have crossed the lines about Montdidier; then on flying north I saw several machines far to the east of us. I suppose there must have been between 15 and 20. At first there seemed to be a lot of 'playing for openings', then came the crash.

A regular dog-fight ensued, and I noticed you [Chick] were well in amongst it. We seemed to be getting on all right, although I knew that with the odds so heavily against us we were in for a tough problem ...

Lieutenant Sellers was hit.

I turned around only to be met with a perfect avalanche of blood. Poor Sellars had got a burst through the head, presumably from a Hun on our left. It was while you [Chick] were having your hands full that I had seen Aspinall go down in flames, so in my predicament I wondered when my hot time would come! However, as nothing like this happened and as Sellars failed to show any signs of consciousness from repeated shakes on my part, I took control ...

Lieutenant Robson managed to steer the aircraft to the ground.

> In some miraculous fashion I was dumped down in a shell
> hole near Pozières, and beyond a cut eye and a swollen face
> I was unhurt, though slightly in a dither. I do not recollect
> what happened for about half an hour afterwards, but I got
> several promises from Hun officers that Sellars would get
> every attention.

Robson had come down well within German lines, having just seen
Aspinall and de la Cour fall to their deaths. Angela immediately
wrote to Lord Stopford, Secretary, Enquiries Branch at the IWGC,
referring to the new evidence.

10th April 1922
22 Hyde Park Square, W.2

Dear Lord Stopford
I understand from the Air Ministry that they forwarded to you,
on Wednesday last, a statement of the circumstances concerning the burial of Lts de la Cour and Aspinall, which throws
doubt on the fact of their being actually the two RAF officers
who were buried under those names in Doullens Cemetery.

This doubt will, I trust, lead you to allow an examination
to be made of the two graves in question, with a view to
establishing once for all if they contain the bodies of these two
officers, or alternatively of my son and his observer.

May I, as a personal favour, and in consideration of the four
years of anxiety and harassing enquiry through which I have
passed, [ask you] to give your urgent attention to this very
pressing question, in order that the doubt may be settled in
one way or another at the earliest possible date.

I am prepared to proceed to Doullens at any time after
Easter, in conformity with the decision to be taken. I beg that

you will not consider my insistence unbearable. I have tried, as you know, on my side, to do all that is humanly possible to locate these graves, and I feel that we should be justified in the examination which I propose. If it should lead to further disappointment, I am fully prepared to start enquiries once more in another direction.

Believe me,
Sincerely yours
Angela Mond

The tone of Angela's letter was a mixture of steadfastness born of confidence and a hint of suppressed excitement: her son was buried in Doullens, she was sure. But much to Angela's anguish, Lord Stopford replied by return stating he was not willing to comply with her wishes. More proof was needed. 'I am afraid I do not see that we have any particular justification for opening these graves,' he wrote.

The particulars given by the Air Ministry are very vague and it does not give any definite proof that Capt. Aspinall and Lieut. de la Cour were brought down in the German lines. I am sure you will understand that before we can open any grave registered in either an officer's or soldier's name, we must have very strong evidence indeed against our registration, otherwise we would be very naturally criticised, and rightly so I think, by the relatives concerned.

On receiving Stopford's letter, Angela presented herself at the Air Ministry to examine the case files herself before returning home to write to Stopford. She did not wait to express her regret at his decision, and she made it clear that she would not back down. Angela was fuming.

I am in circumstances to have every possible sympathy with the feelings of relatives, but I feel also that my own situation is a very painful one. Since 1918 I have spared no effort to repair what a little reasonable care on the part of a Commanding Officer, and a little more human feeling on the part of official heads of the R.A.F. Casualty Dept. might have so easily obviated. As matters now stand I am more than ever determined to continue.

To circumvent Stopford, Angela immediately wrote to Sir Fabian Ware, asking for a 'brief personal interview'. Ware was snowed under with work preparing for the King's imminent visit to France: 'I simply do not know which way to turn so have to refuse to do anything but ordinary routine work.' After the visit he would see her, adding that he had 'for some time been watching the matter … I can assure you that my office is doing everything they can to get the case, a most difficult one I may say, cleared up.' Clearly unaware of Angela's recent communications, Ware finished, 'In the mean-while do come and see Lord Stopford, whom you may have already seen, and who is in close touch with everything that is going on.'

Angela was not interested in seeing Stopford. Instead, she contacted a friend, Sir William Tyrrell, and he too wrote to Sir Fabian Ware. He was a senior British civil servant and diplomat, working in the Foreign Office and the Home Office: in the late 1920s he was appointed British Ambassador to Paris. It is unclear how well he knew Fabian Ware; they had certainly met, but he asked if Sir Fabian would be willing to use his 'powerful assistance' to help Angela in her 'investigations', help that he 'should take as a personal favour'. There is no doubt that Sir William had great sympathy for Angela. He lost both his sons in the Great War, the first, Francis, a loss that had led to a breakdown in 1915, and secondly, Hugo, in 1918.

Despite Stopford's reluctance to retreat from the IWGC's stated position, he was aware or soon to be aware that the Air Ministry, based at Adastral House (where Francis had worked in 1916 and 1917), was ready to concede. In a memo to the IWGC dated 29 April, an Air Ministry officer wrote that the 'Air Ministry

[is] sure that some mistake has occurred and that the bodies are those of Mond and Martyn'. The personal effects file for Aspinall had been found, there was no trace of a file for de la Cour, and in the possessions sent back to Aspinall's family: 'There is no evidence that any of these items were taken from the body of this officer. The effects are, in all probability, those taken from the officer's billet.' It other words, Aspinall's body had not been recovered.

It seemed highly likely that an 11th Squadron tender had taken the bodies to Doullens in the mistaken assumption that they were 'their' men. Armed with this knowledge, it should be relatively easy to track down the two drivers and the man who buried the two airmen, the Reverend Richard Dugdale.

The first news was both sad and disappointing: Reverend Dugdale was dead, killed in the last weeks of fighting in 1918. However, the two drivers were alive: Privates Norman Parkinson and Hampden Pallant, and Pallant, it turned out, had known, at least by sight, Francis Mond.

Dear Madam

Your letter to hand of the 17th [June] and as I am the man who fetched the bodies of Captain Aspinall and Lieutenant de la Cour, I will state as fully as I can all the facts of the case.

In the first place both Capt. Aspinall and Lt de la Cour were personally known to me by being in the Sqdn.

I also knew Captain Mond though not personally but by seeing officers from 57 Sqdn who have had to land at our place for petrol, repairs, etc.

At some time near midnight my C.O. sent for me and told me he had received news that Capt. Aspinall and Lt de la Cour who had been missing had been brought down and their bodies were at a little dressing station at a spot just in front of Corbie at which place the [front] line then ran.

I and Parkinson went to Corbie and hunted about until we found the Dressing Station who told us the bodies were at a little spot further up the road. On reaching the place we found the two bodies under the charge of the R.A.M.C.

I took the two bodies over and signed for them but cannot remember whether I signed for them as Capt. Aspinall and de la Cour or two bodies.

I then asked if there was anything else or could he tell me anything about the case, and all he could tell me was that the bodies were brought from the machine by an Australian and left there. I then looked at the bodies and I am sorry the bodies were not recognisable but as I was told, and no other bodies being there, I took it for granted they were the bodies.

Moreover Capt. Aspinall was a very tall man and that convinced me and also Parkinson that they were them as one was very tall.

This was a strange additional detail as Aspinall was not tall and only slightly taller than de la Cour. If, however, the smaller man was in fact Mond's observer, Martyn, then the gruesome fact that Martyn had lost a large proportion of his head in the crash might help account for the apparent differences in height. Martyn was around 5 foot 8 and Francis Mond around 5 foot 9 inches tall.

Pallant continued:

On arrival at the Squadron, others who were personally acquainted with the officers did their best and came to the same conclusion and after making a couple of rough coffins we buried them. I might add, Madam, that though discs were the order to be worn it does not follow that they were and whoever was i/c of stores would have forwarded to the Headquarters anything that was found on them.

My belief is that these officers were put into the coffins as I brought them back [but] I cannot swear to it, for after handing them over my C.O. ordered me and Parkinson to get some sleep as we had been about 30 hours on the move.

And when I next saw them was at the funeral which took place that afternoon.

I think this is all I can remember and will be pleased to answer any question you care to ask. I am of the opinion that the bodies were Capt. Aspinall and Lt de la Cour, though as I state I could not swear to it.

As regards the machine I expect if you look up records you will find it written off as I do not think it was saved at least not by 11 Sqdn.

I think this is all so will now close.

I am

Dear Madam

Yours truly

H[ampden] Pallant

That Pallant knew Francis Mond by sight might have seemed like an important revelation when it came to distinguishing between his body and Martyn's and those of Aspinall and de la Cour. Yet the known facts surrounding the disappearance of Mond and Martyn were so particular, that despite Pallant's assertions that he identified the two officers from 11 Squadron, he was, believed Angela, surely mistaken.

The tender driver, Norman Parkinson, had driven with Pallant down to Corbie. Parkinson recalled that it was night and the car had become stranded in a shell hole until extricated in the early hours of the morning, the two men arriving at Smith's Farm shortly after dawn. The Corbie-Vaux road was under intermittent fire and unsafe for vehicles in broad daylight.

'The bodies were handed over hurriedly and nothing whatever was said of any effects or anything belonging to the two men.' All they were told was that one man was a captain and the other a lieutenant. 'There were no labels or anything to identify their names that I know of, so naturally, as I was sent to Smith's Farm for two Flying Corps officers, one a captain and the other a lieutenant, I took them to be Captain Aspinall and Lieutenant De La Cour.'

Parkinson could not identify the bodies facially, but, like Pallant, he knew Aspinall well, and he too recalled that he was a 'tall, well made man'. On that basis he assumed that the body was that of Aspinall and therefore the other man must be his observer. 'If your son was not tall,' he wrote to Angela, then 'this man could not have been he', adding:

> The bodies were put in the car and we drove up to Amiens and from thence up to Amiens-Doullens Road to a place just outside Doullens, where our Squadron was stationed, namely [the aerodrome] at Remaisnil. The following day the bodies were interred in Doullens Military Cemetery.
>
> In conclusion I would say that this case stands out very vividly in my memory as Captain Aspinall was a Bradford man.

This was an odd concluding statement as Aspinall was born in Epping in Essex and had grown up in London.

Angela was not convinced by Pallant and Parkinson's testimony. Perhaps they themselves were short, making Aspinall appear tall? Their departure from Smith's Farm had been hurried, in any case, and in the half-light of dawn; did they really take any time to examine the dead? It did not sound like it, and why should they? There was one further detail that neither man mentioned when they saw the two bodies. Aspinall and de la Cour had 'gone down' in flames, according to eyewitnesses – surely there would have been evidence of burning, if not of full immolation?

What their testimony didn't do was back up Angela's certain belief that a terrible error of identification had occurred. More crucially, their evidence would undermine the case she would put before the IWGC for exhumation.

After the evidence given by Lieutenant Robson in his letter of 1919, Angela wrote to Lieutenant Chick, the squadron leader who survived the air skirmish on 15 May. He responded on 30 July, apologising for his slow reply, and extending his sympathy to Angela. 'I can quite imagine what an awful time you have been through trying to trace your son, and I will tell you everything I know that might help you,' he wrote.

> In the 'scrap' two of my machines were shot down, one in flames, and the other with the pilot shot through the head. About a day or so later we received information that the bodies of Captain Aspinall and Lt de la Cour had been picked up in 'No Man's Land', and to send a lorry to bring them back for burial. I could never understand how on earth Captain Aspinall managed to reach 'No Man's Land', as the fight took place well over the lines and he went down apparently east of Mametz, this was then of course well on the German side of the lines. I must tell you frankly that I 'personally' did not see him go down, or the other machine containing Sellars and Robson. I was far too busily engaged in trying to save my own skin. But when I first attacked the Hun formation I saw them dive away down underneath me and I realised that they [Aspinall and de La Cour] had taken themselves right into the trap as another bunch of Huns closed in on top of them from some distance away and above. These people 'did them in', and several other people reported having seen them shot down at that spot. I then found myself all alone with Huns all around, but managed to exist until I was hauled out of it by a formation of Sopwith 'Camels', which dived out of the sun and so frightened the huns that they left me and we then proceeded to follow them down practically to the ground, doing sundry damage. I was then escorted over the lines by the 'Camels' and got back to my aerodrome to find that the other two machines had not returned.
>
> When the information was received that Capt. Aspinall and de la Cour had been picked up, I was amazed, but put

it down to some extraordinary 'fluke', the sort of thing that happened so much in those days. I cannot tell whether they were actually indentified as Capt. Aspinall and de la Cour, but I have reason to believe that no one from 11 Squadron identified them.

Memories do grow weak, but I always remember that particular show very vividly, and *I am certain in my mind that no machine shot down in flames where Captain Aspinall was could have got back to 'No man's Land'* ... [author's italics].

You realise that as an officer I have felt that I am rather 'letting down' Captain Aspinall by <u>perhaps</u> disturbing his people's peace of mind; but you have been very fair in your request and so I cannot see that I can injure anyone in trying to help you. I sympathise very much with you. If there are any other questions you would like to ask me, I will do my best to assist you.

Yours sincerely

John Stanley Chick

In late July, Lieutenant Robson wrote directly to Angela and critically, he placed the action of 15 May behind German lines.

During the flight in that particular evening, I distinctly remember the machine which carried Capt. Aspinall and Lt de la Cour falling in flames east of Mametz, but circumstances would not permit my following them to the point where their machine crashed.

May I quote two passages from a letter dated Jan 10th 1919, which I received from Lieut. J.S. Chick, M.C., the leader of our formation.

'...but that one had been seen to go down with the observer hanging over the side ... and the other was seen to go down in flames. This latter [i.e. the observer] we concluded was you, as we recovered Aspinall and de la Cour.'

It happened to be myself who was 'hanging over the side' and from Lt Chick's account I conclude that the flames in Capt. Aspinall's machine subsequently went out during their downward passage.

The other extract from Chick's letter is as follows:

'Aspinall and de la Cour came down in no man's land with their tail shot off. We fetched them in and they were both buried at Doullens.'

These statements would seem to point to the fact that the recovered bodies were actually those of Aspinall and de la Cour, but of course Lieut. Chick gives no proof that they were positively identified as such ...

I sincerely trust, however, that you will eventually be successful in your devoted enquiries.

Believe me
Yours very truly
C.C. Robson

As an afterthought Robson wrote:

As far as I remember the no.11 Squadron machines more or less followed the River Somme from Corbie to Bray and then struck north towards Mametz. Here the engagement commenced and it had not been in progress many minutes when I noticed Captain Aspinall's machine go down in flames. I should say that the incident actually took place further east than Mametz, as it was about five minutes after this that my pilot Lieutenant H.W. Sellars was killed, and I noted at this time that we were flying at a point a little north of Peronne.

East of Mametz or 'north of Peronne', either way, where Robson was brought down was many miles away from Bouzencourt.

All the letters Angela received, including another from a correspondent identified only as Sergeant Brewster, were submitted to Lord Stopford as further evidence of an error in identification.

I would submit that the evidence I put before you goes far to establish my contention. You will never hear anything from Berlin, in my opinion. It is however established by the records of the Air Ministry that the Germans mention a machine as 'gefallen' [fallen], and the aviator buried by them, as (I think) unknown. Every presumption points to that being the one 'Bristol' [Fighter] which did not return, and was not the one taken prisoner with Robson.

The machine which fell in no man's land [near Bouzencourt] was the D.H.4, flown by my son; I possess the plates with the number and letters and the remains of the machine are in the spot still. Therefore it was not a 'Bristol'.

The men who carried away the presumed bodies of Aspinall and de la Cour from Smith's Farm say they received them from an Australian R.A.M.C. Sergt. That same Australian says only two bodies of aviators passed through his hand at that date. I have given circumstantial detail that Captain Mond and Lt. Martyn were carried to that spot. The C.O. of the 8th Australian Field Ambulance confirms this, saying that his stretcher bearers saw the same bodies there 24 hours later and three days later heard they had been removed, and 'one of the officers came from Sussex'.

(My son gave our Sussex address for all references at that time, as I was mostly down here with my younger children, and nursing convalescent officers in the house. It was therefore to this address the news of his death came, and all the first correspondence.)

Of course, as I have said before, I may be wrong, but I have a very strong conviction that I am right. In any case, I would suggest that my case is a good one and deserves consideration. I must again reiterate my conviction that to rely on definite details from Berlin is to expect almost the impossible.

I am prepared to come up to town at any moment if you wish for a further personal interview.

Angela, ever aware of what she felt was Stopford's obduracy and forearmed with her own personal contact with the head of the Commission, pointedly ended her letter:

> May I ask you to show this letter and enclosures to Sir Fabian Ware?
> Very truly yours
> Angela Mond

Behind the scenes, the Air Ministry was certain of an error but while Stopford agreed that the evidence was strong, he cautioned again that the IWGC would have to tread very carefully before they began opening graves that 'have been registered for some 4 years in the names of others', and he felt certain that the families of Aspinall and de la Cour would oppose any disinterment. To Angela's certain exasperation, Stopford asked again for 'as much confirmation' as possible. Berlin must be given more time to reply and Fabian Ware was away for a month. Angela would have to wait again before the case was set before the General.

Angela agreed: the Germans should be given more time, but she suggested that 'reasonable time' should 'in no sense involve an indefinite postponement of a decision'. She further set on record that she was not only searching for her own son, but was acting on behalf of the Martyn family and his widow. Angela had every sympathy with the families of Aspinall and de la Cour, 'a difficult position that she understood as well as anyone'. She pressed the IWGC to contact the families of Aspinall and de la Cour to raise the doubts over the graves of those two aviators.

Stopford assured her there would be no indefinite postponement of a decision. The families of Aspinall and de la Cour still knew nothing, but that was about to change.

Angela's conviction that nothing would be heard from Berlin was premature. A report was received in the middle of August 1922 from the General Commanding the German Air Force and the Officer Commanding 2nd Air Squadron that a Bristol Fighter was shot down in flames from 5,500 feet on 15 May 1918 at 6.20 pm east of Albert, between Contalmaison and Albert 'on our side of the line'. Attached to the report was a statement by Lieutenant Hans Kirschstein of the 6th German Squadron detailing his eleventh victory. He had attacked the 'lowest' of the British aircraft, concurring with Chick's recollections that he had seen Aspinall and de la Cour dive downwards and into a 'trap'. Kirschstein witnessed the plane go down in flames, confirming that the two dead men were not identified, the wreck of the burning machine lying in 'the shelled area' behind the first front line.

'There appears to be no doubt as to the identity of the two occupants, as detail given i.e: place, time and type of machine of the aeroplane flown by Aspinall-Dormonville de la Cour coincide exactly with those given by Lieut. Kirschstein.' Kirschstein was killed in a crash at his aerodrome on 17 July 1918.

The evidence was as conclusive as it would ever be. Surely the IWGC would agree to an exhumation? Aspinall and de la Cour could not be in adjacent graves in Doullens Cemetery, but did it necessarily follow that Mond and Martyn were there instead?

Map 3

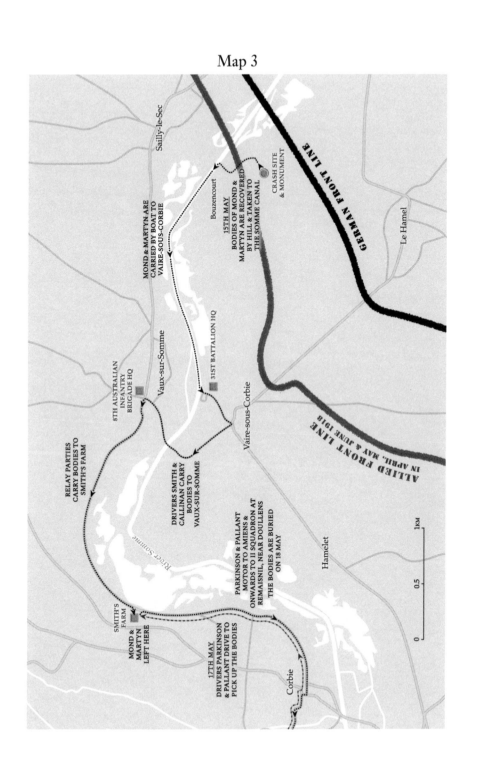

Sailly-le-Sec

GERMAN FRONT LINE

Le Hamel

MOND & MARTYN ARE CARRIED BY BOAT TO VAIRE-SOUS-CORBIE

Bouzencourt

15TH MAY BODIES OF MOND & MARTYN ARE RECOVERED BY HILL & TAKEN TO THE SOMME CANAL

CRASH SITE & MONUMENT

Vaux-sur-Somme

31ST BATTALION HQ

8TH AUSTRALIAN INFANTRY BRIGADE HQ

Vaire-sous-Corbie

RELAY PARTIES CARRY BODIES TO SMITH'S FARM

DRIVERS SMITH & CALLINAN CARRY BODIES TO VAUX-SUR-SOMME

River Somme

PARKINSON & PALLANT MOTOR TO AMIENS & ONWARDS TO II SQUADRON AT REMAISNIL, NEAR DOULLENS THE BODIES ARE BURIED ON 18 MAY

ALLIED FRONT LINE IN APRIL, MAY & JUNE 1918

Hamelet

SMITH'S FARM

MOND & MARTYN LEFT HERE

17TH MAY DRIVERS PARKINSON & PALLANT DRIVE TO PICK UP THE BODIES

Corbie

1км   0.5   0

Chapter Eleven

'I am going back to France to visit again and again that grave where he lies buried. So long as I live myself that hill will be the shrine to which my many pilgrimages will be directed. ... And meanwhile the wild flowers and the long grasses and all the little shrubs will keep watch and ward over him there, and all the other brave soldiers who lie hard by ...'

Harry Lauder, *A Minstrel in France*, 1918

During the war, a number of soldiers predicted a significant influx of visitors – pilgrims – to see the trenches once peace was secured. These civilians, many of them relatives of the fallen, would visit the battlefields, in all likelihood the Western Front, owing to its importance and its close geographical proximity to Britain. These soldiers speculated about the visitors in their diaries and letters, fearing that as many people might come out of ghoulish interest as others who would wish to pay respectful homage. Some imagined, rightly or wrongly, cars criss-crossing the benighted land, dust plumes thrown up by car tyres as drivers sought to meet ambitious tourist timetables so as to 'do' the Somme in a day. Cecil Longley, a gunner in the Royal Field Artillery, was one who predicted battlefield tourism as early as May 1915:

This wood [Ploegsteert Wood] with the awkward halting name will one day be the loving pilgrimage of a few; let us hope it will not become the excursion of the thousand, clamorous, with tightly clasped franc in hand, for admittance to gaze with morbid interest and loud-voiced comment upon the steel-riven wood and the quiet resting-places of those who gave their lives to gain it.

Ploegsteert: that same wood whose owner, a few years later, would threaten to close owing to visitors disturbing his game birds. And yet this wood meant so much to the British. It was 'a hallowed spot in Belgium', avowed Longley. 'I venture to think that those whose honoured dead are lying there could wish them no lovelier spot, consecrated not by the Church, but by the glories of the surroundings and the sacrifice of those who sleep there'. It was why the IWGC maintained that so few war graves should ever be exhumed, and moved only in narrowly prescribed circumstances.

The prediction of battlefield tourism was hardly a revelation: thousands of British civilians had flocked to Waterloo after Wellington's victory in 1815, looking over the celebrated ground, hoping to pick up a souvenir. The difference was that a hundred years later, enquiries about guided excursions to the Western Front began even as the fighting raged. In March 1915, *The Times* reported interest, but scotched any ideas that people would be allowed to go. 'Trips to Battlefields. No "Conducted Tours" Till The War Is Over', it said, while three travel agencies, including Thomas Cook, announced that they had not the 'slightest intention' of arranging tours while the war was on. All three were clearly responding to enquiries.

In the weeks after the Armistice, it would be soldiers who had the near-exclusive run of the battlefields. In a sense they were the first tourists, for trench-fighting men had had only a worm's-eye view of no man's land, venturing over the top after dark, peering through a periscope by day. Their appreciation of the Somme or Passchendaele battlefield was rarely more than 90 metres on either side of where they stood. All of a sudden they could go wherever they wanted, seeking out old dugouts or trenches. On 12 December, Colonel Rowland Feilding took an American doctor to look around the Loos battlefield. Very quickly this seasoned soldier regretted his offer, being put off by his companion's obsession with souvenirs. Feilding wrote to his wife:

It is horrifying to see this sacred ground desecrated in this way and still more so to think of what will happen when the cheap tripper is let loose. ... I know that these things will be collected, and hoarded, and no doubt boasted of, by tourists, – things that no one who has fought would have in his possession. Fortunately, the salvage Corps is busy at work, collecting and burying such trophies.

And when civilians did come, former Scots Guards officer Wilfred Ewart did not hold back his criticism of those with baser intentions, those, he said, who go to gape at a battlefield (from a charabanc) as he would gape at a cathedral or a criminal, his soul being packed in behind with the luggage. 'There are such people – morbid people, inquisitive people,' people who 'in a jolly spirit "run round" to "have a look"'.

These soldiers were troubled by conflicting emotions. They might wish civilians to see this 'other' world in which they had lived for so long, but equally they were anxious that they came for the right reasons, an impossible thing to arbitrate. And yet few civilians had remained untouched by the war. Not every visitor would have suffered loss within their immediate family, but they almost certainly knew some who had not come back – old pals from school, a church friend, mates at work or a neighbour: most would not have identified themselves as tourists but as pilgrims, even if, in the eyes of men like Feilding and Ewart, their behaviour might be insensitive or downright repulsive. Feilding for one feared the 'cheap tripper' who with his 'spit' would 'saturate the ground that has been soaked with the blood of our soldiers'.

The British Army on the Western Front still numbered several hundred thousand men well into 1919. When Ewart walked the battlefields, he had seen far more soldiers than civilians, soldiers 'guarding salvage dumps, guarding each other, making salvage dumps, doing Graves Registration work', and 'cleaning up', as he put it. There was a reason for the paucity of visitors. After the Armistice, the War Office imposed restrictions on civilians travelling to the battlefields. Large areas were 'entirely closed to visitors' during the work of grave exhumation and concentration. In May 1919, the government announced that the ban would remain in force until this work was 'much further advanced'. There was also the issue of transport, the added strain pilgrims would place on the French and Belgian railway network owing to wartime damage, and the army's commitment to demobilisation – not forgetting issues over accommodation – meant that the authorities were not minded to lift the ban. Speaking on behalf of the British government, Captain Frederick Guest told the House of Commons that: 'As soon as conditions improve and it becomes possible to open up parts of the country, public announcements as to the areas accessible for such visits will be made ...' Despite public statements to remain patient, the ban was lifted just a few weeks later. On 1 July, during questions in the House, the government acknowledged that the War Office was no longer imposing any restrictions on travel, but was merely asking people to avoid the areas of cemetery concentration. The appeal was likely to fall on deaf ears. It was not the battlefields per se that drew pilgrims – one ruined battlefield looked pretty much like another – but the associations they had with specific places, towns, villages, woods, even crossroads, the names of which had entered not only the British consciousness but the soul: Mametz Wood, Hellfire Corner, Hill 62, Hooge. These places could not be ignored by pilgrims, bypassed, left for another day. Few Welsh visitors to the Somme would not wish to go to Mametz Wood, for example, the scene of the 38th (Welsh) Division's sternest test, but Mametz Wood, as so many key places, was where the dead lay in greatest profusion.

Though the work of exhumation was far from being concluded, lifting the ban said much about the public clamour to visit the battlefields. To merely stand at places mentioned in a loved one's letters might be recompense enough for the effort made to get there. And as astute as men such as Gunner Longley were, not many predicted the numbers who would want to travel: his expected 'few' were exceeded hundreds of times over. Even old soldiers who imagined flocks of visitors to France and Belgium assumed that their appearance was a one-off event. Former Guardsman Stephen Graham predicted an early peak in visitors followed by the inevitable decline, and with that decline, neglect. 'Brand-new cemeteries' with their gravestones would look beautiful, but then, perhaps within months, increasingly rain-washed and wind-blown before 'falling a little off the straight'. He predicted that as pilgrim numbers thinned out, so some IWGC gardeners would become less conscientious. 'Most of the cemeteries in the more obscure places will be half-forgotten and gone desolate,' Graham forecast. He, amongst others, might have been surprised to know that, in 1938, Fabian Ware put the annual number still travelling to the Western Front at over 100,000, up 5,000 on the year before, an estimate based in part on a IWGC count made of signatures left in cemetery registers, a crude but nonetheless useful indicator of overall numbers. Times were changing, the pilgrims less often the parents and the wives of the fallen: 'It is important to note that nowadays young people, sons or daughters of the dead, [are] visiting the graves,' he told the 15th Meeting of the Anglo-French Mixed Committee in November. As the storm clouds were forming over Europe, perhaps the young as well as the old were keen to remind themselves of the cost of war.

It was then nearly twenty years since the first intrepid visitors had gone across. Back then, the War Office ban may have temporarily halted organised tours but it did not stop those determined to go under their own steam, people who were financially independent and mobile. It is not clear whether there was any attempt to frustrate such unofficial visits; the very first civilians travelled abroad in December 1918.

Sir Edward Poulton went a month after the Armistice, determined that he would see the grave of his son, Ronald, killed in 1915. He knew where he was buried, interred with loving care by his men. Sir Edward also knew that the fighting had been intense in the spring of 1918, flowing over the precise ground where his son lay. It was possible the grave would not be there at all and he had to steel himself for that prospect. The cemetery, he wrote, 'bore many scars of war [with] craters filled with water and trees splintered and broken off. The fence and rustic gateway had disappeared. Ronald's grave was uninjured, although there were four shell-holes within a few feet of it; the oak cross was intact save for two scratches from shell splinters.'

Eighteen-year-old Patricia Wilson went too, shortly after Sir Edward's visit. Her father, Major William Carver, had taken his battalion, the 10th East Yorkshire Regiment, to war in 1915, and he could not wait to go back.

> My father said he must take us and show us where he had been in France, so he took my mother, myself and brother. He wanted to show us all the places where there were trenches, and we went to see where my cousin was buried, who had been in the artillery. The trenches and the atmosphere, it shocked us. My mother didn't like it at all, and you couldn't help feel it was too soon.

Lady Londonderry was another early pilgrim to France; she spent five days on the battlefields in April 1919.

> The only signs of life were salvage parties of men exhuming dead bodies, or burying them, or else digging cemeteries. Two bright splotches of colour caught the eye in the near distance. Flags! Yes. They were union Jacks which lay over the floor of two wagons, they covered poor shapeless lumps of clay carefully placed in sacks, the remains of those who had fought

their last fight on this famous field. I would have preferred myself that the dead had been left to lie in peace where they fell ...

In another place, evidently a machine gun emplacement, lay skulls cut in half, teeth, bones and broken rifles, with belts of cartridges and portions of clothes mixed. The punishment all along the slope must have been deadly. It seemed impossible to realise on this quiet spring evening what a hell the countryside had been so recently.

Visiting was not without significant danger. The epic task of clearing just visible munitions would take years and claim further lives, including eighty-three soldiers and prisoners of war killed and a further 203 injured in the region of the Pas-de-Calais alone between the Armistice and early 1922. In addition, farmers were killed as they ploughed the land, and other civilians seeking to extract the copper from shells or simply hunting for souvenirs. As Rowland Feilding showed the doctor around Loos, he spied one 'respectable' souvenir his acquisitive companion might like to take home. It was a German stick grenade. 'It had been lying about so long that I did not think it could possibly have any sting left. However, I pulled the safety cord to make sure, and immediately there followed a hissing sound.' Feilding called on the doctor to take cover and threw the bomb. It exploded a second later, a splinter hitting the doctor in the hand.

The ground was as encrusted with debris in October 1919 when Wilfred Ewart returned, accompanied this time by his sister. The 'greying' wooden crosses still stood isolated, waiting for the bodies beneath to be exhumed. Helmets, many dented, lay around and shreds of uniforms as well as rusted rifles and gas masks, 'Year-old tragedies lurked on either hand,' he observed. As well as the military equipment, there were 'fragments of letters, photographs of women', which had somehow contrived to survive exposure to twelve months of Picardy weather. And then, incredibly, there is a dugout, probably an artillery officer's, intact, abandoned seemingly at short notice, nothing moved. 'What happened …? A dented enamelled white basin with traces of soapy water stands on a box; shaving tackle all spattered with soil and mud spreads itself upon an improvised table. Something of a meal remains – a marmalade jar with tin plates and rusted knife and fork. A pair of muddy, hardened boots is set down near the entrance.'

Wilfred's sister Angela had lost her husband, Charles Farmer, in the fighting on the Somme in August 1916. She returned to France just the once, with Wilfred, clutching her husband's letters, including one written an hour before he was killed. She wanted to locate where he had fallen near the village of Ginchy and she could do no better than walk with a veteran of the fighting, an expert in picking his way around the land, desolate so that even a map was an 'uncertain guide', the pair correcting their orientation by the 'still visible peak of the Butte de Warlencourt', an ancient burial mound, 'for we know that our friend lies near'. Charles Farmer's body had never been recovered and in time his name would be appear amongst those engraved on the Thiepval Memorial to the Missing.

'I never expected this,' Angela said. 'I have tried to think of him, and of him in it, and of what hell looks like. But I never imagined such loneliness and dreadfulness and sadness in any one place in the world. One cannot imagine it. I thought I knew what it was like, but I only thought. I never felt until now.'

Wilfred Ewart guided his sister towards the mound.

Somewhere he lies near – on that hillside above that shell-stricken wood. … What is the satisfaction of our search? What do we expect to find, and what to feel? It is as though some magnet, some occult, refined sense drew us on. This we could not explain. For, after all, the sunbeams are no more than mocking memories: the reality is underground – a skull, a few bones, a wisp or two of hair, a shred or two of khaki cloth.

But to that we cling. We reach out to within a few feet of what once was. And with every cross we bend down to, puzzling out letters and numbers which time and weather have reduced to mere ciphers, a quick look of hope starts in the eyes ... It is not to be.

So engrossed are we seekers that we do not notice the rapidly westering rays of the afternoon sun or the oncoming of night. We do not even feel the approaching cold. ... Will we find our friend, or do the dead lie too thick – are the crosses too many? We pause in our search, a profound disappointment upon our faces.

Angela Farmer's search was concluded. She would never return, though Ewart discerned a renewed lightness in her outward appearance, though how exactly he should interpret that he was never entirely sure.

Ewart believed that everyone who wished to should go while the battlefields retained their wartime characteristics. People needed to drink in an atmosphere that was necessarily transient, as wildlife recovered and as the ground was cleared. 'There is no time to lose,' he believed. 'The atmosphere is there now but life encroaches, activity multiplies and increases in these waste places. The bitterness and majesty of them diminish, and with every month, with every year, they lose reality and imminence, trending toward their final shape – a legend.'

The best guides were invariably human rather than book, former soldiers like Ewart who travelled from England, or men who had chosen to remain in France to make their livelihoods there.

Lucy Orton journeyed from Bredhurst in Kent in the spring of 1920 to visit the grave of her brother Christopher, killed in April 1918. She went as part of a thirty-strong group, 'all on the same errand to visit a grave', she described in a letter to her local newspaper, the *East Kent Gazette*, following her trip. The group had been led by a former army officer, Mr Coles, a man who had served on the Somme battlefield where Christopher was buried. Mr Coles was 'the most sympathetic, tactful and patient official', she said, a man who 'could answer questions with first-hand knowledge'.

In an article published in May 1920 in the *Evening Standard*, the journalist and pioneering travel writer Henry [H.V.] Morton paid tribute to these former servicemen, 'the type of soldier whose duty it is to help visitors to search for the graves of their boys'.

He went on: 'The men I came in contact with are old soldiers wearing the Mons ribbon and several wound stripes. One man, a private, told me he had been in the first battle of Ypres.

'It's a sad job we've got,' he said, 'and at first I did not like it. But now I know every inch of the town, and I've learnt how not to hurt people's feelings. It's surprising how now and then little thoughtless things you let out, quite innocent like, hurt women. The best thing to do is lead them up to their grave and then disappear. It hurts to see the women who come here, hoping to find graves, walking about reading other people's crosses and crying a bit.'

'When this job is over, what are you going to do?' I asked.

'What I would like to do is to get a permanent job under the Graves Commission and stay out here always in charge of a cemetery. I would get my wife and family here and settle down.'

The ways of officialdom are wonderful and mysterious, but I hope when the men are elected to take care of the Ypres cemetery the claims of these soldiers will be considered first.

There were many literary guides to the battlefields. The Michelin Tyre Company produced the best known and widely recognised books, beginning with a guide to the Marne of 1914, published in 1919. The company opened Information Bureaux, including one in Paris and another at 84 Fulham Road in London (three doors up from their tyre outlet), offering a free service to advise travellers about points of interest, suggested routes and need-to-know rules and regulations when driving abroad. Maps were also sold.

'This volume is the first of a series of guide books,' the foreword began. 'It is offered as a complete and practical guide for tourists who contemplate visiting the scenes where the opening battles in the war were fought ...' The publishers were keen to stress that this was not just a book for sightseers: 'The contemplated visit should be a pilgrimage; not merely a journey across the ravished land. Seeing is not enough, the visitor must understand ...' The book set out the battle's historical context before outlining a suggested itinerary. This, a circuit of 527 miles, could be covered in six days and did not suggest that long contemplative stops were anticipated, but of course the pilgrim or tourist could alter the route and timings at will.

Other Michelin guides followed that same year, including a guide to the Somme with numerous excellent maps and photographs, many snapped during the war, but others, including images of broken tanks, taken in the year of publication. By 1921, Michelin would publish fifteen guides in English, the profits of which were given to aid reconstruction in France and Belgium. It was an astute marketing ploy, given just how many tyres would be required by vehicles hoping to negotiate rutted battlefield roads and tracks. Indeed, the point was not lost on a rival tyre company, B.F. Goodrich, which, not wishing to miss a trick, published its own book, *Guide to the War Regions of France and Belgium*, and included eighteen pages of adverts for their own brand of tyre.

These books put the war into context, reminding readers of the who, where and why. Not everyone wanted such detailed information, some opting simply to take in the sight of the battlefields, to visit as closely as possible where a loved one had fought. Most people found the individual organisation of a trip abroad too daunting, especially when so many had never been abroad before, and that was before the cost was taken into account, prohibitively expensive for most. If families were to visit, then it would be with an organised group, costs shared, responsibility handed to someone else who knew their way around. Such was the demand that tour companies were swift in putting together inexpensive packages. The patriotic sounding Britannic Tours (it began life as Auto Express & Tours Anglo Belge, but soon rebranded) offered tours 'conducted by the boys who served side by side with our brothers who paid the supreme sacrifice'. In case there was any doubt, the 'boys' were 'ALL BRITISH', a key feature when building trust with would-be pilgrims, warning travellers that not every tour was as good as the next. 'Beware of imitations,' it advised, then suborning the line from the popular wartime song 'We don't want to lose you but we think you ought to go' as a last encouragement to book.

Hostels and hotels were rapidly developed to meet demand, mostly hastily erected wooden structures such as the Hotel de Ville in Ypres, built within a wooden garden city on the town's Plaine d'Amour. There were many places to stay by 1920: in Poperinge, for example, a few miles to the west of Ypres, there was 'a sort of anglicised hotel', Ewart wrote, and there were other hotels 'with varying degrees of comfort' in Amiens, Arras and Cambrai. The choice would depend on what a visitor was willing to put up with. At Roisel, east of Péronne, there was the Hotel Silvestre. It sounded attractive but the 'hotel' was little more than a step up from a barrack block, more sleeping quarters than accommodation in the traditional hotel sense, and with an adjoining hut, roofed with corrugated iron, and a sign that optimistically noted that this was the 'Restaurant'. Tellingly, Ewart chose to stay in Lille, firstly because of its central position to the different battlefields and 'secondly, because its hotels are habitable'.

It may have seemed distasteful to some, but the Great War tourist industry grew exponentially and, as with all tourism, packages were offered that suited the pocket. Thomas Cook publicised two tours in the 69th edition of the *Traveller's Gazette*, published in August 1919. The first was a luxury tour, costing 35 guineas, offering the very best in hotel accommodation and travel, the accommodation in hotels presumably some distance away from the scenes of carnage. At the same time, a second, cheaper tour was offered, costing less than 10 guineas, a far more affordable option.

Many of those who travelled to France did so with organisations that had helped the poor and needy during the war, such as the Salvation Army, the Church Army and YMCA. They had offered support and accommodation to families permitted to visit gravely wounded sons, fathers or husbands in hospital on the Western Front, and now, post-war, switched their efforts to helping the bereaved cross to France. As these charitable groups had the infrastructure in place, they were able to respond quickly to the needs of those who wished to travel: the Church Army, for example, took 5,000 family members by the early summer of 1920. Likewise, the Salvation Army helped 18,500 people travel between 1920 and 1923, and the YMCA assisted 60,000 people in the years to 1923.

Yet even the cheapest and shortest trips would cost several pounds, perhaps around £4. In the *Leeds Mercury* in July 1924, one recent visitor to France estimated the cost for two people to the Somme for one week was £20, several weeks' salary for the average male worker, depending to an extent in which industry he worked. For some people, a pilgrimage had been planned from the day they had had received the news of death. The *Nottingham Journal and Express* reported in November 1921 how one woman had gone to the YMCA's Triangle House, and presented them with six sovereigns.

Her boy, she said, had been killed in the early days of the war, and soon after the sad news came through, she and his father determined to save up so that after the war they might visit the place where he fell. After they had saved £6 her husband died, and in spite of many hardships and privations she had kept the little hoard intact for the purpose for which it was designed.

The government was pressed to make some financial accommodation for bereaved families who wished to go to the Western Front but could not afford to. In February 1919, Winston Churchill, speaking in the Commons, reassured MPs that representatives from various voluntary organisations had been called together to form a committee to look at options. In reality, the government did not wish to offer any financial guarantees, estimating that any commitment might cost in excess of £2 million (albeit this was less than one day's military spending during the latter stages of the war). In the event, only a small sum was ever given to these charities to aid the poorest. On the third anniversary of the Armistice, for example, 120 relatives of soldiers buried in France or Belgium had travelled from Nottingham with the YMCA under what was known as the Graves Visitation Scheme, by which expenses were either partially or entirely paid out of the special fund, though whether this was entirely government funded is unclear. Applying for help, proving eligibility through poverty, might not have encouraged many to enquire and undoubtedly not everyone who wished to go to the Western Front, or further afield, ever went.

The number of visitors to the battlefield ebbed and flowed; the initial rush by families began to fall back by the mid-1920s, particularly as the economic climate darkened at home and industrial and agricultural wages were cut. Visitors to the Ulster Tower on the Somme, one of the first permanent memorials to be built – unveiled in 1921 – saw numbers decline from around 300 a week between 1922 and 1924 to around half that number by 1928.

Like their families, there were ex-servicemen who could never go back. Equally there were some who returned once to lay a ghost, to try to settle things in their mind. Former Private James Hudson returned in 1923.

A travel agency sent me a brochure about trips to the battle-fields and on the spur of the moment, I thought I would go. This was on the Monday and I travelled on Friday. ...

There was only one other old soldier on the coach. We got to know each other and together we walked into the cemetery at

Passchendaele, Tyne Cot. It was a lovely summer day, quiet and peaceful, and at the back of the cemetery was a young Belgian fellow with a single plough drawn by a mule, one of ours, for it had an arrow stamped on its backside. The peace, the quiet, the scene had both of us damn nearly in tears. We parted and we were left alone for some time before we could pull ourselves together a bit. It brought back so much.

Veteran organisations such as the Ypres League, founded in September 1920, were heavily involved in pilgrimages. But the League did not just facilitate visits; it campaigned too, led by Beckles Wilson, who had so decried what he saw as the vulgarisation of Ypres. Through the combined efforts of soldiers who had fought in the Salient and the families of those whose loved ones forever remained there, he hoped to keep alive the spirit of fellowship that had grown during the war, while keeping sacrosanct the memory of the town's defence. The League 'organised inexpensive travel' for ex-servicemen and bereaved families, 'maintain[ing] cordial relations with the dwellers of the battlefields'. In 1922, it took 2,000 across, but a year later, it announced in *The Ypres Times*, the journal of the Ypres League, that it would have to scale back the numbers going owing to reduced demand, and a proposed tour the following spring was cancelled.

It is possible that as nature recovered the land, the battlefields appeared less interesting so veterans turned their sights back to families and careers. The British Legion, founded by Field Marshal Haig, was also significantly involved in pilgrimages from the second half of the 1920s, particularly on the occasions when the great memorials to the missing were unveiled, including the Menin Gate in 1927, the Legion's first and relatively small pilgrimage, and the following year, the tenth anniversary of the Armistice, when 11,000 pilgrims travelled to Ypres in an act of national identity and remembrance. Pilgrimages continued throughout the 1930s, with veterans often touring with Regimental Associations to unveil memorials, including on the twenty-fifth anniversary of the Battle of Mons, when dedications took place less than two weeks before the outbreak of the Second World War.

*   *   *

It was in the interests of those who organised pilgrimages to keep tourism relevant as the number of visitors waxed and waned. There were new things to see, they advertised enthusiastically. Reconstruction was changing the landscape, famous buildings, such as the Cloth Hall in Ypres, were, phoenix-like, rising from the rubble and memorials unveiled. Henry Maskell, in his guide *The Soul of Picardy*, beseeched former servicemen to come and have another look, that they might 'find encouragement and consolation in revisiting the stricken fields and viewing what in ten short years of peace has been done to restore hearths and homesteads'. Fields under plough, woods and copses reasserting themselves, roads and paths made good, could all act as a balm to men haunted by the past, softening too the residual anti-German feeling as the damage wrought was made good. As signs of war disappeared under the plough and the trenches were back-filled, a few parts of the battlefields were kept as they were. The tourist trail took in pre-determined routes that included Newfoundland Park on the Somme, Sanctuary Wood and Hill 60 near Ypres and Vimy Ridge near Arras where the trenches and shell holes were preserved in one way or another, with duckboards to walk along, and the barbed wire defences left intact, with all the paraphernalia of war, gun carriages, machine guns, helmets and rusted rifles lying pretty much where they were abandoned. The British Legion amongst others campaigned to protect some of the most visual features, such as the German pillboxes around Ypres, as permanent reminders of the sacrifice made in taking them.

Then there were the cemeteries, oases of calm. These cemeteries had brick walls, and grassed-over pathways, and around the graves, flowers and bushes in profusion – a British garden abroad. Their new rectangular headstones were lined up, rank and file, egalitarian, like battalions on parade, replacing the wooden crosses, crosses that could be acquired for a small fee by families who wished to keep that visceral connection with the original grave.

The expression of the Christian cross, made real in the wooden grave markers, was preferred by some to the headstone, and there had been disquiet amongst small sections of the clergy who would have chosen the maintenance of the physical shape of the cross. By contrast, others pointed out that the cross as a sepulchral monument was, compared to the headstone, a relatively rare sight in Church of England cemeteries.

The sign of the cross would be engraved into each stone, unless specifically opposed by the family, in which case the headstone would remain blank. Requests for variations, such as using Scotland's St Andrew's Cross, were rejected as accommodation would have to be made for 'Christian Scientists, Salvation Army and innumerable dissenting sects', the Commission affirmed in its replies to enquiries. The only permitted variables to the Christian cross were the Sign of David on Jewish headstones and 'appropriate emblems on Mahommedan [Moslem] headstones'. Other requests to engrave insignia such as that belonging to the Freemasons were rejected, the Commission going as far as to say that some emblems and badges might actually cause offence to others. Were private requests acceded to, the work of the IWGC would be hugely complicated, leading to countless errors and a lengthy delay in the preparation and erection of headstones.

As Churchill told the Commons:

Even with this strict standardisation which is being followed, it is calculated that more than ten years will elapse before this task can be completed. If there was to be extra complexity in this task, if, as [other MPs] suggest, 90 per cent of relatives were to exercise an independent judgment, and produce independent memorials, you would not get these graveyards finished within the lifetime of the present generation.

The clear advantage of the headstone was the room it gave for additional information, and not just the man's name and regiment, which was pretty much all that was afforded to French dead. The regimental badge was included, any gallantry awards and, if supplied by the family, the man's age. At the stone's base, the family were afforded room for an inscription of their choosing, a maximum of sixty-six letters (though not all abided by that condition), each letter paid for at the price of three and a half pence: 'PEACE PERFECT PEACE' cost the Allen family of Loughborough four shillings and eleven pence, while Mr Armitage of Halifax paid sixteen shillings for 'LOVED IN LIFE, HONOURED IN DEATH, TREASURED IN MEMORY, ONE OF THE BEST'. Many families struggled to pay these fees, opting for 'R.I.P.' as the cheapest workable option. In time the fees were waived.

The dedications written by families opened a very public window onto their lives. Those left behind had variously recorded their pride, sometimes their hopes for an afterlife, their depth of loss. Even their innermost fears and anxieties were carved into stone. On the Somme, in Delville Wood Military Cemetery, is the grave of Private Albert Cartwright, a regular soldier with almost two years' service on the Western Front. His widowed mother, Maria, paid fourteen shillings for the inscription 'SLEEP ON DEAR SON IN A FAR OFF LAND IN A GRAVE WE MAY NEVER SEE'. When relatively few people held passports, when overseas travel was unusual, France could feel like a very distant shore, far away from her Staffordshire home. She had already lost an elder son in February 1916, buried near Ypres, further complicating a visit taking in two very separate locations. Perhaps a visit was beyond what she could hope to afford. Perhaps her emotional turmoil was such that she could not bring herself to go.

The absence of additional headstone information could conceal, by its non-existence, a powerful human story. The grave of Bombardier Harry Jervis in Roclincourt Military Cemetery has nothing that would make a casual visitor pause for one moment: his headstone is a bare statement of military fact. Only access to the contemporary file held by the IWGC reveals that there is so much more to his case. The paperwork on Ruth Jervis, who challenged the relatives' decision to stop the transfer of bodies to Britain, highlights how she and so many others felt about the struggle over the ownership of their relatives' remains. These were the families who did not buy into the collectivism – socialism some called it – of the IWGC cemeteries, nor the idea of national mourning and remembrance. Ruth Jervis wanted her son back home and rejected everything about the Commission's proposals for British gravestones: 'we are to have a military headstone,' she wrote in disgust to the IWGC,

and if relatives wish to leave an inscription printed thereon, it must not exceed three lines, what next? May I ask how long we may remain at the graveside when we get there?

Then you ask me to be good enough to furnish you with particulars of my son's description. I wonder you have the decency to refer to him as being my son at all since you consider you have the right to withhold his remains from me.

Ruth would neither contribute anything to the headstone nor the records of the IWGC. There is no age on the grave and there is no private inscription at its base. Nor does her name appear in the cemetery register that states only that George Jervis of Doxey, Stafford was Harry's father.

This was by no means a unique stance. In an impassioned House of Commons debate on 4 May 1920, Viscount Wolmer read out a letter written by a father railing against the Commission's refusal to permit a like-for-like replacement of his son's marble cross, a cross paid for by the family in 1915 and destroyed by shell fire. 'I received the usual official bureaucratic reply, the father wrote, adding, 'Should they adhere to their policy, I do not propose to accept their invitation to add anything to what they choose to put upon the stone, as I do not wish to desecrate my son's memory ...'

The care and attention – and the money – spent on memorials and cemeteries reflected the desire to evoke pride in the achievements of all servicemen and women; their loss was not in vain nor sacrificed in a futile cause. In 1928, when the Archbishop of York gave an address at the conclusion of the British Legion's pilgrimage, he stood beneath the Menin Gate and asked, 'Was it all worthwhile?' and then, in answer to his own question: 'Here at this Gate let there be no faltering in the answer, yes, a thousand times yes.' There were those who felt that by over-sanitising the loss by evoking beauty and peace was to obscure an important warning that war was squalid and monumentally tragic. 'Time is already touching those dreadful memories with the rosy finger of romance,' wrote a journalist in the *Daily Herald* newspaper, in response to the Archbishop's words. A number of pilgrims who attended the ceremony supported the newspaper's stance: 'As one just returned from the battlefields I should like to ask his Grace, did he see the scores of armless and legless men not a hundred yards from where he was speaking, soliciting alms?'

Despite the bitterness and violent emotions, the nation had opted for peace and beauty. For former servicemen like James Hudson, these attributes helped him and others on their road to recovery, letting go of the dead in the knowledge that they would be cared for and never forgotten. Another veteran who had been unable to let go was the author Henry Williamson. Prior to going back, he had considered himself 'a foreigner among the living, and half a foreigner to myself'. Travelling to the Western Front, revisiting the places of his youth, walking amongst the graves, put his war firmly in the past. In his book, *The Sun in the Sands*, he recalled that on the final day of the pilgrimage he became 'filled with longing for my home; to see again the lanes, the sea, the barns, the hills, the eyes of my wife, the smile of my little boy listening to the bells on the wind of heaven – the new part of myself overlaying the wrath of that lost forever'.

It was fitting that those who died together should rest together. Just as the IWGC hoped, the sight of maturing cemeteries 'turned' some of those who once pursued the repatriation of bodies. Henry Cook, a widower who lost two sons within three months in 1917, changed his mind. One son, Arthur, would never be found, the other son and namesake, Henry, was buried in Tyne Cot Cemetery. His father wrote to the IWGC after visiting the battlefields to say that while he preferred his son to return to England and the parish cemetery in Guildford, he now understood why all the boys would remain together.

All the arguments about gravestone design left those whose sons and husbands had no known grave wondering if all the heated argument went to only sully the memory of the dead. How wonderful would it be to even have a named grave to visit! In the House of Commons, William Burdett-Coutts read from a letter he had received from none other than Rudyard Kipling. It was marked 'Private', he said.

I do not think he [Kipling] will object to my quoting this sentence, because it applies to the pathetic case of so many relatives, and while coming from him it will touch a chord of sympathy throughout the English-speaking race, that sympathy will cover thousands of other mourners in the same position. The words are these:

You see we shall never have any grave to go to. Our boy was missing at Loos. The ground is of course battered and mined past all hope of any trace being recovered. I wish some of the people who are making this trouble realise how more than fortunate they are to have a name on a headstone in a known place.

* * *

In January 1922, the IWGC's vice chairman, Fabian Ware, issued a statement bringing up to date progress with regard to cemetery construction and the erection of headstones in all theatres of war across the globe. Satisfactory work was continuing on a total of 567 cemeteries and in the case of a further 220 (196 of which were in France and Belgium), the work had been completed. In total, 40,748 headstones had been shipped to France and Belgium, of which 18,953 had been put up, the rest awaiting erection.

This was a monumental effort in every sense of the word, a huge undertaking that had required the IWGC to commission, cut and, in the end, hand-carve over 580,000 headstones to 'known' dead. An entirely new branch within the IWGC had been established, subdivided into three defined areas: one looked after the accuracy of the information gleaned from cemetery reports overseas, one checked the accuracy of the additional information provided by families and one was made responsible for administration, checking and collating the tenders received from contractors.

All the engraved headstones were cut from stone in the United Kingdom and shipped overseas, a major logistical effort. Work had begun back in October 1919 and owing to the low capacity of the majority of monumental masons, the average size of a contract did not exceed 200 headstones. As Winston Churchill reminded MPs during a Commons debate, 'The means for making tombstones in this or any other country are limited – local and limited – and they are more or less proportioned to the ordinary rate of mortality.' Masons were scattered right across the country, underlining how unworkable it would have been to permit personal variations in headstone design. Standardisation was essential.

Captain Trumble, a man with 'mason experience', was appointed by the IWGC to travel around the country, supported by a deputy and assistants, to check on quality control and accuracy. When the stones were completed, the IWGC's director of works was then responsible for their transportation to the continent, a process that remained under constant review to ensure the safest possible method of passage while also keeping one eye on opportunities to save money.

The method favoured was to send headstones, placed in trucks, uncrated and entrained, to Dover. The stones were then packed by civilian staff of the contracted company, placing twenty headstones to a container before they were loaded onto ships owned by the South-Eastern & Chatham Railway company and taken to Calais. The same civilian company that packed the containers at Dover was responsible for ensuring the headstones reached the cemeteries, with any breakages paid for by them. The total cost of carriage worked out at nearly ten shillings each. Given the number of headstones to be cut, engraved and transported, other options were worth considering. Could the stones be taken to Liverpool by rail and shipped in crates from there? Could the Commission charter a smaller vessel to sail from Preston, passing down the Ribble River and out into the sea?

The Commission noted that ships bringing china clay from Cornwall to Preston could be chartered to take back headstones to France. Sailing from Liverpool would cut costs by over a shilling per stone, and from Preston, the cheapest option of all, saving nearly three shillings per stone. The only issue was the problem of breakages. From experience, headstones packed in crates suffered 6 to 6.5 per cent breakages, whereas in containers, it was just .2 per cent. As the Commission would be liable for any breakages suffered from Liverpool or Preston, the saving overall would be negligible, depending on which option was adopted. When it came to efficiency, every money-saving option was considered. Would it make sense for the Commission to purchase their own containers costing £15 each in order to cut costs? Probably not, as containers on the French railways had been frequently damaged during transit even if the stones had arrived intact. In the end, after much consultation, the Commission reverted to their tried and tested method – shipping through Dover.

*   *   *

The natural appearance of flowers amongst the graves on the Western Front, in particular the poppy, captured the public imagination at home. Civilians were inspired by the poem *In Flanders Fields*, written in May 1915 by the Canadian doctor, Lieutenant Colonel John McCrae, who witnessed for himself how quickly they had sprung up amongst the crosses adjacent to an Advanced Dressing Station. To a soldier going up the line, passing a cemetery would hardly be a morale raiser, fortifying his courage, but the sight of well-ordered crosses, cared for and awash with flowers, was at least a soothing sight for sore eyes.

Along with poppies, there were white chamomile and patches of yellow charlock, which in early summer looked serene. Not all flowers were naturally sown; dormant seeds were brought to life by the burial churn of soil. From the spring of 1916, the British Army had sanctioned the foundation of a Horticultural Department, working under the supervision of three officers, to care for cemetery graves. The Joint War Committee of the British Red Cross Society and the Order of St John undertook to provide the funds for the gardening work.

Inevitably, those cemeteries closest to the line and at risk from the gunfire of enemy artillery had precious little dedicated horticultural work, but even these plots were not left entirely to the vagaries of nature, for bags of seeds of mixed annuals were sent up the line to be distributed between cemeteries. In a report entitled *Our Soldiers' Graves*, written by Captain Arthur Hill, the botanical adviser to the IWGC, Hill recalled how the men responsible for each cemetery took it upon themselves to plant 'small shrubs, herbaceous plants or box, brought in from derelict and abandoned gardens, [which] relieved the barrenness of many a wayside burying-ground in Flanders'.

To support the work of the Horticultural Department, nurseries were established in 1917. These were geographically set apart from one another and, so as to avoid confusion, a different British company was chosen to supply each with consignments of trees and shrubs to be propagated. It was hoped that consignments would arrive at set intervals, though as Hill recalls, one horticultural officer complained of receiving simultaneously 56,000 plants, all being unloaded, planted or heeled-in during six days of dedicated effort. In March 1918, two of the nurseries were overrun during the German spring offensive, with years of painstaking work smashed by shell fire. Similarly, a number of cemeteries well behind the lines, where planting of roses, hedges and trees had been carried out, fell into German hands. 'The destruction of work on which so much time, thought, and careful labour had been bestowed must, no doubt, be reckoned among the fortunes of war,' wrote Hill, 'but nevertheless it is a great disappointment to those to whom the work had been a labour of love.'

After the Armistice, the long-term work on the cemeteries began with major horticultural issues addressed for the first time. The number of officers chosen to work on the cemeteries was expanded. All were experts in horticulture, men such as Captain Alfred Melles, a Kew Gardens' employee serving in the Royal Garrison Artillery. He would work with three other officers and former 'kewites', as he described them. 'I leave it to all true gardeners to imagine what a delightful gathering that was – after the terrible days of war. What a time we had polishing up our botanical lore ...' The four men would operate together for the next decade in France and Belgium.

Melles worked in the Ypres area, initially attached to the 6th Graves Registration Unit, helping resurrect cemeteries temporarily abandoned during the Allies' final advance to victory, choked with thistles, knotweed and docks. There was also couch grass, a rapidly growing weed and 'a veritable gardener's nightmare', he recalled, 'literally lorry loads of couch roots were taken out to be burnt'.

Before any grass seeding, each grave mound had to settle. Meanwhile, men drawn from disparate units hastily planted annuals and biennials so as 'to give bright effects', largely for the benefit of civilian pilgrims arriving in increasing numbers during the summer of 1919. Owing to the ongoing shortage of transport, Melles walked or rode a bike between jobs, supervising the work, criss-crossing an area with a 10-mile radius. Only at the end of April 1919 was he given access to a Box Ford car, enabling him to cover much greater ground, as far as St Omer and Bailleul. The car was eventually stolen, crashed and abandoned by a 'joy-rider', Melles asking caustically whether any ride over the Salient's pitted roads and tracks could be considered a joy.

Gardeners' tools were largely obtained from the Labour Corps, occasionally adapted or fashioned by the men for horticultural use. In the temporary absence of lawnmowers, anyone who knew how to scythe was in great demand. Few of the men employed knew anything about gardening, and there were a number of disastrous results when unskilled men were sent on their own to tidy and clean a cemetery, often uprooting or otherwise destroying recently planted annuals. In response, it was decided to try to keep the same men posted at the same cemeteries, thereby giving them a sense of ownership and interest, with at least one knowledgeable gardener left in charge.

By the end of August 1919, Melles and the cemeteries under his control were officially transferred to the IWGC, civilians arriving soon afterwards to form the nucleus of the horticultural staff with the first perennials propagated and planted by the autumn. Temporary drains were laid, fences erected, with cemetery levelling carried out with rollers improvised from steel pipes. The next year, further cemeteries were handed over to the IWGC, each inspected by an officer of the Commission. More civilians were employed, primarily former soldiers who had married locally and remained in Belgium. By 1921, around 200 were employed, mostly as labourers with a view, after a probationary period, of promoting the best by examination to gardeners. This would have the additional effect of deepening the men's interest in their work and fostering 'a much fuller understanding between supervisors and staff than would otherwise have been the case', Melles believed. Not all showed promise: one man, asked to compile a list of herbaceous perennials, wrote 'Flockes, others I forget'; another, asked what was meant by 'deciduous', answered, 'A tree which you have decided where to plant.' Meanwhile, weeding, levelling and sowing continued 'while cemeteries were laid out and planted according to official plans', wrote Melles. 'Old straggling hedges were grubbed out and new ones planted, turf from trench [grave] mounds was lifted and re-laid to new final levels in several cemeteries.'

All the IWGC men working near Ypres were officially stationed near Poperinge and as routines were established, economies of work were introduced, including the formation of Travelling Gardening Parties to cut down on time lost during daily commutes from Poperinge to outlying cemeteries. Ten men, including a cook and driver, worked for a week at remote cemeteries, driving a specially fitted lorry, complete with tools, sleeping tent and rations, their work overseen by the formation of Travelling Supervising Gardeners. Other improvements were introduced, including Area Conferences of senior gardeners to discuss ideas and difficulties encountered and overcome, the work becoming ever more professional and effective. In 1922 and 1923, 439,000 and 393,634 flowering plants, and 65,810 and 98,218 shrubs and trees, respectively, were planted in Ypres Salient cemeteries.

Soil quality – loam – varied significantly in depth, often over-lying chalk, as on the Somme, or clay around Ypres. Where good soil was shallow, it caused problems bedding in plants, such as rhododendrons and azaleas that needed plenty of earth to establish themselves. The fighting had compromised the quality of the soil too. Trench digging and the burial of bodies had frequently brought underlying chalk to the surface, with the topsoil now flipped below ground. This gave the Commission gardeners much additional labour in removing the chalk or, in cemeteries where further burials were carried out, making sure that the quality topsoil was set aside to be replaced after interment. Where cemeteries were within the fighting zone, the ground had been so polluted, so churned up, that finding quality soil proved extremely difficult and it had to be brought in from elsewhere before permanent planting could begin.

Each battlefield presented its own set of problems: there were cemeteries in old orchards, others established on 'bleak hillsides', wrote Hill, and 'with the worst possible aspect and no shelter from the weather'. Near the coast the problems were of a different nature but no less challenging. The presence of dunes close to cemeteries meant that sand had to be held back by planting acres of dense and spiky marram grass, the roots of which stabilised the ground. At Coxyde Military Cemetery on the Belgian coast, gardeners used corrugated iron raised on poles as windbreaks, while a grove of fast-growing pine trees was planted from seed to halt any further encroachment. What little soil there was had mixed with blown sea sand, leaving the gardeners to persevere in trying to establish which plants would 'take' in such conditions. In recognition of the difficult issues, Coxyde was given its own nursery for the propagation of plants and shrubs grown specifically for use in maritime districts. In the end, in 1921, 100 lorry loads of soil were brought to the cemetery and mixed with the sand to obtain a better turf. Then, in 1924, a further 500 tons of soil were brought by train to complete the job, providing 9 inches of topsoil and sand across the entire cemetery, allowing plants to take root. It was a significant investment in time and money for what was only a medium-sized cemetery with just over 1,500 graves.

Since 1915, a French standing order had allowed for 3 square metres of ground for each burial, although the IWGC noted as late as November 1921 that there was a little flexibility in this figure. 'You may rest assured the French and Belgians know the Commission does not feel itself confined to these limits,' it declared in an internal memo. The French allowed extra land too for the cemeteries' architectural 'treatment', but nevertheless, space within a cemetery remained at something of a premium once architects' plans were fully realised. Additional laws, such as those stipulating that no trees could be planted within 2 metres of a boundary wall, or a hedge within half a metre, made planning more difficult still. One of the effects of these French restrictions was to bring horticulturalists into occasional conflict with cemetery architects, including Sir Reginald Blomfield, who complained to the IWGC in November 1920 that his staff were annoyed with what they perceived as unnecessary interference. 'The subject of design in these cemeteries is not to make them a nursery garden of horticultural specimens. ... The [architectural] staff are unanimous in urging that the criticisms of the horticultural advisers should be strictly confined to their proper province of horticulture.' In other words, Blomfield wanted the architect ultimately to have the whip hand over the horticulturalist.

French rules and architects' demands did not always leave much latitude for what Kew's Arthur Hill described as the 'bold treatment' he wished to give cemeteries: on occasions, paths had to be narrowed, graves pushed a little closer together, horticulture simplified, though Hill was at pains to point out that the French authorities were prepared to take a view on any difficulties, allowing for cemetery boundaries to be adjusted so the IWGC 'could prepare a more adequate and dignified design'.

The deployment of trees, shrubs and plants indigenous to the dead soldier's homeland was part and parcel of the horticultural design. Just as the graves of Indian soldiers had been adorned with Iris, Marigolds and Cypress plants, so the Maple tree, native to both east and west coast Canada, was grown from seeds transported across the Atlantic via London and planted near the graves of men who had travelled from towns as distant from each other as Halifax in Nova Scotia and Vancouver in British Columbia. Seeds of the Tasmanian Eucalyptus were sent to France to Australian graves, while cuttings of the Daisy-bush and Veronica traversil were propagated at Kew Gardens and then forwarded to one of the IWGC nurseries for transplantation amongst the graves of New Zealand's dead. Only countries with radically different climates – South Africa, the West Indies and a number of smaller nations – proved hard to represent with perennials on the Western Front, although a consignment of acorns was shipped from South Africa and planted in Delville Wood where the South African Brigade suffered such devastating casualties in 1916.

The dedicated work that went into making cemeteries appear like gardens was demanding, complex and technical. The French gift of land in perpetuity, with permission given for British hegemony over their appearance, 'the right of enjoyment' as it was termed, was far-sighted and generous. And what senior horticulturalists at Kew and on the Western Front made of the government's contemplation of their partial abandonment was all too apparent.

The cemeteries were not abandoned but went from strength to strength. By the mid-1930s, there were over 530 IWGC caretaker gardeners, all former soldiers, all chosen for their horticultural knowledge and experience. By 1938, these men had planted 70 miles of hedges, and 300 miles of borders, populated by a variety of flowers, bushes, shrubs and trees grown in the Commission's three surviving nurseries in Ypres, Albert and Arras: in one twelve-month period, over 1.3 million plants were propagated. Around the gravestones were manicured lawns, 600 acres of grass sown, kept neat and tidy by lawnmowers, each of which rolled across an extraordinary 2,000 miles of cemetery lawns every year, according to the IWGC.

As staff worked, additional graves were dug, on average between fifteen and twenty a week throughout the 1930s. Specific cemeteries were left open to receive bodies, such as the London Cemetery on the Somme and Bedford House Cemetery in the Ypres Salient, which was continually extended in order to meet interments. Most bodies discovered remained unidentified but these dead still required one thousand new headstones and new beds to be planted.

*   *   *

Angela Farmer and Angela Mond both travelled to the battlefields as IWGC gardeners laboured with love to cultivate the sort of cemeteries such pilgrims would be proud to visit. Angela Farmer had gone to France with a vague, unrealistic thought that she might yet find her husband, or rather his lost grave marker above his buried body. Angela Mond had been nothing if not tenacious in her own search, determined to find her son no matter how long it took. Their stories were not the same because the circumstances of their individual loss were not the same. The two women handled their grief in different ways, but in ways they deemed appropriate. Wilfred Ewart recalled that his sister knelt and laid a wreath at a point close to where her husband had died and then she mentally moved on. 'With that we went back into the world again. She chatted blithely all the way to London. Her mind was her own, and it was possible that none should ever peep into it again …' By contrast, Angela Mond felt she could never move on, not until she had found Francis, and now, suddenly, after years of dogged investigation, finding her son appeared unnervingly real.

Chapter Twelve

'There must be something more precious than life since we
are here.'

George Duhamel, *The New Book of Martyrs*

It was important that the IWGC did not rush to judgement in the
pressing case of Mond and Martyn, but equally a decision would
have to be taken and there should be no unnecessary prevarication
for the sake of the families involved. The IWGC was determined to
examine all the evidence with an open mind.

Lieutenant Hans Kirschstein's combat report, as supplied by
the German Air Force to the British Air Ministry, concluded that
Aspinall's Bristol Fighter came down 'about 1km east of Albert'.
'I notice on the last enclosures,' wrote an official at the IWGC, that
'about 1km east of Albert doesn't appear to agree with "between
Contalmaison and Mametz".' That was true, but it was agreed
that any calculation made by Kirschstein was approximate. 'All we
wanted to know was – did A & D come down within the German
lines?' The answer was 'yes'. Taken in the round, the internal
memo confirmed, all 'the evidence warrants the opening of the
grave in question'. And that meant a WGR1, an 'Authority for
Exhumation', would be completed and sent for authorisation.

Fabian Ware would ultimately make the decision to exhume and
as he considered the case, the families of Aspinall and de la Cour
were contacted and the evidence presented to them. Meanwhile,
Angela, and Edgar Martyn's widow, Margaret, were asked to provide
full particulars of the two officers in order to aid identification:

details of teeth, colour of hair, height, build, historic injuries. The exhumation would not take place for some considerable time as the relatives of Aspinall and de la Cour would need to provide details of their own; de la Cour's family lived in South Africa.

On 26 September, Lord Stopford wrote to Angela:

> Your request for the opening of two graves in Doullens Communal Cemetery has recently been considered by General Ware with the result that we are now in communication with the relatives of the two officers buried in these graves, on this matter. ...
>
> If the graves have to be opened, it will be necessary, so as to be certain of getting the right identification, that we should have full particulars if the various officers concerned for identification purposes.
>
> It will, I fear, be rather a shock to the relatives of Captain Aspinall and Lieutenant de la Cour, but I do not see what else we can do than communicate with them. ...
>
> I'm afraid it will be some considerable time before we can get any further with this, as the next of kin of one of the officers, namely, Lieutenant de la Cour, lives in South Africa, so it will take at least seven weeks before we can get a reply from her.

Lord Stopford's letter was courteous and not cordial. Part of his remit was to test the evidence, reasonably requiring a high standard of proof. The evidence was compelling and pointed to an error, with or without Berlin's confirmatory letter. And yet Stopford appeared time and again to drag his feet – 'If the graves have to be opened ...' His letter appeared to lay at Angela's door the upset that disclosure of evidence would cause to the Aspinall and de la Cour families. 'It will, I fear, be rather a shock ...' Of course it would be. Angela knew that; it did not need to be said.

Much to Angela's relief, the Aspinall family agreed to an exhumation. The widow of de la Cour proved much harder to trace, the first letter returned as undelivered. At the end of January 1923, Angela enquired from Stopford whether anything had been heard, her continued frustration at the snail's pace of progress evident. 'I think an answer was anticipated some time in November last, but I have heard nothing … [I] am ready at any time to proceed to France.'

'I was afraid you would be wondering why you did not hear anything from me …' Stopford wrote in reply. De la Cour's widow had remarried, taking a new surname, but she had been located and a reply was forthcoming. Meanwhile, Margaret, the widow of Edgar Martyn, had sent details of her husband's appearance: his dental records with his gold fillings; his hair, fairly light, his eyebrows fairly dark; his head size, about $6\frac{7}{8}$; his height 5 feet 8 inches. He was fairly square-shouldered, the 'inside of knee joints large (commonly called 'knock-kneed')'. She was, it seems, mercifully unaware of the head injuries sustained by her husband in the crash.

A reply from de la Cour's widow arrived on 7 March with the same painful identifying details, plus a lock of his hair. Captain Aspinall's father, 59-year-old Herbert Aspinall, would go to France for the exhumation in the week commencing 19 March, and Angela would be there too. The exhumation was set for Tuesday, 20 March.

Angela knew the bodies were mutilated, that her son's face had been partially shot away, the horror of opening the graves abundantly clear to all concerned. Angela suggested that grave 27 be opened first. If this proved to be the grave of Lieutenant de la Cour, then it would be reasonable to assume that the other body would be Aspinall's and not Mond's or Martyn's, and no further exploration would be necessary. This would be done, as Stopford noted, graciously, 'because Mrs Mond is anxious that Mr Aspinall's feelings can be respected'.

*　*　*

Shortly before 10.30 am on 20 March 1923, Angela Mond and Herbert Aspinall arrived in Doullens Communal Cemetery

Extension No. 2. The morning was cold, and there was an easterly wind.

It was five years, almost to the day, since Angela and Emile had bid farewell to Francis as he returned to active service in France, five years since he had left Greyfriars, his beloved family home for the final time.

A small party clustered around grave 27 and the gravediggers began their work of exhumation.

A wooden casket was found at a depth of 6 feet and the lid prized open. The body was naked and observed to be lying with feet underneath the gravestone. The sample of hair sent by de la Cour's widow from South Africa was less coarse than that found on the body and signs of an old fracture to an arm were absent. Crucially, the body showed no signs of immolation. After careful examination by all parties, the body was deemed not to be that of de la Cour, and after a short conferral between Angela and Herbert Aspinall, it was decided to open grave 29, where a coffin, buried shallower than the first, was discovered; again, the feet were under the headstone. The coffin of grave 28 could be seen as the exhumation proceeded. Coffin 29 was lifted and opened to reveal the body of a male, height 5 foot 9 'approximately' with light brown, medium length hair. The body had been wrapped in a blanket and there was no clothing of any kind, and no identification disc.

Identification of Francis Mond was not made in haste. Although Aspinall's father 'stated at once' that this body was not that of his son, a thorough investigation was made. Dental records had been prepared and the upper and lower jaws were examined for matches.

Top jaw Left side, two molars missing. Right side, two molars missing.

Front teeth very long and prominent. One canine tooth was broken, disclosing a core of whitish substance which might be a dental filling.

3rd molar from back on left side filled with a silver coloured alloy. 2nd molar from back right side filled in the same manner. The condition of the teeth as regards repairs and filling, appeared to correspond with information supplied by a dentist who attended Capt. Mond.

The exception was a gold crown in a tooth in the lower jaw that was probably added by another, later, dentist.

The head was described as being small, broader at the back than the front and the nose smashed, incurred during his last desperate struggles, according to Angela. The body was broad shouldered and, once again, showed no signs of having been burnt.

Angela had found her son.

On conclusive identification of Francis Mond's body, Angela returned immediately to London and proceeded to Baker Street to see Lord Stopford.

He was not available but wrote to Angela later that day.

Dear Mrs Mond

I am sorry I missed seeing you this morning when you called. I was very much interested to hear that your son's body was identified.

We will get the official report no doubt in the course of a day or two.

Yours sincerely

S

The report, as expected, stated conclusively that a case of misidentification had occurred. The body in grave 27 could not be identified as de la Cour, but equally, it could not be identified as Martyn, raising the prospect that Lieutenant W.S. Dann was in grave 27 and Martyn in 28. 'I suggest,' wrote the unnamed official, 'that the bodies were not buried in the order in the reports …' and that 'it was a pity they did not open Grave 28.' It was suggested this could be done at a later date without 'bother[ing] Dann's people'.

Angela was greatly indebted to Herbert Aspinall for agreeing to the exhumation, though he too must have been heavily swayed by the evidence. The headstones so recently erected over what he assumed was his son's and his observer's grave were removed, their names eventually being carved into the Arras Flying Services Memorial. The bodies of Aspinall and de la Cour, buried in May 1918 by the Germans, were never found and identified.

Stopford's sympathy had lain with Herbert Aspinall and only grudgingly, at best, with Angela Mond. On 6 April, in an internal memo, he wrote:

Mrs Mond, to whom I have spoken, is quite convinced that the grave supposed to contain Aspinall contained her son, and apparently Mr Aspinall is satisfied as well. I wrote him a personal note expressing my sympathy with him in the result of the exhumation and have not heard from him, so I do not think there is any doubt in his mind or he would have written.

In the autumn, the headstones were placed above the graves of Mond and Martyn, once Martyn's grave location was finally corroborated. At the bottom of Edgar Martyn's grave was the inscription 'Greater love hath no man than this'; on Francis Mond's grave: 'Killed in Aerial Combat', and then beneath, 'There must be something more precious than life since we are here'. The quotation was taken from a book written by the famous French author George Duhamel. *The New Book of Martyrs* was his wartime memoirs of his service as a surgeon, a copy of which was signed and given to the Mond family by Duhamel.

Angela's search had ended. Finding Francis must have brought with it a great sense of peace and some immediate contentment, but could it bring long-term solace?

In October, Lord Stopford wrote his penultimate letter to Angela. She replied, taking the opportunity diplomatically to smooth over her fractious relationship with him, though what she wrote and how she honestly felt may not have been one and the same.

19 October 1923

Dear Lord Stopford

I am very grateful indeed to you for your kind letter of the 17th inst. in which you inform me that the headstone over my son's grave in Doullens Cemetery is now in position.

This is a source of the deepest satisfaction to me to know that all is now complete; I shall be going out there towards the end of this month. When I was there in the spring, I was deeply impressed by the exquisite care and reverence with which the cemetery was laid out and maintained. Nothing more suitable or more dignified could be imagined.

May I also place on record my deep appreciation of your consideration and courtesy towards me during these difficult years of the search I had undertaken. I fear that I must often have appeared importunate, and it is certain I must have given you and your staff considerable trouble, but I think you will agree that it is a great satisfaction to have arrived at a definite solution of what appeared at one time an insoluble problem.

I trust therefore that you will forgive me every insistence in undertaking what was to me a sacred obligation, and that you will accept my sincerest thanks for all your help you lent me in the success obtained. Without this, my task would have been an impossible one.

Believe me

Sincerely yours

Angela Mond

22nd October, 1923

Dear Mrs Mond

Many thanks for your letter of the 19th instant. I am grateful to you for what you say in appreciation of the small assistance I have been able to render in the matter regarding your son's burial place.

I am very glad to think that this has been so satisfactorily cleared up. It is undoubtedly due to the really strenuous efforts which you made. Do not think for a moment that I consider that you were importunate. I have considerable admiration for the methodical and businesslike way which you employed in your investigations.

Again thanking you for your kind letter.

Yours sincerely

Stopford.

Emile and Angela visited their son as promised the following month, and they were there again in May, their picture taken standing behind Francis's grave, strain and sadness carved into their faces. They went to Doullens at least once every year. Emile made a final visit in August 1938, five months before he died. In the cemetery's visitors' book he wrote: 'This Cemetery is more lovely every time I come to visit the grave of my son. I feel it is a worthy resting place for those who have laid down their lives.'

End Piece

'Francis was the best of them all, my Mother always said so, the best, the brightest, the hope.'

Ursula Mond, born 1928

For all the satisfaction of finding her son, there was no changing the fact that Francis was dead, killed at the age of twenty-three. The quest to locate his body, such a focus for Angela's attention, was suddenly gone. Normal routine reasserted itself, Francis forced into the shadows once more yet an ever-present memory. Her other children, particularly the three surviving boys, Philip, Alfred and Stephen, would, in different ways, struggle too to cope with the after-effects of the Great War and their brother's death.

Ursula, now aged ninety-one, daughter of Philip Mond and almost the sole surviving member of the family to have known Emile and Angela, spent much of her childhood with her grandparents. She witnessed at first hand how unceasing grief affected their home life.

'Neither Angela nor her husband, Emile, was ever the same again after Francis was killed,' she believes. Angela, such a great pre-war socialite, a lady of high culture, threw many parties for London's elite, for actors such as John Gielgud, politicians and diplomats. The great German soprano Elizabeth Schumann gave recitals in Angela's London home.

She loved having people round her, and conversation, and she dressed beautifully. But, it seemed to me, my grandparents always had strange house parties at times, with such people as the art historian Professor Rice, a Chilean lady called Yaya Marshall, the Jacobsens, the family lawyer, it was because my Grandmother liked to fill the house with people and didn't want to be on her own.

There was an aura of tragedy about my grandmother which I never understood. Why? Because no one ever explained anything to me about people being dead, I knew nothing of Francis. The look on her face, her eyes, someone who had gone through something terrible, it was just there. The eyes had had so much weeping, it seemed to me.

I saw quite a lot of my Grandparents until the [Second World] War. We went down to their other house in Slaugham for Easter holidays and often in the Summer which was for us paradise. My Grandmother was what was known as a 'blue stocking' [an educated intellectual woman] in those days, which I found most appreciable as she took me to French films, and she took me to the Comédie-Française when they toured in London, and all sorts of things. She wasn't tactile, but people weren't in the same way back then, but we would discuss books as she loved history and so did I. I used to see her once a week as she would take me out and we'd do something interesting.

Angela dressed in black velvet normally, perhaps with a little red, with a strong smell of gardenia scent. She used to come in the chauffeur-driven car to fetch me, driven by a grumpy chauffeur. She was always sitting down, crippled with the effect of arthritis and would always walk with a stick when we went to the car.

Francis had been the golden boy, the one on whom the greatest talent had been bestowed. His death, and subsequent tragedies, rocked the family and they never regained the equilibrium or the composure they appeared to have had before the war: family relationships faltered, even Angela and Emile's.

Angela and Emile argued the whole time, it was terrible. They would sit at opposite ends of the table at meal times and there was just a perpetual argument. If someone said something was white, the other said it was black; they just did not get on at all anymore. As a little girl, I could not understand why they should get so angry about such trivial details.

And as Angela threw her parties, or took her granddaughter out to the cinema or theatre, so Emile, the chemist, retreated more and more into his laboratory at the top of the house.

Greyfriars, the country home where the family was happiest, was infrequently visited and eventually sold, and the family fell back on 'The Cottage' at Slaugham, where associations with the past did not exist.

Emile was a delightful man and he was very fond of me and used to call me Zuzu and when he was dying, I think of cancer, I was sent for and told to put on my best party frock and go and see him. He wanted to see me before he died. He was already in bed. It was such a shock and I had to say goodbye to him. These things happened, nobody gave anything as to an explanation or preparation for anything and you did not question it.

Emile Mond died on 30 December 1938, a few months after his final visit to France, when it is likely he knew he was very seriously ill.

Angela again visited Doullens Cemetery on 28 July 1939, but with the outbreak of war five weeks later, she was unable to return. She died on 8 November 1941, aged seventy.

Francis was the best of them all, my Mother always said so, the best, the brightest, the hope. I am sure my Grandparents were still happy together when he was alive.

* * *

By the time of their deaths, a fair proportion of the family fortune had been given away. The Mond family had been generous benefactors to various institutions and charities; in 1915, concerned about the educational facilities available to French and Belgian refugee children, they established the Lycée de Londres, which became part of the French Institute. Angela's interest in music and literature had also resulted in substantial gifts. Then, after the war, in memory of Francis they endowed the Francis Mond Professorship of Aeronautical Engineering at Cambridge University, a position still extant today.

One man with whom the family remained firmly in touch was Lieutenant Harold Hill. Post war, he stayed with the Mond family on several occasions, and after returning to Australia and his farm, he remained in contact with the family by letter and telegram. Emile and Angela felt forever in his debt. In the 1920s, in Hill's honour, the family commissioned three statues of the figure of St George by the renowned sculptor Sir George Frampton, one of which was given to Harold. In London, at the Foreign Office, the Mond family paid for a huge frieze showing all the nations that had contributed to the war effort. The Australian figure, it is believed, is also based on Harold Hill.

Although he never met Emile and Angela again after he sailed home for Australia, Harold Hill was always proud of his close friendship with the Mond family.

The friendship lasted a lifetime. At Christmas 1972, he telegrammed May Cippico, Angela and Emile's youngest child:

Dear May, at eighty-four I never cease to remember you at Greyfriars and 22 Hyde Park in 1918. Our abiding love and good wishes that health and goodwill be with you throughout 1972. Bert [Harold] and May.

In December 1974, Albert Harold Hill suffered a serious stroke that left him incapacitated and unable to speak. On Boxing Day, he died, aged eighty-six. May Cippico, the sole surviving child of Emile and Angela, sent a wreath on behalf of the family. It read:

In loving Memory
of
Captain Harold Hill MC & bar
A most gallant soldier
A wonderful friend to Emile and
Angela Mond and family.
Never forgotten, May

Through the Air Ministry in Berlin, Emile and Angela Mond discovered that Lieutenant Kirschstein shot down Captain Aspinall and Lieutenant de la Cour. Did that fact ever pique their interest to know who had shot down their son? It was not entirely irregular for grieving parents to find out. The pilot was 21-year-old Leutnant Johann Janzen, commanding officer of Jasta 6, and his recorded victory on 15 May over the DH4 that was the aircraft flown by Francis Mond was his sixth of what would be thirteen victories. Less than a week before, on 9 May, he was himself shot down by a British pilot, his Triplane spinning to the ground. He survived unhurt, although he was shot down again and captured later that year. He lived into the 1980s.

Unfathomable grief had driven Angela's search to its unlikely conclusion, and Francis had been found, but now what? He was not coming home; he was still dead. Angela and Emile could visit his grave, as they did every year, but there was no closure. On reading the script of this book, one of Angela's two surviving grandchildren was surprised to read that Emile appeared to play so little a part in the search for Francis. Emile supported Angela, but did he also turn to other projects so as to take his attention away from his own grief, leaving Angela to search on her own? Perhaps he chose to look after the other children, recognising Angela's need to focus on her search alone.

The loss of Francis ended the halcyon world in which the Mond family had lived for five decades; nothing was ever the same again. Francis's death seemed to catapult them into an ever-downward spiral. The other children were not happy, their lives in different ways cut short or left seemingly unfulfilled. The greatest mystery surrounds Alfred's suicide in 1929, when aged just twenty-eight, married with a baby son. Drink and divorce blighted two more lives and of the five children, only May lived beyond the age of fifty, dying in 1980 aged seventy-six. Was the Great War's toxic influence directly implicated in these multiple tragedies? It is impossible to say from this distance in time, but the cascading effects of that epoch have been profound on British society and it is hard to image that Francis's death did not play a significant role in how his siblings' lives played out.

As Ursula recalled, Angela and Emile bickered and argued, Emile retreating to his study at the top of the house, Angela entertaining for all she was worth, keeping herself busy and the house full. Yet for all the sadness, both perhaps found some mutual understanding at the end of their lives. The photographs taken in the last year or two of Emile's life seem to show that they had at last learnt to live with their loss. In the last known image, Angela appears a shadow of her former self, outwardly exhausted. She rests her arm on Emile's shoulder while Emile still stands with poise and assurance. Despite all the strife, there is warmth between the two.

Sources and Permissions

Published Memoirs

Ewart, Wilfrid, *When Armageddon Came*, Rich & Cowan Ltd, London, 1933.

Ewart, Wilfrid, *Scots Guard on the Western Front, 1915–1918*, Strong Oak Press, 2001.

Feilding, Rowland, *War Letters to a Wife*, The Medici Society Ltd, London, 1929.

Graham, Stephen, *The Challenge of the Dead*, 1921.

Grinnell-Milne, Duncan, *Wind in the Wires*, Hurst & Blackett Ltd, London, 1933.

Lauder, Harry, *A Minstrel in France*, Hearst's International Library, 1918.

Longley, Cecil, *Battery Flashes*, John Murray, London, 1916.

Seton Hutchison, Graham, *Pilgrimage*, Rich & Cowan, 1935.

Published Books

Clout, Hugh, *After the Ruins*, University of Exeter Press, 1996.

Crane, David, *Empires of the Dead*, William Collins, London, 2013.

Lloyd, David W., *Battlefield Tourism*, Berg, Oxford, 1998.

Longworth, Philip, *The Unending Vigil*, Martin Secker & Warburg, London, 1985.

Maskell, Henry, *The Soul of Picardy*, Ernest Benn, London, 1933.

Michelin Illustrated Guides, *Battlefields of The Marne 1914*, Michelin, New Jersey, 1919.

Unpublished Memoirs and Diaries

Cippico, Aldo Marino, *Chronicle of the Cippico Family 1909–1929*.

Journals and Published Reports

Hill, Arthur, *Our Soldiers' Graves,* Journal of the Royal Horticultural Society, 1919.

Newspapers

Daily Herald
Daily Mail
Evening Standard
Nottingham Journal and Express
The Sunday Express
The Times
Yorkshire Evening News

Websites

www.hansard.parliament.uk
www.longlongtrail.co.uk

Interviews

Interviews conducted by the author with the following people:
  Private James Hudson, 10th The Queen's Own (Royal West Kent
    Regiment).
  Patricia Wilson, daughter of Major William Carver.

Archives

Imperial War Museum

By kind permission of the Department of Documents, Imperial War Museum, London. With grateful thanks to Anthony Richards from the Department of Documents.

Documents 15569, private papers of Lady Londonderry.
Documents 6434, private papers of J. McCauley.

The Commission Archive, Commonwealth War Graves Commission, Maidenhead, Berkshire

Add 1/4/1 Correspondence between F. Ware and HM Treasury re principle that all costs of graves come from public funds, 31 Jan – 8 Feb 1918.

Add 1/3/3 Financial Administration: R. Blomfield re complaint by architects about financial interference in their designs, 2 Nov 1920.

Memorandum of Tour of Inspection by Sir Reginald Blomfield, France, Mar 1922, incl. Thelus Cemetery.

File includes report of staff problems, incl. drunkenness and other disciplinary issues.

Add 1/3/4 Transfer of DGRE work to the Commission, Dec 1920 – Aug 1921.

Further estimates of exhumation costs.

Add 1/1/5 Manufacture of headstones in the United Kingdom.

Organisation of gardening parties in the devastated areas, 1920.

Add 1/3/16 Cemetery Maintenance, Oct 1924.

Add 1/3/17 Cost of Permanent Cemetery Maintenance, Oct 1924.

Add 1/3/20 Cost of Cemetery Maintenance, visit to France, Oct 1924.

Add 1/6/1 A Report on the Cemeteries of the British Expeditionary Force, Feb 1918 by Sir Reginald Blomfield.

CCM/1/474 Francis Mond File incl. extensive correspondence with Angela Mond.

CON 167 Clandestine exhumations.

Also report on the work of battlefield exhumations incl. work of 68 and 126 Labour Company.

F209 Treasury File, 1922–1926 Responsibility for cemeteries. Incl. issue of mis-identification at burial incl. Hooge Crater

Cemetery. Also issue of public access to cemeteries and problems with farmers incl. Berles Cemetery.

Documents on the negotiation with civilians for the purchase of land for memorials.

The Transportation of Headstones to France and Belgium and associated financial costs.

SDC 74 Box 2 A Brief Review of the Development and progress of Horticultural Work in No. 1 Area, Imperial War Graves Commission, by Captain Melles.

WG18 Adornment of Cemeteries: design of graves and cemeteries Jan 1917 – Jan 1919, incl. Policy of equality of treatment and experimental cemeteries.

Graveyards on the Battlefield: report by Edwin Lutyens, Aug 1917.

WG 219/2 Memorials to the Missing – France and Belgium, 14 Aug 1924 – 25 Oct 1929, incl. Thiepval.

WG 219/2 Memorials to the Missing – Tyne Cot and Menin Gate, 5 Nov 1923 – 23 Jul 1929, incl. instances of names inscribed on the wrong memorials.

WG 219/4/2 Memorials to the Missing – Obtaining Correct Lists, 9 Jun 1923 – 19 Nov 1927, incl. problems posed by verification of names.

WG 546/1 Anglo–French Mixed Committee, 2nd Meeting, 8 Apr 1920.

Acquisition and approval of cemetery sites.

WG 546/2 Anglo–French Mixed Committee, 4th Meeting, 16 Nov 1922.

Suppression of cemeteries and local commune demands.

WG 546/5 Anglo–French Mixed Committee, 7th Meeting, 25 Jun 1926.

Objections to some intended monuments, incl. St Quentin and Pozières.

WG 546/6 Anglo-French Mixed Committee, 8th Meeting, 28 Jan 1927.

Modifications to monument-building programme.

WG 546/13 Anglo-French Mixed Committee, 15th Meeting, 14 Nov 1938.

Figures for British visitors to cemeteries.

WG 549 Pt. 1 France – Acquisition of Land, 1916–1920.

WG 549 Pt. 2 France – Acquisition of Land, 1920–1921.

WG 549 Pt. 4 France – Acquisition of Land, Minutes of St Omer Conference, 29 May 1923, incl. requests for regrouping of graves and perpetual concession of graves in France.

Difficulties and slowness of land acquisition; requirements for additional land.

WG 783 British War Graves Association, Pt. 1 (1920–1924) & Pt. 2 (1925–1948).

WG 890/1 Direction Boards – France and Belgium, 20 Sept 1923 – 20 Jul 1932.

WG 909/7 Indian Graves – France and Belgium, 16 Feb 1918 – 10 Jun 1952.

WG 1267 Religious Emblems on Memorials, Jun 1920 – May 1946.

WG 1294/3/1 Exhumation – France and Belgium, 1921, incl. exhumation of isolated bodies. Notes on reinternment, personnel and transport.

Horticultural Maintenance of cemeteries, Oct 1924. Proposals to reduce maintenance of cemeteries and Kew Gardens' response.

WG 1294/3 Pt. 2 Exhumation – France and Belgium – General File, 20 Nov 1919 – 30 Jul 1920, incl. requests from relatives for repatriation of bodies.

WG 1294/3/2 Exhumation – France and Belgium – Army Exhumation Staff 24 Feb 1919 – 6 Oct 1922, incl. public and press criticism of War Office's ending of search work for bodies. Also associated newspaper articles.

WG 1294/3 Pt. 4 Exhumation – France and Belgium – General File, 11 Aug 1920 – 13 Nov 1934. Regrouping of graves in order to economise on land required for cemeteries. Continued issues over the misidentification of remains.

WG 1689 Battle Exploit Memorials, 11th Division.
WG 1708 History of the Commission.

The National Archives, Kew

WO 32/4847 War Memorials France and Flanders & Battle Exploit Memorials Committee.

WO 32/5853 Alfred Mond (Office of Works) response to Churchill proposals for Ypres, 7 Feb 1919.

WO 32/5569 The preservation and reconstruction of Ypres: ongoing discussions, incl. newspaper articles. Letters from Lt Col Beckles Wilson and the Ypres League.

Cab 24/78/92 Winston Churchill and supply of workforce to the IWGC, Feb – May 1919.

T 1/12391 Preparations for the manufacture of headstones, 1919.
T 161/242/15 Minutes from the 103rd meeting of the Finance Committee, IWGC, 13 Nov 1924. Cemetery costs and maintenance.

Photographs

All images are taken from the author's private collection or from the private collection of photographs and documents belonging to the Mond family, unless otherwise stated.

Imperial War Museum, London

Q17486. The Somme Valley near Corbie, 1916, by kind permission of the picture library of the Imperial War Museum.

Pictures of Albert Harold Hill by kind permission of Ian and Robyn Smith.

Picture of Norman McLeod Adam by kind permission of Craig Marshall and Fettes College.

Picture of a Graves Registration Report Form by kind permission of Andrew Fetherston and The Commission Archive, Commonwealth War Graves Commission.

Acknowledgements

I would like to thank the staff at Pen & Sword Books, who gave me such valuable support while I worked on this book, including my great friend Jonathan Wright, who commissioned the work and has encouraged me at all times; I really appreciate your kind words, Jon. I would also like to thank Charles Hewitt for his ongoing belief in my work, and thank you again, Heather Williams and Tara Moran for your outstanding work in production and marketing respectively. Jon Wilkinson has produced a splendid jacket, using his great experience to produce something that we are all delighted with. His brother, Paul Wilkinson, has done an equally excellent job with the picture plate sections, and Dom Allen has produced a first-rate map. As usual, my editor, Linne Matthews, has been superb, picking up many tiny errors or at other times asking questions of the text when questions were needed. Thank you once again, Linne.

Of all those who have contributed to this book, one person was absolutely key, without whose help only a hideously truncated version of this story could have been told. Helen Cippico, the great-granddaughter of Angela and Emile Mond, has been quite simply wonderful. From my first email two years ago, right through to publication, she has been astonishingly generous and helpful. When I first contacted her, outlining what I was hoping to do, she immediately gave me not only access to all the archive materials she held, but also allowed me to take away everything, right down to parts of Francis's aircraft that Angela retrieved from the crash site. Nothing I asked for was too much trouble. I am so grateful to you, Helen.

I would also like to thank Robyn and Ian Smith from New South Wales in Australia. Robyn is Bert Hill's granddaughter and she kindly sent me a number of images, two of which appear in the book. Thank you both for your kind help and patience over the last two years.

I am once again in debt to my wonderful agent, Jane Turnbull, someone who has always been a great source of advice and assistance by email, phone or over a cup of tea at her home in Cornwall. Thank you again, Jane.

As ever, I am enormously grateful to my mum, Joan van Emden. She has answered any number of questions and has read this text through more than once. Her help always makes such a difference and I am indebted to her for all her efforts. My thanks also go to my wife, Anna, and to my son, Benjamin, who have supported me and, when needed, cajoled me into getting on with the job and finishing the book! Thank you again.

I am grateful particularly to Dr Glyn Prysor, Chief Historian at the Commonwealth War Graves Commission, Maidenhead, as well as archivists Andrew Fetherston and Maria Choules, and to Lynelle Howson, former assistant historian at the CWGC. I would also like to thank Chris Baker, Dan Hill, Sarah Ashbridge, Dave Empsom and Lucy Betteridge-Dyson. As usual, I am indebted to Taff Gillingham, my old friend and WW1 expert, who has always been so kind, allowing me to ring up at any time and tap into his astonishing bank of knowledge.

Index